Deconstructing America

Deconstructing America

Representations of the Other

Peter Mason

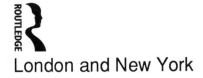

London and New York

for the Dutchess, again

First published 1990
by Routledge
11 New Fetter Lane, London EC4P 4EE

Simultaneously published in the USA and Canada
by Routledge
a division of Routledge, Chapman and Hall, Inc.
29 West 35th Street, New York, NY 10001

© 1990 Peter Mason

Typeset by LaserScript Ltd, Mitcham, Surrey
Printed and bound in Great Britain by
Biddles Ltd, Guildford and King's Lynn

British Library Cataloguing in Publication Data

Mason, Peter
 Deconstructing America: representations of the other.
 1. American culture, history – anthropological perspectives
 I. Title
 306.0973

Library of Congress Cataloging in Publication Data

also available

ISBN 0-415-05260-2

Contents

Illustrations

Acknowledgements

I owe a greater debt than I can say or repay to those who commented on part or all of the manuscript: Florike Egmond, Joanna Overing, Raymond Corbey, Maarten Jansen, Joep Leerssen, Arie de Ruijter. Edmundo Magaña may be said to have initiated and sustained the entire project when my nerve was failing; it was he who introduced me to the field of ethno-ethnology and gave unstintingly of his time and knowledge to make the present volume what it has become. And a big thank you to Heather Gibson from Routledge for taking care of the editorial side.

A version of Chapter Five appeared in *L'Homme* (Paris) as 'De l'articulation' in the Spring of 1990; I am grateful to Jean Pouillon for agreeing to its recycling here for English readers. Chapter Seven is based on my 'Ethnocentrism, euro-centrism, alterity: marginal remarks on Yekuana, Kalapalo and European Myth', published in the first issue of *Revista Indigenista Latinoamericana* (Budapest) in 1988; Luiz Boglár raised no objections to the publication of a substantially extended and revised version here.

Otherwise: a sort of introduction

Any discursive account which has something to say about writing says something about itself. This study has some things to say about alterity, about otherness. At the same time, it is marked by otherness.

Alterity has come very much to the fore in recent studies, as can be seen from a few randomly selected examples. In his analysis of the representation of the other in the work of the Ionian Greek Herodotos, François Hartog has even tried to establish a number of rules governing the rhetoric of alterity (1980: 225–269). The question of alterity poses the question of the border: where is the rupture between self and other to be situated? It thus may have a genuinely geographical sense, and alterity can be one of the procedures at the disposal of the traveller to suggest distance (ibid: 146).

It is in a different sense that Jean-Paul Vernant refers to alterity in connection with the tragic figure of Dionysos (1985). As the incarnation of the Other, Dionysos reveals the possibility of a joyous alterity as another dimension of the human condition. Yet Dionysos does not represent a separate form of existence, according to Vernant. His function is precisely to confuse the boundary line between human and divine, between human and animal, between here and beyond. Dionysos thus also reveals the multiple forms of the Other, the ultimate failure of any attempt to pin the Other down to some simple form of self/other binary opposition.

Not a god but a place is the subject of a pioneering article in this field by Pierre Vidal-Naquet, originally published in 1964 (Vidal-Naquet, 1981: 335–360), in which he seeks to demonstrate that the structure of Atlantis in Greek mythology is a representation dominated by the theme of alterity. The duality he isolates as a characteristic of the location of Atlantis is also shown to be a characteristic of the origin myth of the first inhabitants of Atlantis. The imaginary geography of Atlantis thus leads us into the world of myth.

This link with myth is important, because it has been suggested that myths are narratives of alterity (Smith, 1980: 64). They narrate those collective represent-ations which are not ours and whose underlying causes seem strange to us. As Edmundo Magaña has pointed out (1986: 99), this insight can be applied more widely to the anthropology of the imaginary. In fact, given the problems

1

surrounding the definition of a myth anyway, it might be useful to retain this wider definition of alterity in relation to the imaginary, which may include narratives but is not confined to them (Magaña and Mason, 1986).

So far we have touched on the work of historians and anthropologists. There is another tradition in which alterity is central. I refer to the work of the philosopher Emmanuel Levinas, who perhaps more than any other philosopher has seriously gone about the task of trying to present a phenomenology of the other. In *Totality and Infinity* he introduces a use of 'alterity' which is 'something else entirely', 'absolutely other' (1979: 33), and which is inextricably bound up with Desire:

> Desire is desire for the absolutely other. Besides the hunger one satisfies, the thirst one quenches, and the senses one allays, metaphysics desires the other beyond satisfactions, where no gesture by the body to diminish the aspiration is possible, where it is not possible to sketch out any known caress nor invent any new caress. A desire without satisfaction which, precisely, *understands* [entend] the remoteness, the alterity, and the exteriority of the other. For Desire this alterity, non-adequate to the idea, has a meaning. It is understood as the alterity of the Other and of the Most-High.
>
> (Levinas, 1979: 34)

The word 'understands' is the centre of the problem. For Levinas' concern is to try to understand the other without using the violence of comprehension to do so. To understand the other by comprehension is to reduce other to self. It is to deprive the other precisely of the very alterity by which the other *is* other (cf. Derrida, 1967b: 117–228).

We shall return to this theme in the course of the discussion. But we should remind ourselves that, even if the discovery of the other has to be begun all over again by each individual, it has a history, it has socially and culturally determined forms. Perhaps never has the need to stress the radical alterity of the Other been so urgent as in the present era of monopoly capitalism on a world scale.

The work of Levinas inspired the Bulgarian literary critic Tzvetan Todorov to make a contribution to the discovery of the other in his *La Conquête de l'Amérique: La Question de l'autre* (1982). What led Todorov in doing so to focus on the discovery of *America*? For him, it marks the start of Europe's attempt to assimilate the other, to deprive it of its exteriority and alterity (Todorov, 1982: 251).

Todorov refers to various sorts of otherness: the other in oneself (*je est un autre*); the otherness of groups within the society in which we live to which we do not belong (women as seen by men; men, as seen by women; the rich for the poor; the 'mad' in the eyes of the 'normal'; ...); the otherness of those who are external to us, other in terms of language, customs, etc. (ibid: 11). Like Todorov, I have chosen the otherness of what is external and distant to me (an Englishman living in Amsterdam). Like Todorov, I have chosen to say some things about, *inter alia*, writing and America. But – to reiterate the problem that is central to

Levinas' enterprise – how are we to handle what is other without robbing it of its otherness?

The problem has implications for the way we discuss it, which is why it has to be dealt with here before the reader chooses to proceed (or not). Michel Foucault was faced with a similar problem when he set out to write a history of madness (1961); he wanted to write, not a history of psychiatry, but a history of madness itself, in its vitality, before its enslavement to reason. The desire to write a history of madness itself without repeating the rationalist aggression is admirable, even if it may lay the author open to charges of 'irrationalism of an aesthetic nature' and an 'absolute extraneousness that, in reality, results from the refusal to analyze and interpret' (Ginzburg, 1980: xviii). In persisting in using a European language, are we condemned to persist in violating the very alterity which we seek to convey, to see it crumble under our gaze? Can we follow Nietzsche in linking the arbitrariness of our choice of philosophical concepts to the necessities imposed by our membership of the Indo-European family of languages (cf. Pautrat, 1971: 160–161)? I do no more than repeat the observations of Jacques Derrida when he points out that:

> *All* our European language, the language of everybody who has taken part, from close at hand or from a distance, in the adventure of western reason, is the vast representative of the project defined by Foucault under the title of the enslavement or the objectivisation of madness. *Nothing* in this language and *nobody* among those who speak it can escape the historical guilt [...] which Foucault seems to want to put on trial.
>
> (Derrida, 1967b: 58)

The example of the madman is not fortuitous. Was not the madman the one who confused the categories of alterity, the one who was other in that he failed to respect the signs of resemblance and difference (Foucault, 1966: 63)?

In different terms, Foucault has also written of the madman as the prisoner of the passage between outer and inner (1961: 22). The spatial metaphor of inner and outer links with both the theme of resemblance and difference and that of self and other. It might be as well to be clear about the transcendental nature of discussion of alterity here: we want to provide some sort of account of that which is beyond the boundaries of self and sameness, of that which is *radically and gloriously other*. But if we may be allowed to retain the spatial metaphor for a moment longer, it is not that which is beyond the boundary, for it is unbounded. We cannot even draw such a boundary, for that would be to set a limit to that which supersedes every boundary.

One of the implications of this is the problem of defining our subject matter at all. In the discussion of colonial discourse in the present work, reference to things like 'sexual', 'political' and 'economic' codes might suggest the possibility of some kind of classification of discourses in terms of precisely definable systems and subsystems. However, behind the apparent diversity of the historical forms of 'the economic', 'the sexual' and so on, there is no single and unmediated entity which could be seen as the content of these forms. Form/content, 'the economic (code)' and its variations, are ways of posing the question which already involve a certain foreclosure. They capture 'the economic' within a certain concept of historicity which evades the fundamental point that 'the economic' is itself *an effect*. It is the product of an economic mode of structuring discourse which produces in the act of discourse that very object which it purports to describe. This means that a discourse on 'the economic (code)', through its implication in the object of discourse, precludes the possibility of a discourse-free 'economic code' which would then, 'after the event' as it were, enter discourse as a structuring element. Discourse is economically structured. Hence a discourse on 'the economic' does not allow of a distinction between, say, form and content, because it does not allow any 'clean' distinctions of that kind at all. *Mutatis mutandis*, the same applies to 'the political', 'the ideological', etc. The sexual and economic axes to which we are referring are thus effects of the discourse which were already a part of that discourse itself (cf. Heinzelman, 1980). This means that discourse cannot be classified in terms of the dominance of one 'code' above another. Such structuralist hierarchies, which dominated neo-Marxist theories of the social formation in the 1970s, are unable to do justice to the fuzzy boundary in which one element is parasitic upon another, the 'essential parasitism which opens every system to what is outside it and divides the unity of the line which would mark off its boundary' (Derrida, 1978b: 11).

In approaching our problem, Derrida indicates that the question of the margin cannot be resolved within the terms of inside and outside. The margin obliquely leaves its trace in a text while evading the issue of where it belongs (Derrida, 1972a: vi-vii). As the example of Foucault reminded us, the question of the margin and of alterity demands a different style of writing, a different style of philosophy. For Derrida, it requires conceptually rigorous analyses that are philosophically incapable of treatment *and* the inscription of marks which no longer belong to the field of philosophy, not even to the neighbourhood of its other ... writing otherwise.

For the present study, there seems no other way out. The only way to approach the other by way of a text will be to juxtapose disparate texts. This specific text is inscribed within a general text. Its margin is not blank. On the contrary, it is a tissue of differences of force without a centre (ibid: xix). Our texts will be drawn from accounts of the discovery of America, European witch-trials, the mythology of South American indigenous peoples, the experiences of the European mystics, travels in the Orient... In the *bricolage* of juxtaposition, no *body* of texts will be constituted as the corpus. Instead, like the bodies and their holes discussed in a later chapter, these bodies of texts are fragmentary, fragmented, defective and discontinuous. At times the intervals between them are incomprehensible...

Writing about otherness is thus writing *otherwise*. It is in the nature of things that we cannot now set out a theory and then proceed to verify it, rounding off our remarks with a conclusion. There will be no rounding off here. Most of the edges that do appear will remain jagged. The remarks on theory scattered throughout the text could probably never be put together to form a theory in themselves. In this respect it remains problematical what Derrida meant when he suggested that it should be possible to formalise the rules of the enterprise of deconstruction (1967a: 39); especially as in the later *Eperons* (1978a: 79) he set limits to the process of formalisation. How to formalise rules when the very notion of a rule and its associations is precisely that which is called into question by the method?

Writing otherwise also means a use of language that is often self-effacing. Language is always the language of the other. Hence many of the terms used here should really be put between citation marks to indicate that they involve a temporary shift onto the 'terrain of the opponent'. Since such a typography would be unreadable, the only alternative is to write with the proviso that many of the terms used beg more questions than they solve.

This study's immediate context is thus within a post-structuralist philosophical and semiotic tradition: the work of the 'philosopher of alterity', Emmanuel Levinas; the deconstruction associated with the name of Jacques Derrida; and the wider interest among contemporary historians and social scientists in alterity.

More precisely, the present work is inscribed in the space between Diderot and Derrida. In a work which was published for the first time only in 1830, the French encyclopaedist Diderot compared the fibres of our bodily organs with vibrating chords. These chords have two properties. First of all, the vibrating chord continues to oscillate after it has been set in motion. This oscillation, this sort of resonance, thus has a time span. Second, the vibrating chords set up resonances in others in an unending series, so that it becomes impossible to set a limit to the ideas that are awakened and which evoke others in turn. The spatial span here is immeasurable, the interval is, as Diderot says, incomprehensible (*Entretien entre D'Alembert et Diderot* [1769], in Diderot, 1951: 879).

We shall return to Diderot and his fibres at various points, just as we shall examine in more detail what Derrida (1987b: 137) calls 'the differential vibration of several tonalities'. But resonances, unending series, incomprehensible intervals: perhaps it is not so promising a start after all. If we switch from the musical metaphor Diderot describes to the language he uses, we might seem to be on firmer textual ground. Through time and over space, the resonances refer to other resonances in an unbroken chain. Can we pick up the resonances of his text?

Space and time reappear a few pages later when Diderot writes that interjections are virtually the same in all the dead and living languages. And from where are we to deduce the origin of these conventional sounds? From need and from proximity (1951: 883). At the point of intersection where languages existing in time past and time present meet within the reduced spatial span of proximity, at their point of articulation, we get: inarticulation, the brute interjections that are simultaneously language and non-language, which have a doubtful status somewhere between language and music – not so promising a start either.

Perhaps we should go further afield for the resonances. In his *Essai sur l'origine des langues*, Rousseau also discusses the physical principle of resonance, in an attack on the musical theories of Rameau (Rousseau, 1970: 147ff. and

193 n.1). He accuses Rameau of a false empiricism in his attempts to derive a system of harmony from the physical principles of resonance. He also accuses Rameau of a form of ethnocentrism, in that the treatment of harmony as central belies a vision that is firmly centred in Northern Europe. The isolated, solitary chords are not enough for Rousseau, who insists on the need for a link between what precedes and what follows, for a veritable system of phrases, pauses, periods and punctuation in music, although in the process Rousseau himself seems to lapse into what Derrida (1967a: 301) has called a symmetrical counter-ethnocentrism.

Rousseau's criticism might be appropriate if we were trying to create an ensemble which could genuinely be called single. But the focus of the present study cannot be defined in terms of such a unified whole. As has been indicated above, it belongs within the general text, and from within it is impossible to measure the interval or establish the boundaries or margins which might delimit it from other texts. This is a study of the incomprehensible interval.

All the same, despite the problems raised by the lack of limits, every book has a starting point, and this one starts with America. As for the priority assigned to the discovery of America, Todorov has suggested two justifications for this. First, it is the most astonishing, most intense and most genocidal discovery within the history of human exploration. Second, 1492 marks the beginning of the modern era: from then on the world is closed and mankind has discovered the totality of which it is a part (Todorov, 1982: 12–14). There may even be a correlation between the violent denial of the exterior other in America and the discovery of an inner other within European society and within the European individual (ibid: 252). But the asymmetries which characterise our text do not lend themselves to this kind of correlation.

Some other reasons for the choice might be suggested. A number of the well-known philosophers of Western Europe – Montaigne, Hobbes, Locke, Rousseau, Voltaire, Kant, Hegel – were unable to ignore the challenge presented by the discovery of the New World, reason enough for following this theme in a philosophical study. Moreover, the discipline of social anthropology has a debt to its relation to America. The theme of anthropophagy, for instance, which is so much a part of the stock-in-trade of anthropology (Arens, 1979), is inextricably linked to the iconography of the continent. In particular, the ethnographic centre of gravity in the work of the dominant figure in the field of structural anthropology, Claude Lévi-Strauss, directs our gaze to the American continent too. As for Todorov's closure of the world, perhaps his dating is a little premature. It would be tempting to point to the relics of Russian trading and missionary influence in North America in the nineteenth century, reaching as far south as California (Brotherston, 1979: 58–60) as evidence for the meeting of East with West and for the realisation of Columbus' goal: the eastern route to America.

South America as the other of the United States of America; 'America' as the other of Europe: in the chapters which follow, various strands in the constitution of America are followed to present its alterity within various perspectives. As the interlocutors remark towards the end of Diderot's *Supplément au voyage de Bougainville*, the account is 'shaped a little in the European style' (*un peu modelé à l'européenne*, Diderot, 1951: 992). Simply in terms of the number of pages devoted to the European imaginary in a book which is supposed to be about the deconstruction of *America*, the present study may well appear to be just one big detour which never gets to its destination to some readers. No apologies are made for this. The reader who perseveres to the bitter end will see why.

Before America was discovered it already had a place in the European imaginary. The myth of the Golden Age, the Wild Man and Wild Woman, Atlantis, the travels of Marco Polo, the 'travels' of Sir John Mandeville – these had all prepared the ground for an encounter with the New World in which the New was already familiar.

In previous research on what has been called the construction or the invention of America, considerable attention has been paid to the ways in which the European vision of America was already clouded by particularly European preconceptions. The present study challenges the claim that the European vision of America is a distorted view of some extra-European reality. This is one of the senses in which it lays claim to the title of deconstruction. It also challenges the notion of an 'Enlightenment' in which scientific knowledge about the continent has been steadily accumulating and attaining increasingly higher stages of perfection to arrive at the present state of the art (anthropology). Instead, it stresses the textual construction of America as a figure of discourse. 'America' *is discourse on* 'America'; anthropology is seen as a singularly European product that is itself in need of deconstruction.

The thematic heart of the work lies in the so-called monstrous human races. Known to the Greeks (they are sometimes called the 'Herodotean' races) as well as to the Elder Plinius (they are known as the 'Plinian' races in some discussions), these monstrous races constitute a class apart from both theriomorphic deities and part-human, part-animal hybrids. They are, taken generally, *human races*: human, that is, neither divine nor animal, and races, that is, groups rather than isolated individual cases (the so-called prodigies studied by teratologists). Their monstrosity lies in their deviation from a culturally determined norm in terms of such markers as physique, locality, diet, speech. In four separate chapters these races and some of their tribes are discussed in terms of the relation between their place within the European imaginary and their role as 'translators' of the New World. The sources come from texts and icons of European antiquity and the Middle Ages and from the first European accounts of the Americas.

Chapter One provides a brief account of what ethno-anthropology is. The deconstruction of the real/imaginary and history/myth dichotomies leads to an inability to maintain a distinction between real and imaginary worlds. Ethno-anthropology studies the possible accounts of possible worlds and their inhabitants.

In this context, the referents 'New World' and 'America' belong to systems of names. In borrowing some of their significations from other worlds, they become caught up in the play of signifiers which includes 'Asia', 'the Orient', 'the Indies' and 'Europe'. The failure to find a concrete referent for these names raises the question of the properness of proper names and their improprieties and it creates an uneasiness about classical definitions of the sign. Departing from the de Saussurian formulations, representations are seen to refer to other representations and not to the truth of the represented.

Chapter Two presupposes a distinction between exotic non-European monstrous figures (the 'Plinian' races) and domestic European others: witches, Wild Men, madmen and animals. In this chapter it is the latter group which comes in for scrutiny. Drawing on textual and iconographical sources, a symbolic triangle of anthropophagy–idolatry–sexual excess is isolated and its presence is illustrated for the Americas, continental Europe and seventeenth-century British colonial discourse on Ireland. The interpenetration of European and American themes shows an 'Indianisation' of Europe as the inevitable corollary of the 'Europeanisation' of America. To the lack of an Asia/America distinction is added the lack of an America/Europe distinction. 'America' is not seen through European eyes: it is constructed from European images of Europe's own repressed and outward projected Others.

Chapter Three provides a full-length discussion of the history of the Plinian races from the earliest Greek sources (Hesiodos and Homeros) to the period immediately preceding the 'discovery' of America by Columbus. It serves as a comprehensive introduction to a subject matter that may not be familiar to a number of readers and introduces the races and their names which are taken up in the discussion in Chapter Four.

Chapter Four deals with the ways in which exotic, non-European monstrous races were utilised as models for the inhabitants of the New World. Since there is abundant evidence for the existence of such beliefs among the contemporary Amerindians themselves, the question is raised of possible borrowings between Europe and America. At the same time, the European monopoly of these images is dismissed. In this way the ethnocentrism/eurocentrism and oral/literate distinctions break down. Taking native ontologies seriously lays the ground for a critique of European social anthropology and its a priori inability to grasp what is other in a non-violent way.

Chapter Five traces one of the Plinian races (the Antipodes) in Europe and America. The argument tackles the alleged lack of writing among many Amerindian peoples. The introduction of grammatological considerations breaks down the logocentrism of any oral/literate distinction. The first step toward a syntax of the Plinian races is made.

Chapter Six complements the preceding chapter. It deals with another group of Plinians: those marked in terms of body holes. Contemporary myths from Amazonia and elsewhere in the Americas rejoin Greek sources. Elaborating on the grammatological argument of Chapter Five, the graphical function of holes is presented as being of value for a theory of punctuation.

Chapter Seven follows Todorov's dictum that all research on alterity is necessarily semiotic. A number of Amerindian myths (Yekuana, Kalapalo, Guajiro, Kaliña, etc.) which present an image of other peoples are interrogated within an ethno-ethnographical framework: existent and non-existent members of otherworlds impinge in different ways on the image of self. The image of other, non-Indian peoples, especially Whites, is brought within the scope of these representations. The attempt to compare the modalities of the representation of the other both in Amerindian discourse on Europeans and in European discourse on Amerindians reveals a fundamental asymmetry: the worlds are incommensurate.

The last words attempt to show how this incommensurability comes about. The rhetorical tropes used in the travellers' accounts are discussed to see how they attempt to produce credibility in what they describe. The primary structuring elements of the discourse on America, with strongly marked sexual and economic components, turn out to be the primary structuring elements of discourse as we know it. The deconstruction of 'America' turns out to be the deconstruction of the text. The discovery of America in a voyage 500 years ago is but a moment in the *covering* of America.

Author's note

The spelling of proper names adopted may seem inconsistent to some. On the one hand, there seemed little point in trying to pin down the Plinian races to a fixed orthography in view of the elusiveness of their very contours. In some cases, as is shown in Chapter Three, violence of this kind has resulted in a distorted presentation of the material in the past. Hence the reader will find a variety of spellings (Kynokephaloi, Cynocephali, and so on). On the other hand, here as in other publications Greek and Roman names have been transliterated instead of translated. The Greeks did not know anyone called Aristotle.

Despite the temptation, this is not a picture book. The motives for not including a wide collection of illustrations were largely practical ones, and the provision of an adequate commentary on them would have exceeded my competence. Those whose interests carry them in this direction could do worse than to consult the volumes by Hugh Honour (1975 and 1976), Bernadette Bucher's monograph on de Bry (1981), or the compilations edited by Karl-Heinz Kohl (1982), and by Ulrich Knefelkamp and Hans-Joachim König (1988). Many of the Plinian races are illustrated in John Block Friedman (1981), Claude Kappler (1980), Rudolf Wittkower (1977) and in a number of articles by Edmundo Magaña and myself.

The bibliography was compiled with the following principle in mind: it should help readers to orientate themselves in the mass of literature related to America and the Other, without the pretension of being comprehensive in any sense of the word. Those who look up the recent discussions will find further references to earlier and more specialised debates there.

1   Discovery of the Strait of Magellan

Source: Th. de Bry, *Americae IV*, Frankfurt, 1953. From an engraving by J. Galle after a drawing by J. Stradanus. Reproduced with permission of the University Library, Amsterdam.

Chapter one

Imaginary worlds

In order to *cognize* an object, I must be able to prove its possibility, either from its reality as attested by experience, or a priori, by means of reason. But I can *think* what I please, provided only I do not contradict myself; that is, provided my conception is a possible thought, though I may be unable to answer for the existence of a corresponding object in the sum of possibilities.

> (Kant, Preface to Second Edition of *Critique of Pure Reason*
> [1787], 1934: 16 n.1)

Anthropology produces its object, and it always has (Fabian, 1983). It is not just the selection of the object to be investigated (the Trobriand islands, the pre-industrial societies of Europe, contemporary urban ethnic minorities...) which is the result of a choice made by the anthropologist. The very constitution of that object as an object of anthropological investigation is a result of the labour of anthropological production.[1]

Ethnography, the recording of an *ethnos*, whether in writing or in other forms of recording, is a form of translation and reduction. All ethnography is an experience of the confrontation with the Other set down in writing, an act by which that Other is deprived of its specificity.[2] This writing, this *graphe*, follows specific rules, conforms to certain literary and stylistic conventions, and meets specific expectations. But proper names like 'the Trobriands' remain a product of discourse, a fiction, irrespective – *at a specific level of analysis* – of whether they are to be found in 'empirical reality' or not. In the production of a discourse on the Trobriands, Malinowski was creating a work which is of the same substance, intellectually, as, say, James Joyce's Bloomsday (Ardener, 1985: 57). In a sense, he was defining the form and object which ethnography, and with it anthropology, were going to follow throughout the period of Modernism (which Ardener situates between 1920 and 1975). Malinowski did so by establishing a particular set of rules as the norms (of intense conventionality) for this particular rhetorical genre: the naturalist or realist monograph. Functionalists write realism, 'a discourse as "tropic" as any other' (Boon, 1982: 18). The fall from grace of Frazerian anthropology, usurped from pride of place by its Malinowskian successor, may be due to the fact that 'Frazer's expanding literary allegory was updated by Malinowski until it resembled narrative realism' (ibid: 11).

Ethno-anthropology is the study of anthropologies, explicit or implicit. In the scrutiny of various kinds of anthropological discourse, the question may be bracketed of how far they may be in some way verifiable by some kind of empirical control. If the *Formes Elémentaires* of Durkheim or the *Structures Elémentaires* of Lévi-Strauss make use of defective or misconstrued ethnographic sources, as some critics have alleged, this will not necessarily affect the substance of what they are saying in its quality as a discourse on social phenomena. It only raises problems for a specific and particular branch of anthropology (namely, ethnography) which is concerned with the 'fit' between theory and 'empirical reality'. The intelligible developments described by Durkheim and Lévi-Strauss are not conditional on empirical verification or variation.[3]

Within the perspective followed here, the question of the possible existence of such a gap between theory and observable 'reality' is of little interest. 'Reality' is as much bound up with discourse as theory is. There is no way in which some pre-discursive *factum* might be supposed to escape the bounds of ethnographic discourse. This is not to deny the realist intuition of nature's causal independence from our cognising powers, nor to deny the presence of variable constraints on our powers of imagination.[4] It is simply that we take the gap between words and things seriously. While words and phrases belong within the boundaries of language, objects and their conditions belong to the world of what is visible. By subjecting a Kantian perspective to a linguistic turn, we confine our discourse to phenomena as the only possible objects of discourse about which anything can be said.[5] The opposition between phenomena and noumena itself is incapable of operation or verification, since however close to the margins of phenomena we may suppose ourselves to be, what is beyond the boundaries of discourse simply cannot be said, nor even thought within such a spatial metaphor, as was pointed out in the introduction.

Discourse, including anthropological discourse, does often refer to something that is conceived as external reality. However, such reference has a function internal to discourse. It produces what Barthes called 'l'effet de réel', having as its function the denotation of reality.[6] Although Barthes is referring primarily to so-called literary texts, the reality effect is not just a literary convention. It is an essential part of anthropological discourse. We find it already in the work of Herodotos (Hartog, 1980: 249) with its customary function of encouraging credibility in what the discourse is telling. But the reality effect also tends to divert attention away from the discourse itself (as well as from the narrator). It supports the metaphysical conception by which language is preceded by fact, and discourse is seen as an image (secondary in time and status) of facts.

The world of (anthropological) discourse, however, can be situated within the world of anthropology – it is a part and function of what is presented by discourse. In this sense, discourse is not *re*presentation, for it is not secondary. It is *presentation*; it does not recreate but it creates.

'World' as a referent is thus not an object of knowledge. It evades any kind of reality control. The worlds referred to in this work of construction and reconstruction might be called 'imaginary worlds' if we wished to stress the fact that they are products of thought, and that whatever meaning or intelligibility we might like to confer on them is the result of an arbitrary decision. The term is useful in that it covers both those worlds which are conventionally included within the framework of empirical fact and those worlds which are not. To paraphrase Ardener again, it enables us to treat, say, Thomas More's Utopia and Amerigo Vespucci's America as being of the same substance, intellectually. On the other hand, its use is problematical in so far as it implies that we are able to establish a distinction between what is 'imaginary' and what is not. When Olschki claims that 'the history of America begins, like that of the Ancient World, with legends in which it is not easy to recognise the exact proportion of reality and imagination' (1941: 361), he is operating within the terms of such an opposition, supposing that if we were to strip off the imaginary accretions we would discover the underlying reality. But at what point does the imagination take off from the real world into its free flight? How could we perform the algebra required to settle the proportions between the imaginary and reality? By stressing the fact that reality is constructed through the work of the imagination, we dissolve the opposition between the two.

A similar problem underlies the opposition between myth and reality (or myth and history). The deconstruction of this opposition proceeds along similar lines. Mythology does not consist of imaginary accretions as functions of some underlying (historical) reality; if this were the case, we could follow Pouillon (1980: 90) in raising the following objection: why should we not be satisfied with that (historical) reality, without bothering ourselves with its secondary emanations? On the contrary, there is much to be said for the suggestion that that 'reality' itself is a product of the activity of our imagination (Magaña, 1987b). Within such a conception, it is not the striking empirical realities that we encounter which drive the imagination to mythical excess; on the contrary, it is the selection made by the imagination of certain objects as in some way distinct from others and intrinsically worthy of attention which confers on such objects their striking attributes and leads in turn to their incorporation in myth. Of course, the ethnographical context is not totally irrelevant to the production of myth, for the imagination makes use of what is available within specific and definable ethnographic confines. But it does so in order to produce those very conceptions which go beyond such confines.

It is thus in no way helpful to try to strip off the excess or extravagance of myth – it was Fontenelle who referred in his *De l'origine des fables* (1724) to the myths of the Greeks as extravagances – to get at some supposed non-mythical reality. Mythical worlds are imaginary worlds. They are constructed when the imagination uses the elements available in order to invent such worlds. The question of their possible existence in historical time or space is simply not on the agenda.

Imaginary worlds may serve ideological functions. They may be strongly marked on the symbolic register. They may form part of (and exceed the limits of) representations. But 'imaginary' is not a synonym for 'ideological', 'symbolic' or 'representational' (Le Goff, 1985: i–viii). It is not parasitical on, or secondary to, some 'non-imaginary' reality. For example, the twelfth-century literature connecting marvellous happenings with an urban setting pre-dates the opening up of the marvellous city of Constantinople to the crusaders of the West in 1204 (ibid: 241). Likewise, as we shall see, America occupied a strongly marked place within European discourse as a part of the European imagination already before the arrival of Columbus and Vespucci. The marvellous was in existence as a category of the imagination before it was permitted to bring certain objects of observation under its sway.

To return to the categories with which we began, ethno-anthropology may now be defined as the study of the inhabitants of possible worlds. The question of the verifiable existence of such peoples is suspended. When Plinius the Elder or 'Sir John Mandeville' describe people and their customs, they include exotic peoples who may appear to us to be entirely fictitious alongside less 'mythical' peoples. Examples abound of this juxtaposition of apparently mythical and historical peoples side by side (Magaña, 1982b: 71). Similarly, when sixteenth century travel writers such as Jean de Léry or André Thevet describe the fauna and flora of the New World, they use the same rhetorical techniques of comparison, juxtaposition and difference which inform accounts of patently fictional monstrous constructs (Mason, 1989b). Whatever the case may be, the descriptive procedure followed by their discourses is substantially the same as that followed by anthropologists who study the 'real world', justifying our setting of the question of real existence between parentheses. It is only when the lack of reference to some empirical reality becomes a constitutive and deliberate part of their definition that we have to take it into account.

By laying stress on the creation of imaginary worlds irrespective of the question of their possible correspondence with something called 'reality', we bring to the fore the fact that they are not extra-linguistic realities. The reality of the presence of an imaginary world is not guaranteed by the fact that we talk about it. Nor can its existence be verified by the visible verification (autopsy) which is so important for historians (Hartog, 1980: 271–316; Lestringant, 1987b: 472), for imaginary worlds are not directly visible. They become approachable only through their incorporation within discourse.

An imaginary world cannot be seen, but it can (and must) be named. Its name, in turn, is a part of a network, or rather of different networks, of names. No single name can cover it in its entirety: it is always more than the sum of its parts. As Wittgenstein wrote:

It seems – at least so far as I can see at present [May 1915] – that the matter is not settled by getting rid of names by means of definitions: complex spatial objects, for example, seem to me in some sense to be essentially things – I as it were see them as things. – And the designation of them by means of names seems to be more than a mere trick of language.

(Wittgenstein, 1979: 47)

An imaginary world is thus an ensemble of names. These names interlock with other systems (chronological, topographical, etc.) which all contribute to the establishment of the 'reality' of a particular imaginary world. That is, they have a certain 'reality effect'. Despite the vast number of contexts in which a proper name can occur, it remains invariable from one context to another. It is in this sense that we can say that systems consisting of names of 'objects' and of names of relations between objects designate entities and relations between these entities – what they designate we call a world (Lyotard, 1983: 67). Thus a system of names presents a world, and the entities and relations presented by the contexts in which these names occur are fragments of this world.

In some ways the name of an imaginary world behaves like the expressions called indexicals by some philosophers of language. These expressions, such as 'I', 'here', 'now', designate a reality which appears and disappears with the utterance. A proper name like 'America' behaves to some extent like such an indexical, but there is a rigidity in its designation which means that it is supposed to be the same in all the contexts where it is referred to by name.

If the name of an imaginary world fails to refer to some individual world, this is a *linguistic* failure, not an ontological one. The main idea behind this theory of historical explanation is that:

When a speaker uses a name intending it to refer to an individual and predicate something of it, successful reference will occur when there is an individual that enters into the historically correct explanation of who it is that the speaker intended to predicate something of.

(Donnellan, 1977: 229)

Proper names thus do not conceal definite descriptions. They refer independently of identifying descriptions.

Seen in this light, an imaginary world such as 'America' is a linguistic unity. As a proper name, 'America' has no definition at all (cf. Schwartz, 1977: 30). In fact, its reference is determined very feebly in terms of meaning because of the large number of linguistic contexts in which it can occur. On the other hand, its location in the system of names and of relations between names (worlds) is strongly determined, and it is to this latter aspect that we now turn.

The 'New World'

What does it mean to discover a New World? At any rate, it involves a drastic shift of received opinion, a process which always seems to come up against a good deal of resistance. For example, in some versions of the journey of the Irish monk Brendan, he was condemned to voyage around the world for a number of years as a penance for his disbelief in the wonders of the world which God had created. Augustinus, Bishop of Hippo, on the other hand, saw the individual prodigies and legendary races of the East as evidence of God's power and desire to revitalise man's sense of the marvellous (Friedman, 1981: 3). The same struggle against the unwillingness or inability to accept the challenge to received opinions, summed up in the adage *Noli alta sapere*, which was used as an anti-intellectual maxim from the early Christian Fathers onwards (Ginzburg, 1986: 107ff.), was to motivate José de Acosta in his attempt to 'lay down the causes and reasons for so many novelties and strange things in nature' (Pagden, 1982: 152).

At the time when Columbus set sail for the Indies, one of the books that he annotated and took with him was a copy of Pierre d'Ailly's *Imago Mundi*, a compilation of geographical information culled from Greek, Arabic and Biblical sources, which was first published in 1483. The image of the world presented in this work conforms to the late medieval picture of the *Orbis Terrarum*: the inhabited world is an island surrounded by water. This island was divided into three continents, Europe, Africa and 'India' (i.e. Asia), sometimes represented as a leaf with three segments.[7]

Columbus' landing in 1492 did not disturb this picture. He was convinced that he had discovered a sea route to the Orient. The real break did not come until 1507, with the publication of the new world map by Martin Waldseemüller. This was the first map to use the name of America (*Americi terra*) to refer to the new landmass. From 1507 on, America was recognised as a new continent and no longer as a part of the East.

This disruption of the existing tripartite division altered the image of the world. The closed and stable cosmology of antiquity and the Middle Ages gave way to the challenge of discovering what was beyond the limits of the known world. The discovery of new peoples, like the Turks or the Amerindians, posed problems for the conventional genealogies which derived the races of the world from the three sons of Noah: Ham, Shem and Japhet. There was a new continent in the picture, which had now to be accommodated within a changing geographical and ethnographical system.

The history of this process of invention has been described, with various nuances, many times already (see particularly O'Gorman, 1961). Of course, what is described is not the creation or discovery of the actual existence of a territory called America: 'invention' refers to 'the discovery or production of new *modes of existence*, new forms of apprehending, of projecting or of living in the world' (Derrida, 1987a: 41, with his italics).[8] The following chapters will deal with specific cases illustrating the construction and populating of a new imaginary world, 'America'. But first it is important to consider in more detail the naming of America and the problems that this raises for any anthropology of discovery.

The continent which fails to resemble the three known continents is simply *otro mundo*, 'another world', in the texts of Columbus. It is first referred to as *novus mundus* by Amerigo Vespucci in a letter to Lorenzo di Pietro de' Medici.[9]

Despite uncertainties about which texts may be attributed to Vespucci, it is reasonable to suppose that Vespucci was using the designation *novus mundus* for the American continent around 1500. He treats the term somewhat as a metaphor when he writes:

> I have already written extensively in the past days to you about my return from those new regions [...] which one is justified in calling *novus mundus*, since our predecessors had no knowledge of them and it is a complete novelty to all who hear about it.[10]

In virtually apologising for the use of the expression *novus mundus*, Vespucci uses it in two senses. It refers both to a world which is not recorded in tradition, and to one which is strikingly novel. Later in the same text, he refers to *novas regiones ignotumque mundum*, once again combining the two senses (Vespucci, 1984: 92). Soon, however, the term acquired a utopian flavour in European contexts. In a letter of 1527, Erasmus commented on the violent turn taken by the Lutheran Reformation 'quasi subito novus mundus condi posset' [as if a new world could be established suddenly] (1928, vol. 7: 232–3). By the middle of the sixteenth century it had acquired a firmly utopian flavour.[11] A few decennia later, *nuevo mundo* and *otro nuevo mundo* are used to describe the millennium in the visions of Lucrecia of León, who was active toward the end of the 1580s, but there is now a fusion between the meaning of 'new social order' and the reference to America. For those who believed in a Golden Age vision of America, this New World evoked by Lucrecia could serve as a model of how the new European social order was to be (Milhou, 1983: 18–19).

In the preface to his *Histoire d'un voyage faict en la terre du Brésil*, published in 1578, Jean de Léry based the use of the expression *monde nouveau* on the lack of similarity of the new continent to the three known continents:

> This country of America, where [...] everything that is seen in the way of life of the inhabitants, the appearance of the animals, and in general in the products of the land is unlike what we have in Europe, Asia and Africa can be called a *new world in our opinion*.[12]

The novelty of the New World raised specific problems of recognition. Jean de Léry noted on the quadrupeds of Brazil that 'there is not a single one in this country of Brazil or in America which resembles ours as a whole and in every detail' (1980: 127). The same applies to the flora: with the exception of three plants, de Léry is unable to find a single tree, plant or fruit which is not different from those of the West (ibid: 161). Nor was this a peculiarly sixteenth-century problem. In a work written in 1618 by a sugar planter in Brazil, Ambrósio Fernandes Brandão, the same uncertainties occur: how is he to describe New World corn except in terms of Old World sorghum, or the New World jaguar except in terms of the Old World tiger (Brandão, 1987: 198 [corn]; 278 [jaguar])?[13]

In a sense, the New World was too new and different to be assimilated, which may be one of the reasons why the circulation of descriptions of the Holy Land outnumbered descriptions of the New World in the sixteenth century. The mass of fantastic and familiar features which had accumulated in the popular and learned traditions of Europe provided a source from which the new could be described and accommodated in terms of the old. But when faced with the inadequacy of the old to cover all the material which now presented itself, sixteenth-century observers came up against severe semantic difficulties. The Jesuit José de Acosta (1540–1600), who wrote a *Historia natural y moral de las Indias*, described his own first exposure to the realities of America in *De temporibus novissimis* (1590) in the following terms:

> In my case the things of the Indies seemed after I had had personal experience of them to be both the same as I had heard and not the same.
>
> (cited by Pagden, 1982: 155)

'The same and not the same': this is a scandal for the sixteenth-century *episteme* in which knowledge was acquired through the system of resemblances which connected the elements of the world with one another. By posing resemblance as the link between the sign and what it indicates, sixteenth-century epistemology was condemned to remain bound within a circle of resemblance and identity. On the one hand, it could not know what lay outside this community of words and things; and on the other hand, it could never attain complete knowledge of these words and things because of the never-ending circle in which they followed one another (Foucault, 1966: 44–45).

According to Foucault, the following century witnesses an 'epistemological break' as the infinite play of resemblances comes to be replaced by a stress on the possibility of the absolute knowledge of identity and difference in the work of Descartes and Bacon.[14] The act of comparison is superseded by a breaking down of things into elements in order to establish series. This attempt to create a permanent table of stable differences and delimited identities can be seen as a genesis of difference aimed at the replacement of the sameness of the figures of the sixteenth century. Yet both approaches lead to the same inability to proceed further. In the case of the restrictive figures of similitude, an exegetic apparatus is imposed on the New World to assimilate it to the closed circle of words and things. In the case of the classical analyses of difference, their presuppositions (a self-contained, complete being capable of being broken down into its constituent elements) also exclude what is refractory to such an enterprise and leave it out of account. Monsters and fossils, for example, are the troublesome reminders of the inadequacy of difference or identity to cope with what is the same and not the same (Foucault, 1966: 163–170).

The work of Jean de Léry is a case in point: the very composition of *Histoire d'un voyage faict en la terre du Brésil* reveals a return to a single source of production by a reduction of the other to the same (de Certeau, 1975). We might take as an iconic image of this process the attitude of de Léry towards the food offered to him in the New World. His first response to some of the items is that, from his viewpoint of what is familiar, they are inedible. As he is forced by circumstances to widen his culinary horizons, he goes on to find the strange new stuffs edible. The final stage in this process is that he regards them as quite palatable, on a par with the familiar foods from which he began the work of comparison. From his starting point of the familiar he thus ends up with – the (new) familiar (Whatley, 1984: 395). As M. de Certeau puts it:

> This work is in fact a hermeneutics of the other. It transposes to the New World the Christian exegetical apparatus which, born from a necessary relation with Jewish alterity, was applied time and again to Biblical tradition, Greek and Latin antiquity, and to many other unfamiliar totalities.
>
> (de Certeau 1975: 231)

Sometimes the inability on the part of the European observers of America to go beyond their own familiar frames of reference is a wilful misunderstanding which serves the interests of the observer in acquiring colonies. But, irrespective of the colonising motive, the inability is a conceptual one. It is the inability to perceive likeness and difference simultaneously (Greenblatt, 1976).

It might seem possible to seek a way out of the problem by resorting to non-linguistic means of expression. After all, if it is true that 'the limits of my language mean the limits of my world' (Wittgenstein, 1979: 49), then surely, by simply drawing or painting what they saw, the first observers of America could go beyond the linguistic limits and portray in images what they could not express in words? This was the solution offered by Gonzalo Fernández de Oviedo y Valdés, who, when faced with his inability to describe a tree that he had seen in Hispaniola, said that it should rather be painted (Pagden, 1982: 12).[15] As we shall see in the following chapters, however, the iconographical traditions of European painting worked in a similar way to the literary ones in confining the gaze to what was familiar. In the visual arts, direct observation of reality was normally limited to details, supplementing rather than supplanting the use of traditional schemes, as the medieval artist worked from the *exemplum* rather than from life (Panofsky, 1970: 321).

Even after the close of the Middle Ages, there is still no direct, 'photographic' portrayal in painting. A case in point is that of the paintings of the Indians of Brazil carried out by Eckhout in the seventeenth century.[16] Albert Eckhout was one of the two painters (the other was Frans Post) who accompanied Johan Maurits van Nassau-Siegen as Governor General of the Dutch colony in Brazil from 1637 to 1642 (cf. Joppien, 1979). Among the works produced there is a group of nine large oil paintings depicting a Tupi pair, a 'Tapuya' pair, an African negro pair, a pair of half-bloods, and a 'Tapuya' dance. These paintings certainly reveal a strong ethnographic interest. Indeed, it has been claimed 'nor are there any earlier depictions of the inhabitants of Southern Africa, India or the East Indies of equivalent ethnological validity' (Honour, 1979: 295). Nevertheless, Eckhout orders the Indians in accordance with a scheme that is centred on European canons. The wild dance and the (ethnographically inaccurate) portrayal of the 'Tapuya' as cannibals situate them on the outer ring of wildness. The more 'civilised' Tupi Indians occupy an intermediary position, marked for example by the fact that the Tupi man bears a European knife, and that the landscape behind the Tupi woman contains rows of cultivated palms and a colonial house. The 'civilised' Europeans come implicitly because obviously in the centre as the most attractive and refined people (cf. van den Boogaart, 1979: 538; Vandenbroeck, 1987: 37–38).

The Eckhout paintings relate to distinctions within the various population groups in Dutch Brazil. In the following chapter we shall see how the earliest representations of the Amerindians waver between the positive and negative connotations of the figure of the European Wild Man. At a later stage, however, this uncertainty as to how to classify them is broken down into a dualism that affects the social body of the Amerindians itself. The question of whether the Amerindians are wholly good or wholly bad is thus resolved by claiming that some are worse than others. There are both 'noble' and 'savage' Amerindians. Hence Marc Lescarbot, part of whose work was translated into English as propaganda for the Virginia Company of London in 1609, singled out the tribes of Brazil as being beyònd hope of civilisation (Pennington, 1978: 185). Within the tribes of Brazil, the Eckhout paintings establish further distinctions: the 'Tapuya' are represented as the savage counterparts of the more noble (i.e. closer to European standards) figures of the Tupi. Similarly, in the Caribbean area proper, the words 'Arawak' and 'Carib' are made to conform to the primitive and anti-primitive models of Mediterranean discourse respectively. What appear as ethnographic definitions of Amerindian peoples are in fact labels applying to the *response* of the Amerindians to the presence of the Spaniards in their region: those who accept the Spaniards on the latter's terms are labelled 'Arawak', while those who defend their territory and their way of life are labelled 'Carib' (Hulme, 1986: 72).[17]

We cannot leave the Eckhout paintings without making two further points relating to the question of realism. Firstly, if we compare them with the equally 'realist' portrayal of a (mythical) Wild Man carrying the spoils of his hunt, painted by a contemporary of Eckhout, Jacob Van Oost the Elder (1601–1671),[18] we see that the ethnographical paintings of Eckhout are of the same substance as the mythico-historical painting by Van Oost. The question of reference to reality has to be put between parentheses. Secondly, Eckhout follows contemporary conventions in genre painting in combining observations from life with a moral-ising use of symbols. Perhaps this is nowhere more clearly demonstrated than in the sexually pregnant portrait of a negro woman with child. The presence of conventional erotic symbols shows how Eckhout sets out to produce what is a compilation of borrowed allegory and a personal vision, rather than the portrait of a person encountered in real life (cf. Baumunk, 1982: 191).

An even more desperate attempt to escape the problem was to *bring* the New World to the Old: if drawing and painting failed, small objects at least, if not humans, could be brought to stock the museums and cabinets of Europe.

Columbus, who delivered six 'Indians' to the Spanish king upon his return from his first voyage, is the paragon and precedent that initiated the one-way stream of American artefacts and peoples to the European continent. The Aztecs displayed by Cortés before the court of Charles V in 1529 have come down to us as the earliest known representations of American Indians taken from life in the coloured drawings which Christoph Weiditz made at the time. The stereotype of the exotic Indian became firmly rooted in European soil after a spectacle was held in Rouen (the main French centre for trade in brazil-wood) for the French king and his wife in 1550. Some fifty Brazilian Indians were supposed to give a display of life and battle in an Indian settlement, a task in which they were assisted by 250 French sailors dressed up as Indians. This tradition of spectacles and exhibitions continued right into the twentieth century (Feest, 1987: 613–620; Mason, 1989b).

But the result is the same. When the public of Antwerp paid to see an Indian woman and child who had been brought there in 1565, they were presented with 'a wild woman and her child, who had been taken captive in the mountains, naked, eating only human flesh' (*Chronycke van Antwerpen sedert het jaar 1500 tot 1575*, quoted in Vandenbroeck, 1987: 157 n.163). But the European traditions on the Wild Woman, going back to at least the tenth century,[19] already had the by no means innocent observers in their grip. Observation was still an act of construing the perceived objects in terms of familiar representations. Similarly, when Columbus brought parrots back to Spain, it was as proof that he had reached the East (see below). Torn out of their natural contexts, these artefacts (or persons treated as objects) were readily provided with contexts by their European audiences, who saw in them what they expected to see.

One consequence of this position is that observations in later periods are not necessarily free from the same limitations. In any age, confrontation with the other remains problematical. And the response to this inability remains the stock response of falling back on the familiar figures of tradition. If we proceed from the sixteenth to the eighteenth century, very little has changed. Duchet comments on eighteenth-century travel literature and the writings that it inspired:

> In the case of travel literature, it is hard to avoid the feeling of monotony which it inspires, which is no doubt due to the relatively limited means of expression, but also to the distance which never changes and by which the observer is separated from a world to which s/he remains external and of which s/he has only a superficial knowledge.
>
> (Duchet 1971: 112)

Voltaire can mock the missionaries who see in every statue a devil, in every assembly a sabbath, in every symbolic figure a talisman and in every brahman a sorcerer (*Questions sur l'Encyclopédie*, 'Almanach', cited in Duchet, 1971: 14). Behind such practices is a belief in ethnography as translation, implying the commensurability of the New World with the Old. But the failure to grasp the realities of the New World is not to be explained by a steadfast clinging to out-moded assumptions or prejudices which are supposed to have been cleared up by the time of the eighteenth-century Enlightenment, if not earlier.[20] Such a 'tunnel vision' of the history of ideas, implying at some stage a full correspondence between the observer's perception of reality and that reality itself, is inadmissible (Pagden, 1982: 1–6; Osterhammel, 1989). When observers of America classified in order to perceive, they did what every observer of the unfamiliar does. The innocent eye has never existed. Portrayal always involves at root a degree of betrayal.

Of course, there were changes in the nature and degree of the preselection and the cultural bias. For instance, a shift of emphasis may have taken place from ethnographical interest in the sixteenth century to myth-forming in the seventeenth and eighteenth centuries (cf. Vandenbroeck, 1987: 27 and 145), although the early ethnographical interest was itself already coloured by 'myth' (if we are to use these problematical terms at all).

Another shift involved the changing attitudes by Europe to its own past and to that of other nations. For instance, there was already a marked interest in the past of China on the part of the Jesuit missionaries there, and in some respects their attitude toward America is an intensification of a process that had already been set in motion. With the new presentation of antiquity as less familiar and more exotic (marked for example by Fontenelle), the exotic could be used in turn to cast light on antiquity (Ryan, 1981). While for the Jesuit José de Acosta the Graeco-Roman world remained, except in religious matters, the norm of civilisation, Lafitau's originality lay in his revelation that the Greeks had once been savages too.

A further shift might be labelled as that from a theological to a scientific outlook. To take de Acosta again, his thesis that the Indians had migrated from the Old World to the New was a theological postulate, assuming that the Indians were the descendants of the sons of Japhet, and of course linking the New World directly with the Old. In the eighteenth century, in the work of Buffon, the migration thesis is retained, only this time as a scientific hypothesis (Duchet, 1971: 263).

Despite these shifts, the eighteenth-century Enlightenment, while showing great interest in the new voyages of discovery, remained a world in which classification preceded observation. For example, one of the great popularisers of voyages to the North was Voltaire, who wrote a number of articles for the *Encyclopédie* dealing with these regions. His accounts, however, are already 'processed' and assimilated to the Voltairean scheme of things, which motivates, for example, his refusal to believe in a migration to Lapland, that 'country of Cynocephales, of Himantopodes, of Troglodytes and of Pygmies' (Voltaire, *Encyclopédie* art. 'Laponie', cited in Duchet, 1971: 56). To take a case of preselection, interest in the Southern Seas was centred on the island of Tahiti (Kohl, 1981), which meant that Roggeween's discovery of the spectacular Easter Island in 1721 passed almost unnoticed (Duchet, 1971: 64).

The way in which observers of America resorted to the world that was familiar to them is a timeless response by self when faced with the challenge of the other. In using the elements familiar to them, they were in fact engaged in a double process of reduction and construction. In *constructing* the New World, resemblance was linked with imagination to avoid the endless monotony of the same. The result is a continuing process of construction and reconstruction of a world, which we may therefore call an imaginary world. The frame of reference remains the Old World (though the renaissance was to mean a reconstruction of *that* world too).

The other side of this process is its *reductive* aspect. The perception of the other was not limited to observation from a distance. It was coupled with violence, and the violence carried out against the other was an attempt to *reduce* what was refractory to the bounds of self. We can see this in European attempts to come to grips with the problem of religion in South America. When faced with a world of shamans and spirit beings which they could not understand, the first observers of the Tupinamba of Brazil were quite at a loss as to how to classify the religion of these people. After all, it looked as though they had no religion, unlike the idolatrous city dwellers of Middle America, whose religion was visible to an excessive degree. While the latter could simply be labelled as pagans and assimilated to the Greeks, Egyptians or Chaldeans by counting, identifying and classifying the gods they worshipped, there was no system to which the practices of the Tupinamba could be assimilated in view of the lack of specified places or specified times. True, the Tupinamba clearly had sorcerers and magic, but this was not the same as idols and religion. Hans Staden, who spent some months as a captive of the Tupinamba, could find no evidence for idols apart from the rather unclear beliefs attached to their rattles (*maraca*). De Léry, Thevet and Cardim similarly failed to find evidence for idolatry, as Vespucci had failed to find temples or idolatry in the New World (1984: 100).

In the course of the seventeenth century, however, Cicero's claim that there was no people without religion was taken seriously, and diligent attempts were made to pin down the vague beliefs and practices of the lowland Indians of America to more familiar demonological frameworks.[21] The shamans were recast as idolaters, the spirit beings became devils, and the Tupinamba were fitted into the same framework which was being used to classify the idolaters of Europe (Clastres, 1987).[22] In the process, the freshness of the discovery of a people without religion, without superstition and yet with some notion of a universal God grew stale in the course of its reduction to the familiar. The New World lost its novelty.

The name 'America'

The designation 'New World' did at least serve to point by contrast to the discontinuity with the Old World and thereby to place the continent in a position which could be related, positively or negatively, to the conceptions of antiquity and the Middle Ages. The name 'America', on the other hand, had no predecessors. It was a novelty, coined on the basis of the name of Amerigo Vespucci, who more than Columbus realised the radical novelty of the continent which he claimed to have visited four times.[23] In coupling the name to the observation of the new continent, we detect an emphasis on vision that is typical of this period. It has been suggested that the Middle Ages were predominantly oriented in terms of a triad of seeing, hearing and reading (*visa, audita, lecta*). In the work of Ulisse Aldrovandi, for example, Foucault notes that:

> it is necessary to include within one and the same form of knowledge all that has been *seen* and *heard*, all that has been *narrated* by nature or by men, by the language of the world, of traditions or of poets.
>
> (Foucault, 1966: 54ff.)

In this epoch, 'the great tripartition, so simple in appearance and so direct, of Observation, Document and Fable, did not exist' (ibid: 141). The act of commenting on a text is the same as the act of commenting on reality (Veyne, 1983: 120).

'Seeing, hearing, reading' – the triple alliance, however, is a hierarchy. Throughout the Middle Ages[24] and into the sixteenth century it is vision which is the preferred sense for the acquisition of knowledge. Even when travellers and writers like André Thevet or Bernhard van Breydenbach draw on a complex body of different literary sources for their data, they (disingenuously) stress the predominance of autopsy in their work (cf. Lestringant in Thevet, 1985: XLIXff.). This stress on vision implies an awareness of the world as a terrain waiting to be appropriated, which may be reflected in the rise of landscape painting from the sixteenth century on. The rise of the female nude in painting is yet another aspect of this emphasis, by which the female body becomes the object of scrutiny and penetration.[25] Metonymically, 'mother' earth is caught up in this relation to the world. These are all results of a form of knowledge which seeks to traverse the world with its eyes in order to construct its representation (de Certeau, 1975: 246). Seen against this background, the female name 'America', like Florida, Guiana and, pregnant with significance, Virginia, might be seen to invite the thrust of European masculinity. This metaphor is deployed in a variety of rhetorical tropes by colonialist discourse. Virginia connotes both the virgin land awaiting its English suitors and the lack of cultivators and settled occupation by the natives, and (through a remarkable turn by which the settlers identify themselves with the virginity of the land which has to be defended against their, but not 'her', outsiders) provides the justification for marriage of the land to England as a return to the family fold (Hulme, 1985: 17–18).

In Theodore Galle's engraving of 'America' (after J. Stradanus) which stands at the head of the final chapter, the artist depicts Vespucci in the act of discovering a nude female representing America. There is a sharp contrast between Vespucci's image of serenity, his statuesque pose, his controlled hairstyle, his clothing, and the didactic connotations of his attributes (the compass), on the one hand, and the image of America in movement as she rises from her hammock to speak, on the other. Her flowing hair, her nudity and her simplicity are invitingly erotic - an eroticism which Vespucci and his fellow voyagers found it hard to resist.[26] The figures of Vespucci and (the allegory of) America indicate not just a confrontation between two worlds, for there is a lack of symmetry in their relationship. The female is nameless: it is Vespucci who allegorises her by giving her *his own* name in a feminine declension. For Martin Waldseemüller, who had published a Latin translation of Vespucci's *Lettera al Soderini* under the title *Quattuor navigationes* in his 1507 *Cosmographie Introductio*, it was only natural that America should receive this name from its discoverer, 'since both Europe and Asia have been allotted their names from women'. The onomastics of colonial discourse indicate the way in which Europe's representatives are seen to be recreating the world that they discover in their own terms.

The naming activity of Vespucci neglects the values and names of the culture which he encounters. He assumes that their earth is uninscribed,[27] and to fill this lack he obliges the other to accept the term which he imposes. Perhaps the most baroque version of this trope is that found in an anonymous nineteenth-century author:

America is a female form, long, thin, watery, and at the forty-eighth parallel ice-cold. The degrees of latitude are years – woman becomes old at forty-eight.

(cited in Gerbi, 1973: 417)[28]

If Columbus fails to establish his surname as the base reference for the new continent, he is successful in creating an array of names for a number of locations within that continent. The names which Columbus gives to the places that he discovers, applied to the reality he sees before him, are at the same time a commentary on a text, namely, the text of the various authorities (the Bible, Ptolemy, d'Ailly, 'Sir John Mandeville', Marco Polo, Plinius, Piccolomini, etc.) who had told Columbus what he would find long before he witnessed it with his own eyes. We here witness a reversal of the Aristotelian scheme of things: instead of *mimesis* being a correspondence of an image to reality, reality is made to conform to its (pre-existing) image.

In this respect Columbus is no exception to the practice of other travellers. For example, Pierre Gilles d'Albi (1489–1555), an acquaintaince of the better known sixteenth-century cosmographer André Thevet, wrote an account of his travels in the Thracian Bosporos (the strait between the Black Sea and the Gulf of Marmara) in the middle of the century. His route had already been described long before in the (no longer extant) Greek account of the region written by Dionysos of Byzantium in the second century AD. Pierre Gilles obtained a copy of a Latin translation of this work (*De Bosporo Thracio*), and then set out to find the space which corresponded to his guide – the topographical accounts of Dionysos, the toponyms and the legends. In this case, 'the Bosporos only exists in this osmosis by which an actual landscape is confused with its descriptions and where the present serves the resurgence of antiquity' (Jacob, 1987: 68–69). The hermeneutic of Gilles is rigorously textual. If he has problems in squaring his observations with the Latin text of his illustrious predecessor, his method is to resort to other textual sources in the wealth of ancient travel literature and mythology. It is only in the last instance that this mass of literary material is brought to bear on what he actually observes with his own eyes.

Columbus too is aware that toponyms are themselves embedded in other systems of reference. Unlike Adam in the Garden of Eden, Columbus knows that the names that he gives are not the first names. The first island he comes across he calls San Salvador out of deference to his Spanish overlord, but the Indians already had a name for it: Guanahaní (Colón, 1984: 140). So this naming activity is not the inscription of European names on virgin soil. It is a reinscription over an object which has already received the trace of a name from its earlier discoverers. It is moreover a double inscription, since besides the Indian name of Guanahaní, Columbus also refers to it as an island of the *Lucayos* (ibid: 29), the inhabitants of islands which were traditionally situated in the Asiatic East. Thus the island is named on all three registers: European, American and Asiatic. In this respect, it functions as a palimpsest, that parchment on which 'a text superposes itself on another which it does not dissimulate completely, but lets it be seen by transparence' (G. Genette, cited in Rabasa, 1985: 1). The question of the first name, of the *archè*, is dissolved in the an-archic play of *différance* in which the signifiers refer to one another. As we saw in the first section of this chapter, such representations refer to other representations and not to the truth of the represented (cf. Derrida, 1978b).

The relation of the name 'America' to other proper names takes place along a number of paths. First, it is inscribed in a geographical register. The rigid designation of two places can be achieved with a fixed relation between them in terms of measurable distance. When Pierre d'Ailly claimed that India could be reached by sea in a few days under favourable weather conditions, he was relating Europe to India by means of a quantifiable measure of distance, and he thereby encouraged Columbus to undertake his voyage across the Atlantic. Aristoteles shared the opinion that there may be no great distance between Spain and India by the western ocean:

> For this reason those who imagine that the region around the pillars of Hercules joins onto the regions of India, and that in this way the ocean is one, are not, it would seem, suggesting anything utterly incredible.
> (Aristoteles: *On the Heavens* II.XIV.298a)

This view was certainly known to Columbus (Colón, 1984: 217). Indeed, it has been asserted that 'Aristotle's opinion [...] that there may be no great distance between Spain and India by the western ocean was one of the chief causes which sent Columbus on his voyage of discovery' (D. Ross, 1923: 96 n.3). The presence of signs of measurement in such a context helps to produce an effect of reality. The specification of a series, starting with the speaker and ending with the object of discourse, serves to eliminate any kind of alterity from the picture and to suggest that the object can be included within the terms of the speaker's discourse. Measurement thus functions as a reduction of other to self (Hartog, 1980: 347–348).

The naming activity of Columbus is at times capable of making enormous geographical leaps. In Marco Polo he had read that the city of Zaiton was the port for all the ships that arrive from India laden with costly wares and precious stones and pearls (Polo, 1958: 237), which he promptly identifies with a point on Cuba. He proceeds to identify Hispaniola with Quinsay, the treasury of the empire of the Great Khan. But in the process the 1400 miles separating Quinsay from Zaiton have been reduced to the 18 leagues separating Hispaniola from the Cuban Cabo de Alfa y Omega (Gil, 1984: XLI).

Second, besides its place in the geographical register, 'America' could be related to 'Asia' in terms of its fauna. The Aristotelian passage continues:

> They produce also in support of their contention the fact that elephants are a species found at the extremities of both lands, arguing that this phenomenon at the extremes is due to communication between the two.
>
> (Aristoteles, *On the Heavens* II.XIV.298a)

The elephant could serve as a token of the wealth of the Indies. After the penetration of the Greeks into India in the fourth century BC, and thus contemporary with Aristoteles, the elephant had become a symbol of Asia.[29] Although Isidorus of Sevilla noted a dwindling of the elephant population in Africa in his own time (*Etymologiae* XIV.V.12), the beast retained both its African and its Indian connotations into the Middle Ages. It was doubtless these connotations which prompted Columbus to give the name Cabo de Elefante ('Elephant Cape') to a place in La Hispaniola during his first voyage (Colón, 1984: 73), and on the evidence of Bernardo de Ibarra it was during his third voyage that Columbus was presented with a lump of earth on which an elephant's tracks were supposed to be discernible. In line with these associations, the illustrator to de Bry's *America* depicts an (airborne) elephant in the scene of Magellan's triumphant arrival at the strait which was to bear his name.[30]

In fact, it was so easy to place the elephant in America as well as in Africa and Asia that in Johann George Hertel's allegories of the three continents[31] the so-called 'American' scene contains lions and an elephant, while 'Africa' shows natives with feather headdresses and hammocks in the company of an alligator. Clearly the printed text in this case has been set next to the wrong illustration, but the ground had been laid for such printing errors by the way in which America, from its discovery onwards, was given an 'Asiatic' treatment.[32] The printer's error is a *Fehlleistung*.

The parrot could operate in a similar way to the elephant as a symbol. Parrots belong to a symbolic complex which also includes black natives and tropical heat. We can find them associated, for example, in Marco Polo's description of the Indian realm of Quilon, where the heat is so intense that an egg can be boiled simply by placing in one of the rivers for a short time, and where 'everything is different from what it is with us and excels both in size and beauty' (Polo, 1958: 287–288). Mandeville locates a country where there is an abundance of parrots on the way to the land of Prester John. The parrots are called *psitakes* and can talk like humans: 'those that talk well have long broad tongues, and five toes on each foot; those that do not talk at all – or not much – have only three toes' (Mandeville, 1983: 168–169). This geographical connotation explains why Columbus was eager to find parrots in America and to take them back to Spain (Colón, 1984: 80), for they could serve as proof that he had reached his Oriental destination. Moreover, their presence could serve as a sign of the riches in which he was so interested (Todorov, 1982: 28). This placing of the new continent in terms of its fauna offered an alternative to the quantifiable geographical system. In his *De Orbe Novo Decades Octo*, published in 1530, Petrus Martyr de Angleria refers to the Aristotelian text cited above and then goes on to note that

> Seneca and others who were well acquainted with cosmography declare that the distance via the Western sea route from Spain to the shores of India is not great.
>
> (Petrus Martyr, 1966: 39)

In the same passage, he attaches importance to the fact that, although Columbus' opinion on the size of the globe and its navigable parts seems to contradict tradition on some points,

> the parrots [*psittaci*] brought back from there and many other things indicate that these islands have an Indian flavour, whether from nearness or by nature.

In more general terms, the parrot is not so much a symbol of the East as a symbol of the exotic, wherever that may be located. For instance, there is a painting by Jan Mostaert[33] depicting a West Indian landscape in which an expedition (perhaps Coronado's 1540 expedition) routs the local inhabitants. Mostaert's apparent sympathy with what is exotic and primitive[34] leads him to add the monkey and the parrot to what is otherwise a fully European bestiary in this painting. Like the (ethnographically inappropriate) nudity of the Indians, the exotic additions create a landscape which is undeniably an imaginary one.

We can go on adding to the bestiary. Mandeville mentions the presence of rats as big as dogs on the Indian island of Cana; the men catch them with great mastiffs, for cats are too small (Mandeville, 1983: 121–122). These are the giant rats which Columbus finds on his first voyage (Colón, 1984: 59). Similarly, the apes called 'Paul cats' which Marco Polo recorded as one of the marvels of Comorin, a country of India (Polo, 1958: 288), are the *gatos paulos* which Columbus met with in large numbers on the third and fourth voyages (Colón, 1984: 209).

Another instance of iconographical confusion reinforces the point. In Johannes Stradanus' hunting encyclopaedia, *Venationes Ferarum, Avium, Piscium. Pugnae Bestiariorum et Mutuae Bestiarum*, which dates from the end of the sixteenth century, there is a scene of fishing by means of birds on one of the illustrations (number 91) which Karel de Mallery made for the work. As the Latin subscript indicates:

> Fortunate [or fertile] India has a bird resembling a goose, which knows how to catch fish, its neck being tied with a cord. It is trained not to eat its prey, but to bring it to the nearby banks, to disgorge it and to present it to the Indians.

This use of birds for fishing is known from various travel accounts. For example, in his report on his travels to the Great Khan, J. Nieuhof described the use of a bird, the *Louwa*, by the Chinese for fishing (Nieuhof, 1673: 92). The bird described by Nieuhof, as can be seen from the illustration to the text, is a cormorant. This art of fishing by cormorant in China was known to Europeans from the fourteenth century, and recurs in later accounts too.

In the Latin subscript to Stradanus, the textual reference is to India, and indeed most of the 104 scenes in Stradanus' compilation are taken from Africa and the Orient. Iconographically, however, there are two divergences to note by comparison with the Chinese *Louwa*: the bird is not a cormorant but a member of the pelican family; and the Indians depicted by de Mallery are unmistakably *American* Indians, as is shown, for example, by the fact that they wear feather skirts, an iconographical attribute of the American Indian from the discovery of America far into the nineteenth century (Honour, 1979). Perhaps the confusion of Amerindians with Orientals is due to Stradanus' sources, as K. Achilles has suggested in her discussion of the *Venationes* (1982). In leafing through the pages of some missionary account covering travels both to America and to the Orient, Stradanus may have inadvertently become the victim of a continental shift and have attributed to the New World a well-established fishing practice that was only documented, however, for the Orient. Even if modern scholarship has been able to uncover evidence pointing in the direction of the use of birds for fishing in ancient Peru, this only sets the error of Stradanus right after the event.[35]

This interpenetration of Oriental and American themes may be explained in the case of Columbus by the fact that his conviction that he had discovered an Oriental land had an overdetermining effect on his perceptions. However, Columbus was by no means the only one to collude in this continental confusion. This can be seen not only in relation to the continental bestiaries but also in relation to the kinds of mankind. Somewhere between men and beasts certain intermediate categories were to be located. Some authorities had attempted to interpret hybrid monsters such as satyrs as the result of promiscuous mating of humans with animals,[36] but there were also ethnological attempts to explain them. Within the accounts of the so-called Plinian races, to be discussed in Chapter Three, the distant regions of the globe were populated with various monstrous human races: one-eyed people, people who could cover themselves with their ears, dog-headed races, races with enormous feet, headless races and a host of others. References to such races go back to our earliest Greek sources, and the first catalogue of them can be found in Book Seven of the *Historia Naturalis* of Plinius the Elder. They remained popular throughout the Middle Ages, especially through the well-circulated travels of Sir John Mandeville. Most of these races had always carried a certain Oriental flavour and were sometimes known as Wonders of the East. Hence the documentation for the presence of these races on the American continent (discussed in Chapter Four) was yet another 'proof' of the interpenetration of America and the Orient.

If we pass from the monstrous races of mankind to the more regular ethnological accounts and representations, the same continental blurring emerges. A woodcut commissioned by Maximilian I after Hans Burgkmair the Elder (1517–1518), which depicts 'Die Kalikutischen Leut', mixes Oriental motifs with the American motif of the feathered headdress (Honour, 1979). On a plate from de Bry's *America*, which illustrates the public confession of Japanese pilgrims sitting on a scales that hangs in the air, the supposedly Japanese priests are identical to the Aztec priests who, on other plates in de Bry's compilation, engage in human sacrifice (Bucher, 1981: 19). And the well-known example of poetic justice meted out to the Spaniards, in which their greed for gold was literally satisfied until they choked to death, can be traced back to the words spoken to the Caliph of Baghdad: 'Caliph, since I see that you love treasure so dearly, I will give you your own to eat' (Polo, 1958: 53; cf. Mandeville, 1983: 149).

Geographical and ethnological specificity disappear in this ceaseless transposition of elements from one continent to another. In a later chapter we shall see how the continent of Europe, not surprisingly, is not immune to this play of signifiers. For present purposes, it may lead us to look further into the implications of the naming activity in which the New World/America is caught up from the first.

Naming: proper names and impropriety

At first sight, a proper name like 'America' might seem incapable of providing a meaning contrary to that suggested by the word. After all, within the division of signs into natural and conventional signs, the proper name has always occupied a special place. It forms one extreme of an axis leading from the extreme generality of the adjective, which is capable of being applied to a wide variety of nouns, and having at its centre the common noun (Foucault, 1966: 113). The generality of analogic flow, by which a variety of epithets can be applied to a variety of objects, is temporarily halted by the mediation of the proper name, which might be described as interposing an individuating relationship and cutting the macrocosm of analogy up into manageable pieces (Wagner, 1986: 16). As an extreme case, the proper name thus appears to be that which connotes specificity *par excellence*. Todorov places proper names in this perspective when he draws attention to the penchant of Columbus for naming:

Deprived of meaning, they convey mere denotation and not, directly, human communication; they are addressed to nature (to the referent) and not to humans; they are, like indexicals, direct associations between sequences of sound and segments of the world. That part of human communication which interests Columbus is thus precisely that sector of language which, primarily at least, serves only to designate nature.

(Todorov, 1982: 35)

This purely denotative power of proper names is questionable. In the course of his polemic against Lévi-Strauss' views on native writing, Derrida has also had occasion to consider the question of proper names, but his conclusion is very different to that put forward by Todorov. In his remarks on 'The war of the proper names' (1967a: 157–173), Derrida follows Lévi-Strauss in treating proper names as a part of classification, not of naming as such, but his conclusions are more radical. The very use of the proper name, Derrida argues, is its obliteration as a proper name, because:

[...] the proper name has never been possible, except by its functioning within a classification and thus within a system of differences [...]. When, *in consciousness*, the noun *is called* proper, it is already classified and obliterates itself in the act of naming. It is already nothing but a *soi-disant* proper noun.

(Derrida, 1967a: 159–161)

In more general terms, the individuality of the object, that which can be pointed to, is in fact only accessible through generality, universality, ideas, law. The individual case is already encompassed by a system of relations – in the case under consideration, the system of signs (cf. Staten, 1985: 68ff.).

As a result, proper names such as 'America' cannot be seen to occupy a place apart within a system of signs. By their suspension of the absolute vocative, they enter into the system of what Derrida has called *archi-écriture*, a system of *archi-violence* in which the proper of proper names is lost (Derrida, 1967a: 164). Since they do not in fact just point at something, meaning arises not in the supposed difference between words and the objects to which they would refer, but in the difference between words themselves. In other words, the *signifié* of the de Saussurian system is itself a *signifiant*, and the referent of the sign is: the sign. Hence in the case of 'America', the system of mutual referentiality of 'America' and 'Asia' becomes explicable in terms of the sign itself. The representations of 'America' can easily acquire their Oriental colouring or flavour because they refer to other representations and not to the truth of the represented. At the same time, the lack of the properness of proper names like 'America' means that their identity is dependent on imprints from outside. And given the potential diversity of these imprints, of which the European colonialist idiom is only one of a possible diversity of figures which, like a *stylus,* can leave their trace, then the question of European colonialist discourse can be seen as a question of *style.*

There is thus no concrete referent to which the sign 'America' should be supposed to refer. Like other proper names, it is an 'effect of the real', a representation (cf. Spivak, 1985: 149 n.28). The truth of the represented is elided. To paraphrase what was said earlier, drawing on the work of Lyotard, a system of names presents a world – 'America' – and the entities and relations presented by the contexts ('Asiatic', etc.) in which these names occur are fragments of this world.

In associating the question of the reality of 'America' with the linguistic contexts in which it is placed, we are not denying the native American Indians their historicity. Nor by limiting the discussion to the specifically discursive apparatus of an *episteme* do we intend to hide the fact that the general form of the apparatus is both discursive and non-discursive (Foucault, 1980: 197). Instead, we aim to combine an approach to the text which sees it as a 'praxis on whose surface and in whose interstices a universal grammatological problematic is enacted' with an approach which sees in it 'a praxis whose existence is a fact of highly rarefied and differentiated historical power, associated not only with the univocal authority of the author but with a discourse constituting author, text and subject and giving them a very precise intelligibility and effectiveness' (E. Said, 1983: 214).

This combination of Derrida's insights into the ways in which truth becomes inscribed within the play of signification and Foucault's emphasis on the battle about the status of truth reveals the supplementary excesses of colonial power and its productivity. It may help to reveal how a fictional discourse may induce effects of truth (Foucault, 1980: 193). The content of representations like 'America', though, is not reducible to colonial ideology (Osterhammel, 1989).[37] This ideology is the effect of the means of representation and signification. In other words, it is only after the regulatory and displacing division of the true and the false has taken place (and continues to take place) that the field of the 'true' emerges from analysis at all as a visible effect of knowledge/power.

'America' seems to emerge from our analysis as a lack. As a proper name, it lacks a concrete referent; as an effect of the real, it presents itself as lack to a style which is assured of its ability to penetrate the truth. And, to return to the sexual metaphors (but are they just metaphors?) behind the feminine name, its lack serves as invitation and justification of the metaphysical[38] desire of the colonialist thrust.

In the following chapters, the emphasis is on the Old World obsessions which deny to America its own historicity and which reduce its alterity to a familiar form that is accessible to self. On an intellectual plane, this may be a reproduction of the hegemony that is exerted through colonial power. Of course, colonial discourse is constituted by the power/knowledge complex analysed by Foucault and others. However, in the present analysis this side of the issue is put on one side, and the focus is on those aspects of colonial discourse which can be seen as an effect of the play of signification in which America is caught up. So long as Europe continued to see other societies through categories that were never inclusive, it could recognise and assume the heterogeneity of others without putting them into a taxonomical scale. However, when such taxonomical thought and evolutionist theories became the paradigm for the understanding of the other, this shift was reflected in unifying theories with clear colonial implications. This shift has been dated roughly around the sixteenth century by Jara and Magaña (1982), and has been documented for the attitude of the sixteenth-century chroniclers of Tupinamba religion by H. Clastres (1987), while M. Mustapha (1982) has traced its emergence in the work of the sixteenth-century historians of the New World, relating it to developments in cartography. In a different field, M. Harbsmeier (1986b) contrasts the attitude of Hans Staden and other Germans who travelled to the New World in the sixteenth and early seventeenth centuries with that of their successors: while the earlier travellers linked the incomprehensible utterances of the Amerindians with death, the devil and anthropophagy, those of the Enlightenment period were prepared to view them as a language which could be transcribed for Europeans to read.[39]

Other researchers suggest a similar dividing line between medieval and Renaissance conceptions, on the one hand, and Enlightenment conceptions, on the other. In his attack on the Enlightenment 'uniformitarian view of Man', J. Boon, for instance, sees in the pre-Enlightenment views of human variability evidence for an interpretation of the diversity of behaviour and conditions in the New World as part of the same pattern which existed in Europe. The Enlightenment perspective, by contrast, emphasised geographical distance and otherness to enable the New World to function as an exotic antithesis to European culture (Boon, 1982: 27–49). M. Helms supports a similar dichotomy, though she sees the distinction in slightly different terms:

> In the pre-Enlightenment era, I suggest, the New World was accepted conceptually as part of the cosmographically real world of European Christendom in the same sense that the Orient or far distant realms such as Scandinavia or Russia had been accepted as part of the cosmographically real world, i.e. because they were faraway lands where, as a reflection of their distance, demons or fabulous creatures lived.
>
> (Helms, 1988: 230)

On the other hand, the Enlightenment view depreciates the symbolic value of these fabulous creatures, replacing them with 'the cynical ironies of the concept of the "Noble Savage" and the taxonomies of natural historians' (ibid: 231).

Whatever reservations we may entertain about the usefulness of a periodisation in terms of pre-Enlightenment/Enlightenment, a shift of this kind has obvious relevance for the European reception of the discovery of the New World. In what follows, we come time and time again up against the workings of the machinery of the European *logos* which grinds incessantly within its egocentric circles and at the same time witnesses a constant shifting of the lines along which difference is disseminated.

Notes

1. As James Boon notes 'Perhaps anthropology in any society necessarily produces only what that society's internal conditions require it to conceptualize as *other than* itself' (1982: 6).
2. One of the earliest statements of this theme (from the second century AD) can be found in Lucian's dialogue on friendship, in which the Greeks talk and the Skythians act. There is a complementary relationship between the two: the 'barbarian' Skythians cannot speak for themselves, since it is the Greeks who are best at that; but the Skythians master in practice what the Greeks want to express. (This is one of the 'para-anthropological' texts discussed by Harbsmeier, 1986a.)
3. In a similar way, J.-P. Sartre criticised Engels for having tried to change Marx's conception of history from an intelligible process to a scheme corresponding to empirical facts. See Marx and Engels, 1973–, Vol. 6: 482 and Sartre, 1960: 216, and compare the remarks in Derrida, 1967b: 422ff.
4. Needham (1978) has discussed under the name of 'primary factors' such constraints as opposition, number and colour.
5. The relation between phenomenology and epistemology, and the break with a Heideggerian intentionality which the position adopted here implies, derive from the work of Michel Foucault: see the pertinent remarks in Deleuze (1986: 116–117).
6. For instance, in the description of Rouen in *Madame Bovary*, what matters is not *Rouen* itself but *reality* – Rouen loses its specificity and becomes interchangeable with other cities, in that they are in themselves insignificant; their significance as places (connoting reality) is subordinated to their significance as pointers towards, or indices of, the reality they come to denote (Bal, 1984: 91). And if the choice of *Madame Bovary* seems *recherché* to some readers, it is worth recalling A.I. Richards' account of the way in which Malinowski's work seemed lively and stimulating and enabled the reader to visualise himself/herself in the field; 'Richards read Malinowski as Emma Bovary read novels' (Boon, 1982: 11).
7. A three-leafed clover from H. Bünting's *Itinerarium sacrae scripturae* (Wittenberg, 1588) is illustrated as Abb. 1 in Kohl (ed.), 1982.
8. Derrida also refers here to an interesting passage from Kant's *Anthropologie in pragmatischer Hinsicht* on the notion of invention.
9. First printed (in Latin) under the title *Mundus novus* late in 1503 or early in 1504, probably in Florence, to be followed by numerous printed editions. It was further translated into five modern languages and had run into 30 printed editions by 1515.
10. Superioribus diebus satis ample tibi scripsi de reditu meo ab novis illis regionibus [...] quasque novum mundum appellare licet. Quando apud maiores nostros nulla de ipsis fuerit habita cognitio et audientibus omnibus sit novissima res (Vespucci, 1984: 88).
11. The term came to designate both the peasant utopia of the land of Cockaigne in the anonymous *Capitolo* dating from the mid-sixteenth century, and the sober urban utopia of Anton Francesco Doni's *Un mondo nuovo* of 1552 (Ginzburg, 1980: 81–86). For the interaction between the theme of the land of Cockaigne and the travels of discovery of the sixteenth century, see Boiteux (1987). In the seventeenth century, I. Burchoorn wrote a work entitled *Nieuwe Werelt vol Gecken, Opgepronckt Met een selfsbedriegelijck Onverstandt door Den belagchelijcken Duyvel* (The Hague, 1641), which links the name of the New World to the European traditions on fools going back to Sebastian Brandt's *Ship of Fools*.
12. Ce pays d'Amérique auquel, comme je déduirai, tout ce qui s'y voit, soit en la façon de vivre des habitants, forme des animaux, et en général en ce que la terre produit étant DISSEMBLABLE de ce que nous avons en Europe, Asia et Afrique, peut bien être appelé monde NOUVEAU à notre égard.
13. Pagden (1982: 11 and n.8) provides other examples of this kind from the work of

Gonzalo Fernández de Oviedo. The author's very brief chapter on 'The problem of recognition' (ibid: 10–14) is full of suggestive observations in this respect.

14. Through, as Pagden (1982: 5) points out, the thought described by Foucault is only that of a very few; most people in the seventeenth and the beginning of the eighteenth centuries were still searching for the 'restrictive figures of similitude' in human behaviour.

15. In addition to many drawings of plants and animals, Oviedo prepared at least 20 ethnographic illustrations relating to Hispaniola, Central America, Peru and Patagonia. Their originality is certain; indeed, no previous models are known for any of them (Sturtevant, 1976: 424). The 'Plinius of the late 16th century', Ulisse Aldrovandi, similarly planned to send an army of writers *and painters* to compile a vast encyclopaedic work on the New World (see his *Discorso naturale* of 1572/73, reproduced in S. Tugnoli Pattaro, 1981: 173ff.).

16. These paintings are reproduced and discussed in more detail elsewhere: see Mason, 1989c.

17. An important aspect of this work of colonial classification is the theme of intrusion. As Hulme notes (1986: 53), the group of natives which shows itself to be the most aggressive (i.e. the most resistant to colonial domination) is designated as the group of intruders with respect to a more docile group. The gains for colonial ideology are obvious: in carrying out the task of colonial expansion, the colonisers can use the excuse that they are setting things right again by expelling the intruders and restoring the security of the more docile, 'autochthonous' group.

18. Illustration in Vandenbroeck, 1987: colour plate I, catalogue no. 8; Mason, 1989c, ill.10.

19. As proved by the penance of a bread and water diet laid down by Burchard of Worms around the year 1000 for those who believed in Wild Women [*agrestes feminae*] (cf. Lecouteux, 1982, I: 18).

20. Colin, for example, sees the disappearance of the Wild Man from the visual arts and literature by the end of the sixteenth century as a sign that the world was 'gradually more attuned to reality' (1987: 29).

21. The same process is at work in the first European accounts of the Hindu gods. Ludovico di Varthema's description of the idol known as Deumo, who was worshipped by the King of Calicut, dating from between 1503 and 1508, owed far more to European demonological conceptions than to perception of Indian gods (Mitter, 1977: 16ff.). In its impact on later travellers, Varthema's description supplanted what they actually saw from their own experience.

22. The framework in use on the European continent was itself caught up in a process of restructuring. A case in point is the reinterpretation of the Biblical episode of the sorceress of Endor (*I Kings* 28): while the early Christian fathers voiced various opinions as to her status, by the end of the Middle Ages necromancy and black magic had become synonymous, and she was unequivocally described and portrayed as a witch (Schmitt, 1987).

23. The number of Vespucci's voyages is uncertain and their chronology is muddled: the accounts presented in the *Mundus novus*, in the *Lettera al Soderini*, and in the three letters to Lorenzo di Pierfrancesco de' Medici (dated July 1500, June 1501 and 1502) do not tally.

24. In a polemic against the work of Norbert Elias, H.-P. Duerr (1985: 52ff.) argues the case for an awakening of all the senses, but especially the sense of vision, in the middle of the fourteenth century.

25. See Ginzburg (1986: 152) for the emergence of vision as the privileged erotic sense in the sixteenth century.

26. For Vespucci's obsessive preoccupation with the naked Indian women, see the

voyeuristic remarks in Vespucci, 1984: 100, 104, 134–135. Of course, Vespucci puts the blame on the ceaseless and insatiable sexual longings of the women. I return to this theme in the last chapter of the present work and elsewhere (forthcoming b).

27. This is implied in the designation *terra nullius* to be found on some maps.

28. The anonymous author may have been a follower of the Schellingian Henrik Steffens. The text is cited by Humboldt in a letter to Varnhagen von Ense of 28 April 1841.

29. On a set of playing cards from 1644, the four continents are represented by female personifications seated on chariots drawn by animals. 'America' is drawn by two armadillos, 'Africa' by lions, 'Europe' by horses and 'Asia' by elephants. See Kohl (ed.), 1982: 32 and 330 [8/15].

30. The elephant is in fact in the grips of a giant bird. Wittkower (1977: 93–96) has convincingly shown the origins of the scene in oriental conceptions of the bird known as the 'roc'.

31. Illustrated in Kohl (ed.), 1982, ills. 185 and 186.

32. On another eighteenth-century allegory of America, by Johann Wolfgang Baumgartner, we find in one painting not only the alligator, but also a camel and an elephant's tusk, which point to an African provenance.

33. Now in the Frans Hals Museum in Haarlem, the Netherlands.

34. This attitude to the exotic has been compared to the sympathy for the primitive displayed in the paintings of Piero di Cosimo (Snyder, 1976).

35. For more details on the sources, illustrations and a fuller discussion, see P. Mason (1987a).

    In his *Histoire Générale des Antilles habitées par les françois* of 1667, Jean-Baptiste du Tertre mentions the use of birds for fishing among the Island Caribs and explicitly compares it with the use made of cormorants elsewhere (cited in: Cárdenas Ruíz, 1981: 464). Another seventeenth-century writer on the Caribbean, S. de la Borde, attributed the alleged melancholic nature of the Caribs to fishing (ibid: 511). But it remains uncertain how reliable such authorities are as ethnographic records. (I am grateful to Edmundo Magaña for bringing these texts to my attention.)

36. Piero di Cosimo (1461–1521) had interpreted hybrid monsters such as satyrs as the result of promiscuous mating of humans with animals (Panofsky, 1962: 55 n.60).

37. It is for this reason that stereotypes of the other cannot be reduced to the effects of the colonial or imperialist thrust. As Boon points out (1982: 280 n.10), the Dutch, for example, were well aware of the differences between Hindu and Islamic societies as well of the differences between Hindu and Islamic societies as well of the differences of both types *vis-à-vis* Dutch society. Moreover, these Eastern societies in turn produced stereotypes of each other. The implications of this for a possible distinction between ethnocentrism and eurocentrism are discussed in Chapter Seven.

38. Compare Derrida's remarks on the sexual politics of metaphysics in his *Eperons: Les Styles de Nietzsche* (1987a), as well as my notes on de Sade and America (forthcoming b).

39. Duchet (1985: 221) has suggested that the study of kinship relations, pioneered in the work of Morgan, marked a break with such Enlightenment conceptions, in that the catalogue of kinship relations could be seen as equivalent to the art of writing by which the West created its own conception of history.

2 Distribution of boiled parts among women and children in Brazil

Source: Th. de Bry, *Americae III*, Frankfurt, 1592. Reproduced with permission of the University Library, Amsterdam.

Chapter two

Popular culture and the internal other

When faced with the task of classifying and assimilating the unfamiliar, Europe was caught up in a double movement. On the one hand, it could fall back upon traditional representations in order to accommodate the new. These represent-ations then served as parameters by which to organise the initially refractory material. The self of Europe could thereby reduce and assimilate the other that it encountered outside Europe. On the other hand, Europe had its own internal other, and this it could project onto the New World outside the confines of Europe. The encounter with the New World thus served as the point of articul-ation of the demands of the European unifying *logos* with the external projection of European fantasies, fears and desires (Kohl, 1981: 19).

In the following chapter we shall concentrate on the tradition relating to non-European exotic peoples, the so-called Plinian races. They are other to Europe in their distant location. But another main source of inspiration for the construction of America was firmly planted within the confines of Europe, and it is to this tradition that we now turn.

The images discussed in this chapter are all products of a process of exclusion: witches, Wild Men, madmen and animals are aspects of the European self that self cannot tolerate. They are caught up in the play of alterity and marked as other through the work of difference. Todorov introduces his analysis of the discovery of America in a similar way:

I want to speak about the discovery of *other* by *self*. The subject is immense. It is hardly formulated as a general question before it breaks down into different categories and in multiple, infinite directions. We can discover the others in ourselves and realise that we are not homogeneous and are radically foreign to all that is not self: *je est un autre*. But others are egos too: subjects like me, separated and distinguished from me only by my point of view, which places them all *over there* and me *here*. I can conceive these others as an abstraction, as an instance of the psychical configuration of every individual, as Other, other or another in relation to *me*; or as a concrete social group to which we do not belong. This group may be internal to society: women for men, the rich for the poor, the mad for the 'normal'; or it may be external, another society, near or far: beings closely resembling us culturally, morally and historically; or else unknown beings, strangers whose language or customs are incomprehensible for me, so strange that, – at the limit – I hesitate to recognise that we belong to the same species.

(Todorov, 1982: 11)

Todorov sees his choice of the discovery of America as an option for the *external, distant* society. In this chapter, on the contrary, we shall see how the New World is articulated with the other that is *internal* to *Europe's own society.*

Inevitably, the European self is amenable to further analysis in terms of categories like 'learned culture' and 'popular culture'. *Le savoir de gens*, as Foucault calls it, is defined as:

A particular, local, regional knowledge, a differential knowledge incapable of unanimity and which owes its force only to the harshness with which it is opposed by everything surrounding it.

(Foucault, 1980: 82)

'Popular culture' is thus definable in negative terms. It refers to the lack of a legitimate status in the culture of the traditional society for a specific set of practices. Foucault's primary concern may be seen as the act and criteria of exclusion, of what has to be excluded from self and what thereby comes to occupy the place of other. This process of exclusion is also one of secretion: popular culture is the product of a constant drawing and redrawing of the boundary between popular and learned culture. There is thus no inherent fixity in the elements which might come to find themselves on one or other side of the boundary. They could in the course of time change hands from one class or stratum to another. For instance, while learned opinion persecuted witches in the fifteenth century, and thus gave credibility to their existence, it should not be forgotten that the dominant view of the Church from the tenth to the fourteenth centuries was that belief in witches itself was a superstition that deserved to be punished (Hirst, 1985).

The terms 'learned' and 'popular' refer to the forces at work in the battle over knowledge/power, and not to the cultural products themselves. Most of these are in fact composite, constantly shifting forms in which elements from learned and popular culture are combined. While Cohn set out to reconstruct the history of the witches' sabbat and arrived at the conclusion that the sabbat was a revival of ancient, negative stereotypes that had been projected onto various groups in the past - Jews, early Christians and medieval heretics (Cohn, 1975), Ginzburg sees the image of the witches' sabbat as a composite formation; he distinguishes in it both popular and learned elements, and goes on to claim that 'the emergence of this compromise forms a good example of the interrelations between learned and popular culture in preindustrial Europe' (Ginzburg, 1984: 40, cf. Ginzburg, 1989: passim).[1]

Wild Men and Wild Women

We begin with an example to indicate the difficulties of providing a visual imagery for popular beliefs which lacked points of reference in the world of the educated classes. European popular belief speaks of the Wild Horde, first recorded in Ordericus Vitalis' *Ecclesiastic History* of ca. 1140. In January 1091 a priest of St. Aubin de Bonneval was walking at night when he heard a noise like that of an army on the march. A giant armed with a huge club appeared, followed by a crowd of men and women who were subject to various torments. The priest saw in this crowd some Ethiopians, women, priests and soldiers. This is a version of the widespread European myth of the wild hunt or wild army, in which the dead appear at night in a noisy group, led by a goddess (Perchta, Holda, Diana, Hekate) or a male figure (Herlechinus). The later development of this myth was considerably influenced by the new ideas on purgatory which began to gain concrete form in clerical circles in the second half of the twelfth century (Le Goff, 1981), and at an even later stage the horde of wandering dead became transformed into the inquisitorial image of the witches' sabbat (Ginzburg, 1981; Duerr, 1985: 5–6 and *passim*).

One of the Strasbourg sermons of Geiler van Kaisersberg, which were collected under the title *Die Emeis*, deals with the Furious Horde. Since the Horde, despite its borrowings from long-established ideas on a community of the living and the dead,[2] was a relatively new phenomenon, there was no hallowed iconographical tradition on which artists could draw to illustrate the *familia Herlechini*. In the first edition of *Die Emeis* (Strasbourg, 1516), the sermon on the Horde is accompanied by an engraving of a satyr, Silenus and Bacchus.[3] For the second edition of *Die Emeis* (Strasbourg, 1517), this illustration was replaced by one[4] showing a wagon load of fools (Ginzburg, 1983: 45-47).

This example shows the difficulty facing artists who for the first time had to depict what had not been illustrated before.[5] They could fall back on to traditional images that originally belonged in a different context, as in the case of these two illustrations from *Die Emeis,* and transpose them to the new setting in an act of *bricolage*. In the case of the sermon on the Horde, the artist had to portray something that was new. The choice was made out of a pool of various available European images which had in common the fact that they belong to the representations of Europe's others.

The illustrations to *Die Emeis* indicate a certain degree of mutual interchangeability between the image of the fool and that of the Wild Man. Besides these images, the European Middle Ages were also familiar with the image of the wandering beggar and with that of the peasant. Though these images belong to distinct (but at times overlapping) genres, they have in common their role as the negative self-definition of European non-popular culture. In an age when culture was hard to define, but when its boundaries were being drawn more and more tightly (the process described in detail by Norbert Elias), those in Europe who saw themselves as the bearers of culture defined themselves and the culture they defended in a way resembling that of the photographic negative: by portraying everything that they were *not*, they created – by antithesis – an implicit image of what they in fact *were* – or rather, thought themselves to be.[6] The behaviour which was no longer tolerated in the upper echelons of society was extruded from them and attributed to their social subordinates (Vandenbroeck, 1987).[7] As we shall see, the cultures of America were thus defined in the eyes of the European discoverers as the very non-existence of social institutions and cultural elements. To a certain extent, they appeared as an ensemble of negations (Kohl, 1987: 69).

The giant armed with a club is the iconographical type of the Wild Man. In fact, the earliest, tenth-century references to this tradition refer to Wild *Women* (Burchard of Worms), who appear to men, have sex with them and then vanish again (Lecouteux, 1982, I: 18). The literary evidence for the Wild Man mainly post-dates the twelfth century, and the first artistic representations date from the middle of the following century, rising to a period of particular popularity from the second half of the fourteenth century (Bernheimer, 1952: 21; Vandenbroeck, 1987: 8). By the end of the sixteenth century this wave of popularity had died out in Europe, perhaps because of the monopoly of images of the Wild Man as images of the American Indian by that time.

Any definition of the Wild Man is arbitrary and ethnocentric, for it is the very essence of this figure to articulate the relation between a specific society and that society's vision of the other (Le Goff, 1985: 166). The contours of the Wild Man are thus as fluid and intangible as those of the other.[8] Given the mediatory function of this figure, it is not surprising that we find Wild Men from the Epic of Gilgamesh (Enkidu) and the Homeric Odyssey (the Kyklops) onwards. The *silvestres homines* of the Greco-Roman tradition were thought to live in the woods and mountains far removed from the open spaces and plains on which the activities of rational men took place. They had as their companions various woodland gods and demi-gods: fauns, centaurs, satyrs, Silvanus and Silenus. The etymological link between forest and savage (*silva* and *silvaticus* in Latin, *Wald* and *Wild* in German[9]) directly connects the lack of civilisation to the woodland residence of the Wild Men. The opposition in terms of inner/outer which this implies is firmly rooted in the Indo-European heritage (Benveniste, 1969, I: 311–314). Moreover, it is one of the two axes (the other being upper/lower)[10] by which medieval civilisation tended to classify its cosmos (Le Goff, 1985: 134). The inner/outer opposition served to articulate the distinction between self and other in terms of the domestic inner world and the untamed, wild outside world.

In view of the way in which the image of the Wild Man and Wild Woman served to relate self to other, it is easy to understand a certain degree of contamination in the image of the Wild Man under the influence of the exotic, non-European monstrous human races which were also others in opposition to self. Both European peasants and exotic, non-European gypsies could serve as the internal negative self-definition of the European upper classes. The term 'heathen' could cover both European Wild Men (as well as peasants, gypsies and beggars) and exotic races from abroad. The European and exotic traditions meet in the *Mabinogion,* where there is a black, one-eyed and one-footed Wild Man (Bernheimer, 1952: 31). Similarly, just as we find certain saints associated with the exotic dog-headed Cynocephali (see Chapter Three), so we find a legend of Chrysostomos in which the Pope becomes a European Wild Man and only by miraculous divine intervention retraces his steps to civilised life to become a saint (Colin, 1987). Sometimes the text follows the European pattern while the illustration follows the exotic models: thus in the *Apollonius von Tyrland* dating from around 1300, the text presents Kolkan as a Wild Man, but the miniature in the Heidelberg manuscript depicts a dog-headed figure with a boar's tusks (Lecouteux, 1982, II: 101–102). In Thomas of Cantimpré's *Liber de natura rerum,* the *homines silvestres* are located in the Orient, indicating a similar (con)fusion of European and exotic themes. There is a comparable juxtaposition of the theme of the Wild Man with an exotic location in a tapestry which combines exotic elements (camel, oriental landscape) with two hairy wild men (Vandenbroeck, 1987: 137).

From the fourteenth century onward there is also contamination with the figure of the madman, who is depicted from the twelfth century as an ugly and deformed naked man with long hair, armed with a club as the symbol of his brutishness, living in a meaningless world without redemption, his lawless life devoted to gluttony, luxury and felony (Blum, 1983).[11] Iconographically, there is a marked increase in interest in the fool around the end of the fifteenth and the beginning of the sixteenth centuries (Vandenbroeck, 1987: 56), and it is in this period that the congruence between the figures of the Wild Man and the madman can be seen in the illustration copied from the *Ship of Fools* for use in the 1517 edition of *Die Emeis* (cf. Pleij, 1979: 146).

Despite the variety of sub-types which lie behind the image of the Wild Man and Wild Woman, the vagueness of the contours and the arbitrariness of any single definition of the Wild Man, there was a tendency towards a more rigid definition and a tightening up of the tradition in the years preceding Columbus' voyage (Vandenbroeck, 1987: 8).[12] For the main type established in this period we can follow Bernheimer (1952: 1ff.) in seeing the presence of one or more of the following elements as the main, though not exclusive, iconographical means of identifying the Wild Man and the Wild Woman:[13] long hair;[14] hair covering the body except for the face, feet, hands and the breasts of the female;[15] human and animal traits;[16] nudity, or clad only in animal skins; a heavy club or tree as a weapon.[17]

For a physical portrait of such a being we can quote the composite figure of the giant herdsman in the *Yvain* of Chrétien de Troyes (lines 276–285): he is a peasant who looks like a Moor, he is extremely ugly and hideous, and is seventeen feet tall. His backbone is long, but twisted and hunched. His forehead is wider than two *espanz* (i.e. two hand-spans), a detail which serves to stress his reality, since he can be measured in a recognisable way. The portrait is further composed of metonymic animal comparisons: his head is bigger than that of a horse or any other animal, he has the ears of an elephant, the eyes of an owl, the nose of a cat, the mouth of a wolf and the teeth of a wild boar. Contrary to appearance, however, he is human and is able to speak.[18]

The Wild Man has ambiguous connotations.[19] On the negative side, Wild Men were creatures who lurked in woodlands and mountain passes ready to seize upon the unwary traveller, and they were a continual threat to the civilisation of the cities. Their association with the fauna of the woods tended to give them an animal quality, as if birds of a feather always flock together. Their mode of hunting and gathering set them apart from the sedentary agriculture of civilised society and brought them close to the life of the peasant (Le Goff, 1977: 131–144). Iconographically, we can see this in the association of the Wild Man with the peasant on the north portal of the thirteenth century church of Notre Dame in Semur-en-Auxois (Bernheimer, 1952: 39), as well as in some of the features of the Wild Man of Chrétien, such as his bent back. The existence of a diet of raw vegetables and meat bring them close to bestiality. Insatiability and lack of discrimination characterise both their dietary and their sexual behaviour. The latter is a salient feature in a number of accounts. For instance, in the Alexandros legend, Alexandros tests the humanity of a Wild Man he meets by stripping a young girl in his presence to see how he reacts. The Wild Women may be assigned a similarly voracious sexual appetite: a night with Ruel la Forte (the wife of the giant Feroz in the *Wigalois*) is enough to age a man prematurely (Lecouteux, 1982, II: 103). In this respect the Wild Woman was a match for her male counterpart. This might also be illustrated by two figures among the hundred and ten snowmen which adorned the streets of Brussels in the cold winter of 1511: a Wild Man and a Beguine. The latter were noted for their lasciviousness, and the pairing of the two types is a fitting match for what had become symbols of unbridled male and female lust. Who could be a better candidate to watch over the *lollepot* (brazier/vagina) of the Beguine than her male counterpart, the Wild Man (Pleij, 1988: 92–93)?

Although it comes from a later period than the rest of our sources, it is worth looking briefly at the legend of an eighteenth-century Wild Man, Blaise Ferrage, for the persistence of these themes. According to the report in the *Mercure de France* for 1783, Blaise Ferrage was a mason who was small but very strong. He was dark-skinned, vicious and a sexual menace. Moreover, he was rumoured to rub a special herb into his hair to give himself a Samson-like strength. At the age of twenty-two he retired to the Auré mountains, where he lived in a cave like a bear.[20] He raped passing girls and women and then proceeded to cut off their breasts and thighs and to eat their intestines and liver (Gaignebet and Lajoux, 1985: 242–244). In his pigmentation, habitat, sexual mores and anthropophagy, Blaise Ferrage is a true descendant of the medieval Wild Men.[21]

On the positive side, the Wild Man is considered by some to be capable of becoming civilised, and the taming of the Wild Man was a popular theme in the century preceding the discovery of the New World. He could serve as a symbol of an idyllic life of freedom and happiness, unconstrained by the bonds of civilisation. In this respect the Wild Man could appeal to the nobility which was still supporting traditional rural values against those of the new urban civilisation, and the combination of savagery, hunting and the exotic was exalted in contrast to the domesticated, familiar life of peasants and pastoralists (cf. Pouchelle, 1981). His association with the beasts of the forest could have positive as well as negative connotations, for he was also a master of beasts, able to hunt them and to utilise the various fauna and flora of the forest for his own ends. As a repository of (folk) wisdom, like the Centaur Phoinix before him, he could thus come to share some of the prestige of those other inhabitants of the deserts and forests of the Middle Ages, the hermits (Le Goff, 1985: 72). Indeed, in some contexts he even appears as a supernatural helper (ibid: 167), like the Wild Man whom Alexandros begged to consult the oracle trees of the sun and the moon, or like the modern shaman (Taussig, 1987).

Late medieval representations reflect this ambiguous status. A print by Master bxg dating from the last quarter of the fifteenth century, depicting a Wild Man and Wild Woman with two wild children, was interpreted as a depiction of Adam and Eve by nineteenth-century print connoisseurs because of the idyllic life evoked by the print (Filedt Kok, 1985: 196). On a number of prints from the same period by Martin Schongauer, Wild Men and Wild Women supporting coats of arms are depicted in similarly idyllic poses (ibid: 179). In contemporary prints of Wild Men and Wild Women by the Master of the Amsterdam Cabinet, they are completely at home in their natural surroundings as they ride on stags or unicorns. Incidentally, the unicorn itself can convey positive and negative values: as an unmistakable phallic symbol, it evokes the aggressive sexuality of the Wild Man, but the legend that the unicorn could be tamed only by a virgin suggests a view of the Wild Man in which he is at least capable of being domesticated (ibid: 144–145).

The prints on which Wild Men or Wild Women support a shield bearing a coat of arms may be intended to suggest that the Wild Men convey extra strength to the family whose arms they are supporting. At the same time, these pictures can be seen as symbolic expressions of the taming or domestication of the wild by the West. In a New World setting, the sixteenth-century façade of Casa del Montejo in Mérida, Mexico, and the Wild Men supporting the arms of Charles V at Tlaxcala (Bernheimer, 1952: 180–185) are rather symbols of the western domination of the New World. The negative portrayal of the New World in the early representations could serve the interests of a colonialist attitude, which was only too ready to domesticate the continent and to tame the wildness of its inhabitants. In this sense, the portrayals with the coat of arms may be seen as a piece of wishful thinking, if not a confirmation of geopolitical practice.

The appeal of the North American Indian as Noble Savage to those who had become disenchanted with European civilisation in the Enlightenment has been amply documented (e.g. Kohl, 1981; Sheehan, 1980: ch. 1). For the period immediately before and after the discovery in 1492, however, it is the European image of the Wild Man, with its positive and negative characteristics, which influences European perceptions and representations of the New World.[22] In fact,

47

this influence is overwhelming. We find a more or less classic description of the Wild Man in Columbus' picture of Indians whom he encountered during his first voyage:

> ...They found certain men with bows and arrows [...] and asked one of them to come and speak with the Admiral [...]. He was more ugly in appearance than the others that he had seen. His face was painted with charcoal [...]; his hair was very long, gathered and tied behind, bound up with parrot feathers, and he was as naked as the others. The Admiral assumed that he was one of the Caribs who eat men [...].
>
> (Colón, 1984: 114)

The earliest portrayal of American Indians is to be found on the woodcut frontispiece to the metric version of Columbus' letter by Giuliano Dati (*La lettera dell isole che ha trovato nuovamente il Re di Spagna*) of 1493. The scene is portrayed as an episode in a romance, with King Ferdinand II in the foreground and a mass of naked men and women on land. Both the men and the women are naked and have long hair. The fact that the men are bearded is not in accordance with ethnographical reality, however: borrowed from the iconography of the European Wild Man, it is a sign of the fact that, from the first, the European representations of America were to be shaped in accordance with European conventions.[23] Indeed, it is the astonishment of the Europeans at the Amerindians' lack of body hair which reveals their preconceptions: they had expected to find the hairy Wild Men of the European tradition (Gerbi, 1973: 73).

This woodcut was copied for the 1495 edition of Dati's poem and, in reverse, for the frontispiece to the first edition of Vespucci's *Lettera delle isole nuovamente trovate* (also known as the letter to Soderini), published in 1504–1505 in Florence. Eighteen of the thirty editions of Vespucci's letters that appeared before 1516 are illustrated, and, as Susi Colin has recently shown in detail (1987), both the descriptions in the text and the illustrations depicting the population of the New World in these editions show a number of qualities characteristic of the Wild Man and Woman of the European pictorial and literary tradition. If we wonder why Vespucci was astonished that none of the Indian women had flabby breasts (Vespucci, 1984: 104, 135), this needs to be seen against the background of the European representations of the Wild Woman with hanging breasts, as in the image of Luxuria in the porch of the twelfth-century church of St. Pierre, Moissac (Bernheimer, 1952: 39). Vespucci stresses the lack of body hair of the American Indians, but hairiness was not a necessary attribute of the Wild Man.[24] The bow and arrow of the Indians (Vespucci, 1984: 102) is an alternative to the stout club within the European tradition too, though it may carry connotations of inferiority (Lestringant, 1987b: 483; Le Goff, 1985: 157–161). As for the sexual advances made by the Wild Woman, these are illustrated in the woodcut from Grüninger's 1509 edition of Vespucci showing a young member of the crew who is solicited by a group of native women, while another woman stands behind him with a club ready to fell him (Vespucci, 1984: 164–165; illustrated in Colin, 1987: 14). The text of Vespucci also relates the use of venomous insects and spices by Indian women to enlarge the penises of their mates (Vespucci, 1984: 100), once again a sign of the sexual lasciviousness assigned to the European Wild Women, as well as referring to the power of European witches to cause impotence in males (Kohl, 1987: 69).

The woodcut showing the attack on the young Spaniard is one of a set depicting the cannibalism of the Indians which were specially designed for the 1509 German translation of Vespucci's letters published by Johannes Grüninger in Strassburg.[25] The second depicts a group of two men and a woman with child, which in their harmony recall the idyllic wild family depicted by the Master bxg; to their right a man is shown urinating in public without any embarrassment. In the background a man is engaged in butchering, what are unmistakably, human limbs on a chopping block, while a woman looks on and caresses herself. This woodcut combines the two views of the Wild Man: the idyllic family life is contrasted with the bestiality of a cannibal diet. Urination in public seems to occupy an intermediate position between the two extremes, for though explicitly condemned by Vespucci in the text (Vespucci, 1984: 134), it might be seen as an expression of both lack of civilisation and a freedom from the bounds of civilisation, a double function which it also carries in depictions of the European peasant.

The positive and negative views, with certain qualifications, pervade the early representations of the Amerindians, which Kohl has labelled 'zwischen Verteufelung und Idealisierung' (1987: 86).[26] In the coloured woodcut to the 1505 Leipzig edition of Vespucci the American Indians are not cannibals, but in general their cannibalism is stressed.[27] A woodcut from a broadsheet of 1505–1506, probably printed by Johann Froschauer in Augsburg, depicts American Indians with feather headdresses and feather skirts[28] standing around a wooden construction from which human limbs hang 'as we hang up hams', as Vespucci wrote (1984: 102). Two figures and the severed human head and arm are borrowed from it for a scene in the description of both Vespucci's voyage and that of Hans Springer to the East published by Jan van Doesborch in Antwerp around 1520 (Honour, 1979: 271). If we compare these family scenes with, for example, the idyllic life of a wild family in a cave from a manuscript illumination of around 1500 (Colin, 1987: 27), we note that the addition of attributes of cannibalism gives the American illustrations a grim note that is missing from the European images.

The way in which printers transposed illustrations from one context to another may be seen to have had a conservative influence on the European reaction to the discovery of America, for they invariably translated the New World into Old World terms (cf. Hirsch, 1976; T.R. Adams, 1976). At the same time, their borrowings led to a lack of specificity. The repetition of one virtually unaltered image to represent Damascus, Ferrara, Mantua and Milan in the woodcuts which Wohlgemut made for Hartmann Schedel's *Nuremberg Weltchronik* (1493), or the depiction of Athens as a typically German city in the same work, implies that none of these images need correspond to a specific location (Gombrich, 1959: 60).[29] Or rather, it implies that was what at issue was the delineation of a single, common culture (that of Western Europe) in contradistinction to the non-European rest of the world. Hence the lack of specificity did not particularly disturb the illustrators, as is evident from the warning appended by de Bry to the plate illustrating the departure of Benzoni from Sevilla: as the engraver did not have a correct image of the town of Sevilla at hand, he 'has in stead drawn the town of some seaport or other after his own invention'. The same point has been made for sixteenth-century images of Bali. In the first South Asianised images of the island, it was seen as a mere extension of the Indian continent. What was of primary importance was to distinguish Bali from Holland or Portugal or anything else Western European readers were likely to measure it against. The representations were tightened only when they became ambiguous, when they appeared to confuse two forms – Bali and Hindu India – that according to newly emerging criteria were eventually conceived as distinct (Boon, 1977: 18).

The same process can be detected in the printing of texts themselves. Commenting on chapbooks from the first half of the sixteenth century, Chartier notes:

> The same text successively recounts the death of Marguerite de la Rivère, executed at Padua in December 1596, that of Catherine de la Critonnière, executed in the same town in September 1607, again that of Marguerite de la Rivère executed at Padua (but this time in December 1617), and lastly the same heroine executed at Metz in November 1623.
>
> (Chartier, 1984)

In transposing European images to a new setting, the artists often inserted them in new contexts where the original connotations jarred with the new setting, introducing, whether deliberately or not, an element of irony.

This irony is evident in the portrayal of the poles of the ambivalent attitude to the New World: paradise and purgatory. When Jacob Winter was looking for woodcuts for his Low German translation of the Vespucci letters (Magdeburg, 1506), he combined an image of King Solomon and a scene depicting the expulsion of Adam and Eve from the Garden of Eden, which had appeared as separate woodcuts in Martin Brandis' *Van der clage on ansprake de Belyal*, to produce a composite title page representing the naked people of the New World and the Portuguese king (Colin, 1987: 25–26). Perhaps Winter selected the woodcut of Adam and Eve only because he needed a representation of a naked couple. But he may have had the intention of thereby suggesting that the inhabitants of the New World were living in a terrestrial paradise, as Vespucci and Columbus both called it. Whatever his intentions may have been, we are faced with the fact that the use of a depiction of Adam and Eve was not considered incompatible with the requirements of a New World context by the readership for which Winter's book was intended.

Culinary, religious and sexual perversion

A similar transposition takes us back not to the Garden of Eden but to purgatory.[30] In the woodcuts illustrating the marvellous travels of the Irish monk Brendan we find one (in the 1499 Strasbourg edition of *Die wunderbare Meerfahrt des heiligen Brandan* printed by Matthis Hüpfuff) depicting the island where Brendan saw human forms walking over the sea, while they were alternately tormented with heat and cold. These he discovered to be the souls of servants who had kept the food that was to be distributed among the poor for themselves.[31] Seven years later, the identical woodcut was used to illustrate the Strasburg German and Latin editions of the letter from Vespucci's third voyage (*Von den nüwen Insulen vnd Landen so yetz kürtlichen erfunden synt durch den Künig von Portugall*). Once again, whatever the intentions of the printer may have been in recycling a woodcut in a different context, it is significant that readers of his text were expected to have had no difficulty in supposing that the inhabitants of the newly discovered continent of America bore a resemblance to the sinners who were now located in a place which closely resembles the European view of what purgatory was like (Le Goff, 1981).

Michel de Certeau complained that travel literature has unfortunately not been studied systematically as a vast complement and displacement of demonology. The same structures, he claimed, are found in both (1975: 244 n.53). One way to document this convergence of images is via the Wild Man and other European categories which could sustain both American and diabolical connotations. First, we might begin with Bernheimer's remark (1952: 59-60) that the association of the Wild Man with devils is first mentioned in Sebastian Franck's *Weltbuch* (1534) in a description of a pageant of mummers; and Geiler of Kaisersberg had treated devils as a sub-species of the Wild Man in his *Die Emeis*; but the association must surely be older. One of the names for the Wild Man is *ork* (Latin *orcus*), but the name can cover a much wider spectrum of beings, including devils, beggars, peasants and fools (Vandenbroeck, 1987: 136). Harlequin, the leader of the Wild Horde (*familia Herlechini*), appears with diabolical attributes in seventeenth-century painting, but his clothing points towards devil's costumes which already feature in fifteenth-century archives (ibid: 134). Second, the exotic Plinian races, whose American connotations are discussed in Chapter Four, could also be seen as diabolical in some accounts. André Thevet, for instance, claims that they formerly existed as the work of the devil, but that in his time they are no longer to be found except in Africa (1983: ch. 31). Aldrovandi similarly explained satyrs as demons who assumed their special appearance to deceive men, but stated that they no longer existed in his time thanks to the prevalence of the true faith (Céard, 1977: 457f.). Third, there are diabolical associations with the fool: a sixteenth-century Protestant satirical print from the Netherlands shows a Pope's head with a devil's head as its reverse, with the text: *Ecclesia perversa tenet faciem diaboli* ['the perverse church has the devil's face'] (Vandenbroeck, 1987: 52 and n.281).

In a play by John Rastell, *A New Interlude and Mercy of the Nature of the iiii Elements*, published around 1517, it was stated of the inhabitants of the New World that 'they nother knowe god nor the deveil, Nor never harde tell of hevyn nor hell'. All the same, one of the first representations to link the Indians of America with the devil is an oil painting of the Inferno, attributed to Jorge Afonso and dated around the middle of the sixteenth century. The Indians are here portrayed as devil-worshippers, and Brazilian feather work is worn by one of the devil's assistants and by the presiding devil (Honour, 1975).[32] Another sign of the infernalisation of the American Indians is the depiction of grilling on a bonfire in the late-sixteenth-century engravings of de Bry illustrating the practices of the Tupinamba. In fact, the Tupinamba did not cook in this way, as they used a slow fire, but this ethnographical distortion fitted in with a view of cannibal cooking as hellfire (Bucher, 1981: 194 n.6). By the early seventeenth century, Crispijn de Passe's 'America' allegory emphasises the cannibalism of its inhabitants, who are engaged in human sacrifice, but who are also portrayed as devil worshippers. The Aztec deity Huitzilopochtli enters European literature under the name of Vitzlipuitzli in the familiar form of Satan in Montanus' *The New and Unknown World* of 1671 (cf. Kohl, ed., 1982: ill. 216).

The representations of Wild Men and Women, exotic Plinian races, devils and fools that we have considered so far all tended to exert a mutual attraction on one another. Iconographically, the image of the madman could easily shade into that of the Wild Man, which in turn could be given diabolical colouring. An intellectual justification of these kinds of overlap is provided by the famous disputes between Bartolomé de Las Casas and his opponent, Juan Ginés de Sepúlveda, conducted in Valladolid in 1550–1551 (for which see Pagden, 1982: 109–118). De Sepúlveda's *Democrates secundus* – 'the most virulent and uncompromising argument for the inferiority of the American Indian ever written' (Pagden, 1982: 109) - was built around contrasting opposites which, following Todorov (1982: 159) we might list as follows:[33]

Spaniards	Indians
adults	children
men	women
gentle	savage
form	matter
soul	body
reason	appetite
continent	incontinent
human	animal
good	bad

The result of De Sepúlveda's diatribe can be described thus:

The acerbity of this language - the use of images of inversion, commonly reserved for witches and other deviants, and of such descriptive terms as *homunculus*, which suggests not only stunted growth but, since *homunculi* were things created by magic, also unnatural biological origins, the persistent reference to animal symbolism, monkeys, pigs and beasts in general – was intended to create an image of a half-man creature whose world was the very reverse of the 'human' world of those who by their 'magnanimity, temperance, humanity and religion' were the Indians' natural masters.

(Pagden, 1982: 117–118)

If we look at the right hand side of the list, we see the basis for the interchangeability of terms for the Indians: they are savage and incontinent (like the Wild Men and Wild Women), and unable to manage their own affairs because of their child-like mentality (a foreshadowing of the conflation of the categories 'primitive' and 'childlike' which was to play such an important role in the nineteenth century). This last point reinforces the solidarity between images of the Wild Man and those of the mad fool. A similar point was made a few years earlier by Francisco de Vitoria, who had argued that, if the Indians were not actually foolish (*amentes*), they were not far from being so.[34]

The central feature of their near foolishness was their alleged inability to discriminate. This lay behind their culinary habits: the consumption of human flesh and of lower species of animals or plants (rats, snakes, locusts, worms, roots, berries, etc.) were indications of a failure to respond to the presence of pollution and to make satisfactory distinctions between the edible and the inedible (cf. Pagden, 1982: 87). It also lay behind their devil worship: through their inability to perceive the world correctly, the American Indians failed to distinguish between the genuine faith and a set of false beliefs, a problem that was only aggravated for them by Satan's own cunning in imitating confession, communion and the feast of Corpus Christi for his own diabolical ends (ibid: 175). Thus although observers were forced to admit the high level of complexity of Mexican religion, they saw in this a ruse of Satan by which the ceremonies of the ancient religion were usurped and put to fiendish ends.

A similar inability to make the correct distinctions lay behind their sexual deviations, which will be discussed later on. Indeed, there is a relation between the two: anthropophagy as the eating of like by like (with its limit case in the phenomenon of autophagy) implies a similar short-circuit in the culinary circle to the block that incest constitutes in the social circle. Such a lack of discriminatory capacities cannot help recalling Foucault's account of the perception of the madman down to the eighteenth century, according to which he is alienated in analogy: he is other in that he fails to respect the signs of resemblance and difference (Foucault, 1966: 63).

The theme of cannibalism belongs to this complex as a sign of the lack of discrimination of the Amerindians in the choice of their items of consumption.[35] But it had much wider ramifications. There is a striking contrast between the numerous reference to anthropophagy in various regions of the world, which have been subjected to scrutiny by W. Arens (1979), and his failure to find one single eye-witness account of a cannibal feast nor a single description which does not rely on elements taken from classical accounts of anthropophagy. Specifically commenting on island Carib cannibalism, R. Myers (1984: 141) concludes that 'if the Caribs were on trial for cannibalism, they would be acquitted'.[36]

Whatever the verdict may be on the existence or not of isolated cases, the strong points in Arens' argument are those which explicate the mechanisms by which self constructs its anthropophagous others. For it is impossible here to make a distinction between image and reality. From the first, anthropophagy was a practice that carried coherent religious and social symbolic connotations. In many alleged cases of actual anthropophagy, anthropologists come into the field only to find that anthropophagy died out just before their arrival; or to find that it is not practised by the people in question but by their neighbours, who, when questioned in turn, deny its existence among themselves but can readily point to neighbours of their own who are anthropophagous... And sometimes the anthropophagous neighbours turn out to be Europeans, an ironic comment on the colonial presence (cf. Magaña, forthcoming). Contemporary anthropological experience is borne out by ancient Greek ethnography, which already reveals the same mechanism at work in allegations of human sacrifice: it is always *foreign* nations who are presumed to practise human sacrifice (Skythians, Egyptians, Cypriots, Celts, Carthaginians, Germans and some Arab peoples, according to Henrichs, 1980: 233 n.4). And, as Plinius pointed out, it is but a slight step from human sacrifice to anthropophagy.[37] And to move on to the Renaissance, despite the differences in their visions, both Catholics and Protestants made much of the alleged anthropophagy of their respective opponents in the heated discussions of the sixteenth and seventeenth centuries (Lestringant, 1982).[38]

Following the same procedure, Columbus happily situated immense wealth in gold and anthropophagi, which were coupled in the Old World traditions, on the island of the Caribs *which he failed to visit* (Hulme, 1978). Similarly, Vespucci's reference to an island people of *cambali* in a letter of 1500 (Vespucci, 1984: 62) is based on information gathered from the neighbours of these alleged anthropophagi. Despite the obvious unreliability of such reports based on hearsay, by 1505 anthropophagous Amerindians appear on a woodcut to the Vespucci letters, and this was to remain one of the main iconographical attributes of America. In the 1611 edition of Cesare Ripa's *Iconologia*, which was to be the standard work for artists to consult on iconographical questions, the decapitated head at the feet of the figure of America continues to bear the same grim message. It became such a part of the stock-in-trade for describing America that, when Pigafetta recorded having comes across 'giants' at the Río de la Plata in his journal of the voyage of the Vittoria, one of Magellan's ships, he could not resist the temptation to label them as 'cannibals' (P.G. Adams, 1980: 22). In the illustrations to de Bry's *America*, the appearance of cannibalism in Book Three marks the end of the idyllic relations between Indians and Europeans which had marked the first two books.

On the European continent, the popular classes could at least be suspected of harbouring desires to eat the rich, even if they were unable to put these wishes into practice during the 1579 uprising at Romans (Le Roy Ladurie, 1979: 203 and 233; Davis, 1975: 324 n.100). Six years earlier, though, a case of cannibalism was reported from the siege of Sancerre, where the unfortunate victim was a three-year old girl. Jean de Léry, who included it in his account of the siege, was familiar with cannibalism from his account of it among the Tupinamba of Brazil. Besides this isolated case of siege cannibalism in the context of a besieged town where all other edible and potentially edible stuffs had been used up, however, there is a specific European group which was believed to have engaged repeatedly and with pleasure in anthropophagy: the witches. They are the inheritors to the title of anthropophagi in a long line of dissidents, stretching from the early Christians to the Paulicians (Cohn, 1975; Moore, 1987). In his *Italia Illustrata* of 1482, Biondo credited the Fraticelli with the eating of the ashes of babies. Ritual anthropophagy was attacked by Johannes Nider in the late fourteenth century in his *Formicarius* (Ginzburg, 1984). This belief in a widespread group in Europe which practised anthropophagy prepared the ground for acceptance of the belief that such practices were also typical of the native peoples of America.

In the Sancerre report by de Léry, he stresses in particular the role of the old woman in the act of cannibalism (Whatley, 1984), and in the same author's report on Brazil, he again notes that it is especially the old women who are greedy for human meat (de Léry, 1980: 176). In European iconography, the witches are often (though not invariably) portrayed as old hags (cf. Held, 1987), with sagging breasts. Though this was also a feature of some of the predecessors of the Wild Women,[39] the sagging breasts crop up particularly in European accounts of vampires, witches and demons, from the sagging breasts of the figure of Luxuria on the twelfth-century porch of St. Pierre in Moissac, France to the seventeenth-century *Pentamerone* of Basile and the post-medieval Swiss ogre known as the Faengge (Bernheimer, 1952: 33, 38, 39, 195 n.26).[40] B. Bucher (1981) has devoted a monograph on de Bry to the iconography of the savage woman with sagging breasts (the French title was *La Sauvage aux seins pendants*). The motif is to be found on various illustrations to de Bry's *America*: hags engaged in a cannibal feast (cf. Bucher, 1982); the tempter in the garden of Eden; the old hag with Pandora's box; the Indian women of Cumará; and the idols (*zemis*) worshipped by the Arawak (Bucher, 1981). In a later volume of de Bry's *Great Voyages* (Part 13, published in 1627), the Indian woman depicted in the ornamental architecture is clearly a witch (Colin, 1987: 30 n.8). Her breasts hang down below the navel and the nipples are unusually long. Moreover, her skin is pierced with holes and distorted by the weight of inserted ornaments, such as the dead frog hanging from her ear lobe. Moving further into the century, we may add the sagging breasts of the negro slaves of Surinam in a mid-seventeenth century painting by Dirck van Valckenburg (Vandenbroeck, 1987: 34).

Besides the Old World tradition of witches, and the projection of this vision on to the New World (what we have called the 'Europeanisation' of America), as well as the reactive process by which the popular classes of the European continent came to be tarred with the same brush as the Amerindian peoples (the 'Indianisation' of Europe), there is also copious material on anthropophagous monsters in the mythical representations collected among contemporary indigenous American peoples (cf. Magaña, 1982a and b). And if the documents which date from soon after the Spanish conquest of America are to be trusted as the bearers of genuine Mesoamerican beliefs, then it is also worth noting the women called *mometzcopinque* who flew with fireballs through the air and sucked the blood of babies (López Austin, 1980: 42).[41]

According to Aristoteles, intemperance was not a feature of the senses of smell, vision or hearing, but only where there is contact by touch: eating, drinking and sexual contact (*Nicomachean Ethics* III.10.1.118a–b).[42] Not surprisingly, the Middle Ages followed him in seeing sexual perversions as a corollary of the intemperance attested by the cannibalistic feasts.[43] The link between cannibalism and female (auto)eroticism is already present in the Vespucci woodcuts (cf. Kohl, 1987: 82), and, once again, the illustrations to de Bry are revealing. A woodcut from the first edition of Hans Staden's *Warhaftige Historia* (Marburg, 1557), which depicts a scene of women and children enjoying such a feast, is taken up on a scene in de Bry's illustrations to Staden's account, but in the space of the years between the two publications the women have acquired the added characteristic of sexual perversion (lesbianism and auto-eroticism: Bucher, 1982).[44] In the de Bry illustration of *zemi* worship, the procession of women who flock to the ceremony of worship are clearly depicted in various 'lesbian' poses. Moreover, the very nakedness of the women had diabolical and witchcraft connotations for North Europeans in the sixteenth and seventeenth centuries; in portrayals of European witches they are almost invariably naked.

To this deviance on the part of their womenfolk corresponded deviance by their men. In the Fifth Book of his *Historia General y Natural de las Indias* (1535), Gonzalo Fernández de Oviedo referred to what were in his eyes the perversities of anal intercourse by men with members of both sexes, as well as to the luxury and promiscuity of Anacaona as an example of a perverted female.[45] Despite the absence of any evidence from which we might conclude that the Cueva Indians were particularly disposed to homosexuality (Bucher, 1981: 200 n.11), both Petrus Martyr and Francisco López de Gomara report that the conquistador, Vasco Núñez de Valboa, had some forty Indians thrown to the dogs on charges of sodomy.[46] In line with this is the tendency to display exaggerated sexual traits on the part of Amerindian women and reduced genitals for the men.

Intemperance and appetite were set off against moderation and reason in the *Democrates Secundus* of de Sepúlveda, as we saw above. Jean de Léry similarly made the connection between cannibalism and sodomy: excess in the one semantic field connoted excess in the other, an easy correlation given the identity of the words for 'eat' and 'copulate' in a large number of languages (Lévi-Strauss, 1984: 47). For Aquinas, these were both areas susceptible of excess, by which he understood the consumption of human flesh, bestiality[47] and sodomy (Pagden, 1982: 217 n.174).

These allegations of sexual excess proceeded from Old World assumptions. After discussing the unnatural sexual vices of the Indians, de Oviedo went on to consider the polygamy of the Indians. He compared them to the Thrakians in this. At this point, his source led him to the alleged human sacrifices of the Thrakians, which in turn leads him back to the cannibalism of the Indians. He is prepared to accept the accounts of their cannibalism because Plinius claimed that 'the Cyclopes' of Italy and Sicily practised human sacrifice (*Historia Naturalis* 7.2). We witness here a constant to and fro movement between Europe and America. On the one hand, de Oviedo uses the American 'evidence' to quell doubts raised by the European Isidorus of Sevilla about the genuine existence of human sacrifice among the Thrakians, while on the other hand he uses the 'evidence' of Plinius the Elder to support his rather shaky 'American' evidence.

The method followed by de Oviedo presupposes a correspondence between the barbarism of the Indians and the barbarism of the Old World (cf. Ryan, 1981). In other words, Thrakians are to Greeks as Amerindians are to Europeans.[48] On the basis of this supposed correspondence, which is intended to be taken literally rather than metaphorically, he fills in many missing details by 'reading them off', as it were, from the better documented Old World examples. This procedure was described by Descartes as the common practice by which, when certain resemblances are found between two things, they are both attributed with what has been found to be true for only one of them, even on the points on which they differ in reality (cf. Foucault, 1966). M. Duchet sees in this process a 'hyper-historicity' motivated by a *horror vacui*:

In deducing the unfamiliar from the familiar, in establishing archives through homologous series, a reassuring and harmonious image of human history appears in its continuity and its finality. Half-way between ethnology and history, comparativism is the best operator of this sort of hyper-historicity based on a horror of emptiness.

(Duchet, 1985: 221)

However, De Oviedo does not restrict barbarism to the outer recesses of the civilised world. In this movement of come and go, a certain interpenetration of American and European themes takes place. He praises the Indians of America for observing the incest taboo more strictly than the natives of Spain, and the barbarian can be found in the midst of de Oviedo's own countrymen, even among the ranks of the clergy, a theme which was to be developed with great alacrity in anti-clerical circles in the eighteenth century.

If we follow de Oviedo's lead and turn to the European continent, we find sexual orgies associated with the early Christians, Montanists, Manichaeans, Paulicians, Gnostics, Waldensians, Thrakian Bogomiles, Fraticelli, Cathars, Knights Templar and the Euchitians, to name but a few. Similarly, Nider's 'new' witches are accredited with sexual orgies as well as ritual anthropophagy. The two are first connected directly with one another in the eighth-century sermons of John of Ojun, in which it is the sexual orgies and incest practised by the Paulicians which lead to the birth of illegitimate babies, who are in turn alleged to be consumed by the heretics (Cohn, 1975: 18).[49] The sexual malpractices of the witches included copulation with the devil or one of his satellites, and the sexual overtones of the smearing of ointment between their legs to enable them to fly on broomsticks (cf. Duerr, 1985) are evident in Hans Baldung Grien's depiction of such a scene.

There is no difficulty in adding evidence for devil worship to the picture. Just as the Amerindians were seen as idolaters, so the witches of Europe – like another persecuted group, the Jews (Moore, 1987) – were supposed to be bound in a pact with the devil. Images of American idols thus follow the diabolical conventions of European iconography, bearing out Michel de Certeau's claim that there is a homology between the structures of European demonology and the perceptions of the New World (1975: 244 n.53). We can see this process at work even in the most 'ethnographic' portrayals of American Indians, the paintings of Brazilian Indians by the seventeenth-century Dutch artist, Albert Eckhout, which were discussed in the previous chapter. European preconceptions of both devil worship and pagan deities seem to have coloured the imagery of the paintings (Baumunk, 1982; Mason, 1989c). In the same way, the attempts at Dutch co-operation with the Tarairiu Indians of Brazil were thwarted by the suspicion with which the Europeans viewed their potential allies: the strange ceremonies which the Tarairiu held every evening were construed by the agents of the West India Company as evidence for contact with the devil (van den Boogaart, 1979: 527).

One aspect of this diabolical colouring that is worth singling out is the theme of *inversion*. In the practices surrounding European carnival customs, and particularly in representations of the Wild Man and Wild Woman, the mad fool, the beggar and the peasant, the difference between self and other is not measured: it is set up absolutely by inversion, which is thus a privileged form of utopian discourse. It is the absence of any nuances in this difference which gives inversion such a strong rhetorical force (Hartog, 1980: 267–268), since it allows of no alternatives other than Self and the Other as anti-self. Seen in these terms, the American world was an inversion of the hallowed norms, both in social and in religious terms. Thus the level of complexity attained by Mexican religion, and other features of American religion, were tricks by which the symbols of the Christian religion were mimicked while its values were inverted (Pagden, 1982: 175). In European thought of the time, the play of opposites was such an essential element that demons were in fact necessary as proof of the existence of God (Clarke, 1980). These inversions, it should be noted, were not confined to the implicit or unconscious level at which anthropologists are wont to locate them, but they form an explicit component of discourse about the real world at this period. Iconographically, perhaps the strongest expression of the upside down world of the European witches (cf. Duerr, 1985) is Albrecht Dürer's copper engraving of a witch mounted on a ram from ca. 1500–1501: she rides the beast seated in reverse; her hair unnaturally streams *against* the wind; and one of the putti who accompany her tries to look between his legs, a symbolic gesture which may also be brought into association with the theme of the topsy-turvy world (cf. Dresen-Coenders, 1985: 76 and note).[50]

It was a feature of the witches of Europe that they could transform themselves into animals, and the European traditions on the Wild Man oscillate between an animal and a human designation (Bernheimer, 1952: 5). In the case of criminal acts perpetrated by animals, the question could thus always arise of whether one was dealing with an animal or a transformed witch. In other words, we come up against both the 'animalisation' of the human and the 'humanisation' of the animal (Affergan, 1977, Mason, 1988). Combined with a tradition of animal trials going back at least to the ninth century (Evans, 1987: 265), it is not surprising to find that a certain degree of fusion in the fifteenth century between the popular traditions on sorcery and the learned doctrines about diabolism led to an overlapping between the exorcism of animals and the exorcism of witches. Both phenomena have an epicentre in Switzerland and the neighbouring parts of Italy and France around the middle of the fifteenth century (Cohen, 1986: 33). By the end of the following century, the same formulae are being used to exorcise witches and animals, and the best known work on animal trials in its time, the *Tractatus de exorcismis* of the Swiss jurist Felix Malleolus, was included as a companion to the collection of tractates on witchcraft and demonology, the *Malleus maleficarum*, in the 1582 edition published in Frankfurt and in later editions. These animal trials soon became a part of the 'Europeanisation' of America: in the early eighteenth century an application was made to the bishop of the province of Piedade no Maranhão in Brazil for an act of interdiction and excommunication to deal with a plague of ants which had consumed the food and damaged the furniture of the Franciscan friars of the cloister of St. Anthony (Mason, forthcoming a).[51]

The animal comparison introduced by the witches is frequent in our sources dealing with the Americas too (cf. Sheehan, 1980: 65ff.).[52] The sexual perversities of the anthropophagous women in the illustrations to de Bry are imitated by, or from, monkeys (Bucher, 1982). De Sepúlveda, in the dichotomy between Spaniards and Indians, had included in his 'table' the opposition between humans and monkeys. The privileged role assigned to the monkey in these accounts is due to the marginal status which this animal occupied in European thought from Aristoteles to Buffon, Linnaeus and Rousseau. Opinions differed on whether the orang-utang was an animal or a human being. Linnaeus saw in it a form of the Wild Man (*homo silvestris*), which Rousseau in turn took to be evidence for the existence of the first stage of human evolution which he had postulated in the second *Discours*. The use of the monkey in the American context could thus throw doubt on the humanity of the native peoples. Iconographically, the ape was a symbol in European art for everything subhuman in man: lust, greed, gluttony and shamelessness in the widest possible sense (Panofsky, 1962: 195; Janson,

1952). Besides, it could also be a symbol for the Devil: Lafitau refers to 'the Demon, who has always been the monkey of the Divinity', who inverts the meaning of the Christian sacraments.[53]

The Europeanisation of Amerindia and the Indianisation of Europe

The above examples all bear witness to a convergence between the European image of the Amerindian and the European image of its own 'popular culture'. Tylor had already tried to establish the existence of a similar convergence between Europe and another continent when he wrote:

> [...] we may draw a picture where there shall be scarce a hand's breadth difference between an English ploughman and a negro of Central Africa.
>
> (Tylor, 1871, I: 7)

The significant point is that Amerindia is not identified with European culture in general, but with that of its subaltern classes.[54] The extension of the hegemony which learned culture exercised over its European others to their non-European counterparts could thus be justified by a process of analogy. In the eyes of Voltaire, this meant that the judgement of 'primitive' peoples was to be carried out in terms of their ability to resist European influence (Kohl, 1981: 167). This analogy had already been made in the sixteenth century, when Vitoria in his *Relectio de Indis* argued that the American Indians were not to be conceived as 'natural men', but that they were like all other men:

> The 'barbarian', by definition an 'outsider', had now been brought 'in'; 'in', it is true, at the lowest possible social and human levels: socially as a peasant, a brutish creature living outside the discrete web of affiliations, patterns of behaviour, modes of speech and of expression, which made up the life of the civil man; psychologically as a child, that unreflective, passion-dominated, half-reasoning being. But 'in' none the less.
>
> (Pagden, 1982: 105)

One implication of such a view was the notion of 'the tropicalisation of the white man'. Assuming that the low level of civilisation of the American Indians was due to the enervating effects of the climate, and given the basic affinity between Europeans and American Indians, it followed that Europeans who were exposed to the rigours of the tropical climate for any length of time would sink to the level of their Indian counterparts (Gerbi, 1973: 571–576).

Once the analogy was accepted, the 'Europeanisation' of America could soon be followed by the 'Indianisation' of Europe. As Pagden notes (1982: 97–98):

> The word 'Indies' soon became a term to describe any environment in which men lived in ignorance of the Christian faith and of the proper modes of human life. Jesuit missionaries spoke constantly of 'these Indies' of Asturias, of Calabria and Sicily, of the Abruzzi, regions where, they

claimed, the country people lived like 'savages', polygynous and apparently polytheistic.

In the eighteenth century, Voltaire was to present the following portrait of the 'savages' of Europe:

> Rustics living in huts with their mates and a few animals, ceaselessly exposed to all intemperance of the seasons; knowing only the earth which feeds them and the market [...] speaking a jargon which is not understood in the towns; having few ideas, and consequently few expressions.
>
> (Voltaire, 1963: 22)[55]

It was even possible for the term 'Indians' to be applied to those who deviated from the orthodox faith (Pagden, 1982: 220 n.235), just as the Protestant Jean de Léry could refer to the Catholics as idolaters, and others could identify the Catholic interpretation of the mass as a condonation of anthropophagy (Lestringant, 1982). By this time, of course, 'Indian' included native North American Indians as well as their Southern counterparts, so that in the early eighteenth century the term 'Mohock' (Mohawk) even came to be applied to a class of aristocratic ruffians who infested the streets of London at night (Hamell, 1987: 189).[56] In the following century, Eugène Sue's account of the slums of Paris in *Les Mystères de Paris* explicitly claimed inspiration from Fenimore Cooper's descriptions of North American Indians.[57] We could even go on into the present century, when Roger Casement referred to the peasants of Connemara in Ireland as 'white Indians' (Taussig, 1987: 19).

The symbolic to and fro between Europe and America came to become aligned with a theory of the solar course of history which implied a transfer of culture from the East to the West (Gerbi, 1973: 129–145). In line with this, Bartolomé de Las Casas established an apocalyptic relation between the destruction of Spain in the time of Rodrigo, the destruction of the Americas, the second destruction of Spain as a punishment for the Conquista, and the translation or restoration of Christianity on the American continent (Milhou, 1981–83). In the visions of Lucrecia of León, who was active in the period 1587–1590, there is a use of terms with an American flavour in her visions of the millennium. Following a sixteenth-century tradition implying the transfer of the Church from the East to America, she links this transfer with the theme of the destruction of Spain and of European Christianity. In its place she prophesies that after a period of torment 'you will see your longed-for Indies which will be the golden age and the time of God as some of the prophets say' (cited from Milhou, 1981–83). Unlike de Las Casas, who placed the new millennium in the New World, in this vision of January 26 1590, Lucrecia describes the establishment of the millennium *in Spain*, but this millennial age takes the form of *vuestras Indias deseadas*: your longed-for Indies. The Indianisation of Europe is seen as the culmination of world history.

It is not only the rural population of Europe which is affected. Voltaire, following in the line of Montaigne and de Léry, found levels of cruelty in Europe which equalled or surpassed those with which the peoples of South America were credited, but in this case it is not the peasants but their masters who are the barbarians. They may act like cannibals *metaphorically*, as the usurers do. Or they may act as cannibals *metonymically*, consuming their prey by means of an intermediate instrument (such as wild beasts) (Lestringant, 1982: 235). It is the Jesuits who are the real Iroquois, consuming their fellowmen like cannibals, the Inquisitors, the Conquistadores and those entangled in the wars of religion (Duchet, 1971: 313). And by a strange paradox, while the Conquistadores fall on the American peoples like wolves falling on sheep (the image is from Las Casas),[58] it is the sheep in England and Spain which, through the policies of enclosure which were being pursued at the time of the discovery of America, bring about the downfall of the European peasants in the phase of what Marx referred to as the so-called primitive accumulation of capital. It was this dispossessed class which was able to furnish the crews for overseas voyages, as in the case of the recruits for Columbus' third voyage, who were taken from Spanish prisons. In turn, the fulmination against these practices to be found in Thomas More's *Utopia* was to influence Vasco de Quiroga in his plans to reorganise Indian life on experimental communities in Mexico.

The fixing of the status of the American Indians at the level of that of the lowest echelons of European society had implications for the attitudes of the European ruling classes towards their colonies abroad as well as towards their own rural classes. The link between Ireland and America posed a challenge to the division between domestic events and those abroad, as initially the English view of the 'wild Irish' resembled to some extent the English view of the American Indian (Bottigheimer, 1978: 61; Pennington, 1978: 179; Sheehan, 1980: 54–56). In the course of time, however, in searching for an image for the Irish, British colonial rule could no longer resort to the images that had been appropriate for the American Indians, for they were now too 'European':

> An Indian will be taken with any thing that is neat, handsome or usefull, if given, return thanks for it, if not so, purchase it if he can; if the Irish be more brutish than the Indians, why may it not be reasonable to tame such wilde beasts had they never been in any kinde so cruell and bloody to the English.
> *(The Moderate Intelligencer*, 26 April–2 May 1649,
> cited by Carlin, 1985: 94)

In British anti-Irish propaganda of the middle of the seventeenth century, we find the same complex of accusations that had been levelled against the American Indians. Spenser makes them descendants of the ancient Skythians,[59] a barbarian people in the eyes of the ancient Greeks, just as Columbus asserted of the Americans (Gil, 1984: XLIII). Their land is uninhabited and uncultivated, thereby making it fit for expropriation: the same theme and its use as a justification of colonialism is found in the American context (Hulme, 1985) and elsewhere (Boon, 1982: 168–173). Spenser's complaint against the excessive influence exercised by Irish women echoes de Oviedo's objections to Anacaona and her like. Spenser claimed that the Irish drink human blood, and a traveller's account of the 1590 famine relates:

> a most horrible spectacle of three children [...] all eating and gnawing with their teeth at the entrails of their dead mother.
>
> (cited by Carlin, 1985: 100)

And in a defence of the English right of reconquest in America, William Strachey had this to say of the earlier inhabitants of England before the Roman conquest, who in his eyes were no different from the Celtic inhabitants of Scotland, who were of course related to the Irish:

> [...] overgrown Satyrs, rude and untutred, wandring in the woodes, dwelling in Caves, and hunting for our dynners [...] prostetuting our daughters to strangers, sacrificing our children to Idolls, nay eating our owne children [...].
>
> (W. Strachey, *The Historie of Travell into Virginia Britania* (1612), cited by Carlin, 1985: 104)

Cannibalism, idolatry, sexual excess: the same triangle of vices that were projected on to the American Indians reappear in the seventeenth-century ideology of British domination of Ireland, together with a (slightly) higher ranking of the Indians on the scale of European civilisation. Such internal divisions within the definition of the Other are a feature of ancient Greek ethnography too. The Skythians could be useful as mirror images of negative self-definition for Athens: the Skythians were what the Athenians were not. But was not Herodotos' account of Egypt based on the supposition that it was an inversion of Greek mores? And if so, what was one to make of the relations between the Egyptians and the Skythians (Hartog, 1980)?

The Irish example is a similar case. Within the Other, there may be gradations of otherness. What must be clear for the European ruling classes in this case, at all events, is that the Other is not Self. Whatever the proliferation of the Other may entail, both Europe's inner demons and the demons that it finds abroad are conceived and maintained through the structures of alterity.

Notes

1. For another study of the way in which learned traditions of demonology came into uncomprehending contact with popular magical beliefs, see Ginzburg's study of a witchcraft trial from Modena in 1519 (1986: 3–28). Ginzburg speaks of a 'hiatus' between the beliefs of the accused and those of the judge, a hiatus which the inquisitor tries to dissolve by getting the statements of the accused to conform to his own vision of reality. In the same way, we might regard the attempts to fit the New World into an Old World framework as attempts to do away with such a hiatus.
2. This community between the living and the dead is evidenced in medieval law, in which the dead could act as prosecutors or defendants, and could be punished. The

notion of the dangerous corpse and the fear of the dead is a relatively recent phenomenon: see the detailed discussion in Oexle (1983).

3. This engraving is copied from a 1502 edition of Vergilius.

4. This one is copied from Sebastian Brant's *Stultifera navis* of 1497.

5. For a similar problem in the depiction of Indian religion, see Mitter's discussion (1977: 3–5) of a fourteenth-century French illumination intended to depict consecrated Indian maidens dancing before an idol: there is hardly any physical resemblance between these blonde nuns and Indian consecrated maidens, or between the dark-skinned effigy and Indian religious images. We might also compare the difficulties faced by artists when they tried to illustrate ghosts. Around the twelfth century, there was a sudden increase in interest regarding an afterlife in another world and the possible localisation of its inhabitants (Schmitt, 1982; Le Goff, 1981). Despite the controversies about the existence of such spirits, artists could do little else than portray ghosts like other beings, perhaps adding a tombstone as an iconic indication of the defunct status of the beings concerned (Schmitt, 1987). The portrayal of the macabre and the fantastic had not yet come into its own.

6. There is a congruence between this mechanism of projection and that which lies at the heart of ethnology:

> Die postulierte Nähe zum 'Ursprung', das Vorherrschen des affektiven, die 'Verkehrte Welt', in der alles ganz anders is – das sind Vorstellungen, die eher dem Diktat jener Phantasien als der Realität der fremden Kultur folgen.
>
> (Erdheim and Nadig, 1987: 172)

7. This process is not confined to the inner experience of Europe. In a similar vein, J. Leerssen (1986: 109) has demonstrated the ways in which Europe's others (Asia Minor, the Mediterranean, and – closer to home – Ireland) could be used 'not to throw Europe from the centre stage, but to silhouette it, to circumscribe it, even to define it. Europe is defined in its periphery and by its margins, in its contacts with the unknown past and the alien outer world.'

8. Cf. Lecouteux (1982, I: 24):

> L'homme sauvage est l'antithèse du chevalier. Par son aspect, sa pilosité, sa taille, ses moeurs et ses armes il s'oppose à toutes les valeurs de l'univers courtois.

9. *De wilder man* is *der waltman* first in the *Iwein* (Lecouteux, 1982, II: 106).

10. On the upper/lower distinction, see too Ginzburg (1986: 107–132).

11. Compare the picture of Robert of Arbrissel, who had been commissioned by the Pope to preach the crusade in the 1090s. He wore skins, went barefoot, had staring eyes and unkempt hair, 'wanting only a club to complete the outfit of a lunatic', as Bishop Marbod of Rennes put it (Moore, 1987: 19).

12. Various scholars have drawn attention to the correlation between the conceptual bracketing of 'marginal' social groups and the tightening up of political administration e.g. Moore, 1987 (heretics, Jews, lepers in the eleventh and twelfth centuries); Egmond, 1987 (bandits from the eighteenth century).

13. There are a number of illustrations of various types of Wild Men in Gaignebet and Lajoux, 1985: 120–127.

14. Long hair was sometimes the only distinguishing element between a Wild Man and a giant, and in the case of the Wild Woman the distinction becomes even harder to make (Lecouteux, 1982, I: 20 and 24 n.1).

On the other hand, the long-haired *pilosi* to whom Thomas of Cantimpré refers as *homines silvestres* (*Liber de natura rerum* IV.90) are half-human, half-animal, thereby resembling the satyrs, fauns and incubi.

15. Though in the *Göttweiger Trojanerkrieg* of Ps.-Wolfram, the wild men whom Odysseus meets are so hairy that their mouths and eyes cannot be seen (Lecouteux, 1982, I: 22; II: 107).

16. For example, the Wild Men mentioned in the previous note have horns.

17. The savage club is replaced by a bat in the iconography of Herlechinus (Ginzburg, 1983: 49).

18. The humanity of one of the earliest figures of the Wild Man, the Homeric Kyklops, is demonstrated in a difference of language: while epithets like 'wild' are applied to animals as a form of personification, the term is only applied to Polyphemos with the addition of the substantive 'man' (cf. Duala-M'bedy, 1977: 40–41).

19. The figure of the Centaur among the ancient Greeks carries a similar ambiguity. In the fifth century BC we encounter only aggressive male Centaurs, whose continuation depends on the rape of human females through a lack of suitable partners of their own kind. Zeuxis, however, painted a 'domestic' Centaur family comprising a father, mother and little centaurs. Cheiron, the Centaur who was a repository of wisdom, also belongs to this more civilised model. See further von Blanckenhagen (1987).

20. Kolkan (in *Apollonius von Tyrland*) is thirty years old and lives in a cave in the mountains (Lecouteux, 1982, II: 101). The comparison with the bear is not fortuitous: in a number of European festivals the figures of the Wild Man and the bear overlapped (Vandenbroeck, 1987: 9).

21. Compare, for instance, the Wild Men of *Apollonius von Tyrland* who have carried off a young woman and her son. The woman is expected to cook her son for their meal (Lecouteux, 1982, II: 104).

22. Friedman notes that the Wild Man of the woods came to be regarded at the end of the Middle Ages as a kind of noble savage, but he assumes this to belong to later phases that lie beyond the scope of his book (1981: 164).

23. In the seventeenth-century illustrations to his *El Primer Nueva Corónica y Buen Gobierno*, Guaman Poma de Ayala remains true to the norm in portraying Indian males without beards. Of the two exceptions, one is a compatriot and personal enemy of Guaman Poma whose ugly, cat-like face whiskers may be interpreted as a sign of his European-style debauchery (Adorno, 1981: 105 n.14).

24. The body hair on some of the Tupinamba in the illustrations to Hans Staden's narrative of his period in captivity in Brazil may be a misinterpretation of body paint by the designer of the woodcuts (Colin, 1987: 12).

25. Grüninger went against the common practice of his time in his refusal to lend or borrow woodcuts or printing clichés (Colin, 1987: 31 n.11).

26. This posed a dilemma for the writers of propaganda designed to encourage colonisation in the New World. On the one hand, tales of barbarism, cannibalism and so on attracted a large reading public but were less attractive for potential investors or settlers; on the other hand, portrayals of the American Indian as (relatively) civilised made it harder to justify the act of colonialism itself (Pennington, 1978: 178–179).

27. Examples: the 1505 Nuremberg edition of the letters, the 1509 German translation, or the decorations after Hans Holbein the younger to the Grynaeus map of 1532 showing *canibali* in South America.

28. The feather skirt as an element in the iconography of the American Indian may have helped to foster the identification of Indians with the Wild Men. The portrayal of the body hair of the latter is often done in a manner suggesting feathers rather than hair. This is evident in the setting of an Indian in feather skirt side by side with a hairy wild man wearing a bird mask on one of a series of prints from around 1600 illustrating various masked ball costumes by Jacques de Gheyn (Vandenbroeck, 1987: 35, ill. 34).

29. Though as Mitter (1977: 287 n.7) points out, the portrayal of Nuremberg does in fact bear some resemblance to the actual topography of the city, despite the presence of fanciful elements.
30. Is it more than coincidence that both purgatory and the Garden of Eden might be seen as transitional locations, the former as a point between life on earth and life in heaven, the latter as a stage between the creation and the 'ordinary' world?
31. An earlier woodcut of this scene from the 1476 Augsburg edition (which was still being used in editions of the 1490s) is the prototype; it differs from the later version in depicting six figures instead of four, and in its omission of the figure in the background who brings the good news (!) of the arrival of the Portuguese (cf. Kohl, 1987: 71 and note). For the earlier type see Gerritsen *et al.*, 1986: 106; the 1499 version is reproduced there on p. 66.
32. Compare from the same period Gerardsbergen's *Last Judgement*, where an Indian appears in the guise of a devil (Vandenbroeck, 1987: 158 n.181).
33. A striking parallel to this list can be found in the European images of black Africans as child-like, irrational, animal-like, etc.: see the recent important study by R. Corbey (1989).
34. In his *Relectio de Indis*, delivered in 1539, Vitoria raised the question of whether the Indians, though not natural slaves, might yet be 'so little removed from the foolish (*amentes*) that they are not able to constitute nor administer a legitimate republic in civil or human terms' (cf. Pagden, 1982: 79–80).
35. Strabon claims that the Irish were both *anthropophagoi* and *polyphagoi*. Surely these two epithets should be taken together: they consume human flesh and they are indiscriminating in what they eat (they will eat *anything*). In a number of Amerindian myths, anthropophagy is similarly linked to a lack of discrimination: compare e.g. Jara, 1988: 68 (a Gê myth).
36. Not all anthropologists are convinced by Arens' *tour de force*. Lévi-Strauss concludes that the massive documentation makes it impossible to deny the existence of some form of anthropophagy in South America (1984: 141), and despite the unreliability of Spanish sources, the evidence of non-Spanish sources on the taking of human trophies and the ritual cannibalism of war captives among the Caribs and the Arawak or Tupinamba have been regarded as credible by N. Whitehead (1984).

   Without ruling out the possibility that some forms of anthropophagy on this scale may have been practised, we here wish to stress two points. First, the Old World traditions played an undeniably crucial role in the *construction* of the image of anthropophagi. Second, the generalisation of possible isolated incidents to convey the impression that the American Indians did little else besides preparing the next meal of human flesh involves the creation of a stereotypical persuasive definition that can have little to do with anything in reality.
37. *Quod paulum a mandendo abest*, Plinius, *Historia Naturalis* 7.2.9.
38. The Protestant Samuel Purchas, the compiler of a vast and rambling collection of ethnographic material embedded within a Jacobean perspective, first published in 1625, associated giants, sodomy and devil worship with the Antichrist as embodied in the Pope (cf. Boon, 1982: 37–38 and 165–166).
39. For instance, in the *Wigalois* the breasts of Ruel la Forte hang like bags, while those of Berille in the *Heldenbuch* are so long that she bumps into them with her feet when she walks (Lecouteux, 1982, I: 35). For male equivalents, compare the men of the land of Hormuz in the metrical version of the *Travels* of Sir John Mandeville, whose 'ballokis hangeth binethe hir knee'.
40. The sagging breasts are also a feature of the iconography of Death, Heresy and Famine.
41. In view of the resemblance of the latter to Spanish imaginary beings of the time,

however, it is uncertain whether we are here dealing with genuine pre-Conquest representations or not.

42. According to Ginzburg (1986: 152 and n.43), it was in the sixteenth century that vision came to gain the upper hand over touch as the dominant erotic mode. But the history of the senses has yet to be written...

43. Aristoteles employed the same mechanism of deflecting charges of deviancy on to the foreign neighbours that his predecessors had employed. Hence the Celts, an anthropophagous people for some ancient authors, are reported by Aristoteles to be inclined to homosexuality, despite the fact that 'until the second century BC the Greeks knew deplorably little about the Celtic world' (Momigliano, 1975: 58).

44. Another indication of the deterioration in the European estimation of the Amerindians in the period between Staden and de Bry can be seen in the references to manioc and tobacco cultivation by the Tupinamba in Staden's book. By the time of de Bry these references have been eliminated as the portrayal of the Tupinamba becomes more 'savage'.

45. For the incestuous connotations of Anacaona see Sued-Badillo (1986: 19).

46. The prevalence of homosexuality in the Americas was to become a commonplace in the eighteenth century. Buffon saw it as due to physical causes and correlated it with the Indians' lack of body hair. For Voltaire, the presence of 'Socratic love' in America was proof of the fact that it was not contrary to nature. For Diderot, it was a result of the climate (Duchet, 1971: 264–265, 304, 446; Gerbi, 1973: 6, 44).

47. Accusations of bestiality, sodomy and idolatry, generally practised only by males, tended to go together. This is supported by the mass of bestiality trials in seventeenth- and eighteenth-century Sweden that are currently being studied by J. Liliequist.

48. For Cornelius de Pauw (*Recherches sur les Grecs*, 1787), the Americans corresponded to the Spartans. But then convention has it that the Spartans were barbarian Greeks – it was the *Athenians* who were the civilised Greeks (Gerbi, 1973: 350).

49. The figure of de Sepúlveda reappears in this context, for he attributed nocturnal orgies, the killing and burning of babies and the mixing of their ashes with communion wine to certain Fraticelli in the mid-fourteenth century in his *De vita et rebus gestis Aegidii Albornotii Carrilli*. He is repeating details which are traceable within a literary tradition stretching back to John of Ojun (Cohn, 1975).

50. Many of the features detailed here with respect to European witches can be found outside this geographical area too. Needham (1978: 41), for instance, lists opposition, inversion, darkness, colour, animals, flight and nocturnal lights as factors which are variously and sporadically combined into the synthetic image of the witch in a much wider spectrum of cultures.

51. Father Gilij also resorted to exorcism to rid his house of a plague of ants – with success (1987, II: 233).

52. There is a further interesting convergence, based on the homology between 'primitive' contemporaries and 'primitive' ancestors, between this discussion and the question of man's apish ancestors.

53. 'Le Démon, qui a toujours été le singe de la Divinité, avoit affecté de faire retenir aux Idolâtres les usages qu'ils avoient pris de la vraye Religion' (Lafitau, 1724, I: 416).

54. Father Gilij, a Jesuit exile from Orenoco, also compared the Amerindians to the European peasants in the four volumes of his *Saggio di storia americana* (Rome, 1780–84) (Gerbi, 1973: 232).

55. For eighteenth-century writers on this theme see Kohl (1981: 132, 166–167 and 273 n.94).

56. These are perhaps related to the visit of three Mohawk 'kings' from Canajoharie and Fort Hunter to Queen Anne in London in 1710.

57. Sue's vision was adopted by Alexandre Dumas (*Les Mohicans de Paris*) and Victor

Hugo (*Les Misérables*). Balzac wrote of the peasants of Brittany in similar terms in *Les Chouans* and Michelet's account of the Vendée uprising makes use of similar figures.

58. On the earlier history of this symbolism and its use by Lucrecia of León, see Milhou (1981: 25–47 and 1983: 11–54).

59. For the implications of this Skythian derivation for later antiquarian views of Irish origins, see Leerssen (1986).

der welt Das ·xii· blat

ben on einichem suchen des leibs. Item ein geschlecht der menschen Soiite genannt. die der
fluß arabis von den inderen scheydt. kennen kein andere speyß dann der fisch die sy mit den
nagelen zerteylen. vnd an der sunnen dörren vnd also prot bar auß machen. Item in den ey-
nöden Affrice kommen menschen gestaltnuß den leüten entgegen vnd verschwinden in eim
augenplick widerumb. als dann vil kriechischer geschichtbeschreiber von den hieuorgeschri-
ben wunderperlichen vnd seltzamen gestaltnussen schreiben vn meldung thün also das die
sünnreich natur zu endöckung jrs gewalts solche vnd der gleyche gestaltnuß vnd form vns
wunderperlich beduncke ende gemacht hat. vnderden öttlich hernach entwoiffenn geschen
werden.

Un mancherley gestaltnus der menschenn
schreyben plinius Augustinus vnnd ysido
rus die hernach gemeltenn dinng. In dem
land india sind menschenn mit hundsköpffen vnnd
reden pellende. nön sich mitt fogelgefeng vnnd kley
den sich mit thierheütten. Item öttlich habenn allein
eyn aug an der stirm ob der nasen vnnd essen aliein
thierfleisch. Item in dem land libia werdenn öttlich
on haubt gepoien vnnd haben mund vnnd augenn.
Ettlich sind bederley geschlechts. die recht pinst ist jn
manlich vnnd die linck weybisch vnnd vermischen
sich vndereinander vnnd geperen. Item gegen dem
paradeys bey dem fluß Ganges sind öttlich mensch-
en die essen nichts. dañ sy haben so kleine mund das
sy das getranck mit einem halm einfloessen. vnnd leben vom geschmack der öpffel vnnd plümen. vnnd
sterbenn pald von bösem geschmack. Daselbst sind
auch leüt on nasen eins öbnen angesichts. Erlich ha
ben vnden so groß lefftzen das sy das gantz angesicht
damie bedöcken. Item öttlich on zungenn die deüten
einander jr meynung mit wincken als die clösterleüt.
Item in dem land Sicilia haben öttlich so grosse oun
das sy den gantzen leib damie bedöcken. Item in dem
lannd Ethiopia wanderen öttlich nidergebogen als
das vih. vnd öttlich leben vierhundert iar. Item ött-
liche haben hörner lang nasen vnd geyßfüeß das fin
destu in sant Anthonius gantzer legend. Item in ethi
opia gen dem nidergang sind leüt mie einem preyten
füß. vnnd so schnell das sy die wilden thier erfolgenn.
Item in dem lannd Scithia habenn sy menschen ge
stale mit pferds füß. Item alda sind auch leüt fünff
ölnpogen lanck vnd werden nie kranck bis zum tode
Item in den geschichten des grossen Alexanders liset
man das in india menschen seyen mit öchß henden

6 ij

Source: Hartmann Schedel, *Das Buch der Croniken unnd geschichten*, 1500.
Reproduced with permission of the University Library, Amsterdam.

Chapter three

The monstrous human races

By the time that Columbus was about to set out for the New World, one of the texts that he probably studied for information on China was the *Travels* of 'Sir John Mandeville'.[1] Mandeville's book first began to circulate in Europe in the mid-fourteenth century (it was written around 1346), and it had run into numerous manuscript and printed copies by the end of the fifteenth. Some 250 manuscripts of the work exist in ten different languages, and there are around 180 printed editions known in the same number of languages. It was widely utilised for maps and encyclopedic works, and has no equal in the travel literature for its lasting and widespread influence on European images of what lay outside the European continent (cf. Deluz, 1987). The fact that it was known to the circle of Menocchio the miller (the hero of Carlo Ginzburg's *The Cheese and the Worms*), who used it as an authority for the relativity of beliefs (Ginzburg, 1980: 45) indicates to what extent it had penetrated the European popular classes by the sixteenth century.

The largest portion of the work is devoted to the Holy Land and its neighbouring countries, but shortly after a section on the circumnavigation of the globe, which must have been of special interest to Columbus in view of his cosmographical beliefs (discussed above in Chapter One), the writer goes on to describe the palace of the King of Java and 'other marvels and customs in the environing isles'. It is in this rather vaguely designated geographical region that we come across the following description of marvellous human races.

> There are many different kinds of people in these isles [the Andaman Islands]. In one, there is a race of great stature, like giants, foul and horrible to look at; they have one eye only, in the middle of their foreheads. They eat raw flesh and raw fish. In another part, there are ugly folk without heads, who have eyes in each shoulder; their mouths are round, like a horseshoe, in the middle of their chest. In yet another part there are headless men whose eyes and mouths are on their backs. And there are in another place folk with flat faces, without noses or eyes; but they have two small holes instead of eyes, and a flat lipless mouth. In another isle there are ugly fellows whose upper lip is so big that when they sleep in the sun they cover

all their faces with it. In another there are people of small stature, like dwarfs, a little bigger than pygmies. They have no mouth, but instead a little hole, and so when they must eat they suck their food through a reed or pipe. They have no tongues, and hiss and make signs as monks do, to each other, and each of them understands what the other means. In another isle there are people whose ears are so big that they hang down to their knees. In another, people have feet like horses, and run so swiftly on them that they overtake wild beasts and kill them for their food. In another isle there are people who walk on their hands and their feet like four-footed beasts; they are hairy and climb up trees as readily as apes. There is another isle where the people are hermaphrodite, having the parts of each sex, and each has a breast on one side. When they use the male member, they beget children; and when they use the female, they bear children. There is another isle where the folk move on their knees marvellously, and it seems as if at each step they would fall; on each foot they have eight toes. There is still another isle where the people have only one foot, which is so broad that it will cover all the body and shade it from the sun. They will run so fast on this one foot that it is a marvel to see them. There is also another isle where the people live just on the smell of a kind of apple; and if they lost that smell, they would die forthwith. Many other kinds of folk there are in other isles about there, which are too numerous to relate.

(Mandeville, 1983: 137)

Where did this array of monstrous races come from? What is their genealogy, and what are they doing on the Andaman Islands? What is the relation of these exotic peoples to the negative self-definition of European culture discussed in the previous chapter? What is their ethno-ethnological import?

In the present chapter the sources from which we derive our information about them will be reviewed, from the earliest Greek texts in which they make their appearance to contemporary versions that have been collected in Latin America.[2] This is followed by a description of the various 'races'. and their geographical locations. The concluding remarks concern the principles of classification into which the races are divided.

We can take the account in Mandeville as representing a rough picture of the knowledge about the monstrous races that was available to European readers immediately prior to Columbus' voyages. The present chapter is confined to the pre-Columbian phase of the European tradition. The following chapter deals with the fate of these monstrous races in the post-Columbian tradition.

The first reference to such monstrous races is preserved by the first century BC geographer Strabon:

Yet no one could charge Hesiodos with ignorance when he speaks of 'men who are half-dog', of 'long-headed men' and of 'Pygmies'; no more should one charge Homeros with ignorance when he tells these mythical stories of his, one of which is that of these very pygmies; nor Alkman when he tells about 'web-footed men'; nor Aischylos when he speaks of 'dog-headed men', or of 'men with eyes in their breasts', or of 'one-eyed men'.

(Strabon, 1.2.35)

The works attributed to Hesiodos, Homeros and Alkman are among the earliest texts in Greek to have come down to us. Without necessarily ascribing pride of chronological place to Homeros, we start with one of the most familiar of these monstrous human races that can be traced back to the *Odyssey:* the race of the Kyklopes. When Odysseus and his companions come to the land of the Kyklopes, Odysseus sets out with the crew of his own boat to establish relations of friendship and hospitality by the exchange of gifts (in the Maussian sense). They make contact with the monstrous Kyklops Polyphemos in his cave, where he proceeds to hold Odysseus and his men captive and to kill and eat a number of them. Odysseus and the rest escape only after blinding Polyphemos with a stake and leaving his cave bound or clinging to the bellies of the Kyklops' rams.

The *Odyssey* establishes a clear division between the 'real' world of the Greeks and the 'magical' imaginary world peopled by Kalypso, Kirke, the anthropophagous Laistrygones, the Sirens (half-woman, half-bird in the post-Homeric tradition), the Lotus Eaters and others, and it is to the latter that the Kyklopes belong. In the Homeric text (most of *Odyssey* Book 9), there is a further duality within the world of the Kyklopes themselves. On the one hand, they live in a Golden Age and do not need to work to gain their food. They have only to trust in the immortal gods. The Kyklops Polyphemos is in fact a relative of one of the gods, Poseidon. On the other hand, it is the same Polyphemos who replies to Odysseus that the Kyklopes pay no regard to the blessed gods nor to Zeus, and who eats his meal of human flesh raw, like a savage (cf. Shaw, 1982–1983). This duality in the world of the Kyklopes (cf. Kirk, 1970: 162–171; Vidal-Naquet, 1981: 50–53) is a feature of Greek conceptions of the Golden Age in general: it is an ambiguous state in which an apparently untroubled life, free at any rate from the need to engage in agriculture or pastoral labour, is coupled with rawness and anthropophagy (Mason, 1987b).

The Homeric Kyklops is defined along a number of parameters which may be said to constitute the more or less rigid framework of Greek and Roman accounts of the monstrous human races (Müller, 1972: 57; Friedman, 1981: 26–36; Magaña, 1982a: 223). Besides the food and dietary practices, we can also note the possession of articulate language, which allows Odysseus to converse with him; the lack of 'civic institutions', of religion and of technological advancements (agriculture and ship-building); and of course the physical attributes: the very name Kyklops refers to the roundness of the single eye, to which we should add his gigantic stature. Polyphemos stands at the head of a tradition of one-eyed monstrous humans, called *monoculi* in Latin.[3]

There is another human race mentioned by Homeros which resembles the Kyklopes of the *Odyssey*, namely the Abioi mentioned in the *Iliad* (13.5–6). They are a vegetarian people living in the far North. They are noted not only for their vegetarian diet but also for their justness, which is not a result of their diet (as it is in later writers) but of the communism they practise. The Odyssean version of the Kyklopes was to colour the later accounts of the Abioi, but despite the resemblances, the Abioi do not have the lack of one eye which makes the Kyklopes monstrous human figures. As for the Homeric pygmies to which Strabon refers, they were engaged in a battle with cranes, but their appearance in the *Iliad* is only a summary one within a simile (*Iliad* 3.6).

The Boiotian farmer-poet Hesiodos mentions a number of mythological creatures in his *Theogony*, but it is in works which have not been preserved in the manuscript tradition[4] that he referred to 'men who are half-dog', 'long-headed men' and 'pygmies'. The seventh-century poet Alkman, of whom little is known or preserved, mentioned 'web-footed men', but we know nothing of the context, and it would be rash to assume (as some translators have done) that these are the same as the 'shadow-footed men' (Skiapodes) to whom we shall come in a moment.

Another shadowy figure from the seventh century is the shaman-like Aristeas of Prokonnesos, whose *Arimaspeia* would have provided us with more information about the monstrous races if it had not already been lost before the Alexandrian era (Bolton, 1962). If the fragment preserved by the Byzantine Tzetzes (*Chiliades* vii 690–691) is genuine, the people referred to as Arimaspoi are described in terms similar to those used for the Homeric Kyklopes:

> Each has one eye in his comely forehead
> They are shaggy-haired, toughest of all men.

The last of the ancient authorities referred to by Strabon, the dramatist Aischylos, belongs firmly in the fifth century BC. The dog-headed race to which he referred is not to be found in his extant works. In Aischylos' *Prometheus Bound*,[5] however, the prophecy of the wanderings of Io delivered by Prometheus describes the three swan-shaped[6] Graiai, daughters of Phorkys, who have one eye and one tooth between them. Their sisters and neighbours are the three Gorgons, after whom Io will meet the army of the one-eyed Arimaspoi (*Prometheus Bound*, 795–805). It is worth noting that these monstrous figures are situated in the Asiatic wanderings of Io, while the figures she encounters in her European wanderings are less remote and exotic.

Though he is not strictly relevant for ethno-anthropological purposes, it is worth noting that another fifth century figure, Empedokles, claimed to have found a solution to the problem of the existence of legendary hybrids like the Minotaur and the Centaurs. Within a cyclic cosmological scheme, he argued that the elements were separated under the control of Strife. As they began to come together with the entry and advance of Love, the unattached limbs were formed:

> Here many heads sprang up without necks, bare arms were wandering without shoulders, and eyes needing foreheads strayed singly (fr. 57 D–K).

These heads, arms and eyes combined in various monstrous unions:

Many creatures with a face and breasts on both sides were produced, man-faced bulls arose and again bull-headed men, others with male and female nature combined, and the bodies they had were dark (fr. 61 D–K).

Gradually, under the increasing influence of Love, these combinations became less abnormal, and monstrous births occurring in the author's own time were attributed, not to a badly matched combination of separate limbs, but to some defect in the seed or fault in its motion.[7]

The expansion of the Greek world from the seventh century on gave travellers the opportunity to widen their horizons in the literal sense. From this point on in the tradition, it becomes possible to note the recurrence of certain monstrous races in different authorities and to trace the first occurrence of a particular variety in the sources which have come down to us.[8] The sixth century BC traveller Skylax, who travelled through the Middle East and India, composed an account of his travels in which a long-headed people, a people who used their huge feet as parasols, one-eyed people and a people with very long ears all figured. Some of these races recur in the work of another Ionian Greek, Hekataios, who was one of the first to make a map of the known world and on whom Herodotos in turn was to draw.

With the Ionian historian Herodotos, we encounter a number of the races which are already familiar from the above mentioned literature, such as the pygmies, whom he locates in the African interior (2.32.6), the one-eyed Arimaspoi and the dog-headed Kynokephaloi, to which Herodotos adds the Akephaloi, a people without heads who have eyes in their chest (4.191), although the summary way in which Herodotos introduces them suggests a certain familiarity with them on the part of his audience. He also mentions a goat-footed people among the Greeks' northern neighbours, but attaches little credibility to the report himself (4.25).

The grid according to which Herodotos places these peoples can be shown to be Greek-centred: Greece is 'the domain of measure, while the extremities of the earth are the domain of extreme riches (gold) and of the extremely bizarre' (Lévêque and Vidal-Naquet, 1973: 81 n.1). Increasing geographical remoteness is coupled to remoteness in terms of dietary practices, sexual customs and cultural faculties (cf. Rossellini and Saïd, 1978), a schema which is followed by Herodotos' successors too (S. Saïd, 1985). The symmetrical play of opposition by which this grid is organised (cf. Hartog, 1980) suggests that the 'ethnographical' details furnished by Herodotos should be seen rather in the light of differences which are 'good to think with', and that it is more rewarding to examine these patterns in the light of Greek thought about non-Greeks than to try to track down the 'lost tribes' which might be supposed to conform to such descriptions.

A number of fragments have been preserved in the *Bibliotheka* by the ninth century AD Byzantine Photios from the work of Ktesias of Knidos, a court physician to the kings of Persia around 400 BC. Though it is by no means certain that the tales recorded by Ktesias are more than armchair romance, his *Indika* did at any rate serve as a source book for knowledge about the East and enjoyed widespread popularity. Here one could read about the people who slept under the shadow of their foot, the people with long ears, the one-eyed races, the pygmies, the dog-headed people, as well as being introduced to those with eight fingers and eight toes. In this way, elements of Indian tradition found their way into Greek literature, and could even be incorporated into Greek philosophical discussions; the fifth-century sophist Antiphon, for example, supported his arguments with the existence of a number of these human races.

The relatively limited number of these early monstrous human races came to be increased extensively from the fourth century BC through the activities of Alexandros in the East. Combining science and exoticism, rather as Johan Maurits van Nassau-Siegen was to do in seventeenth-century Brazil, Alexandros took an army of experts with him (Kallisthenes, Onesikritos, Nearchos, Ptolemaios, Aristoboulos) to report on the wonders of his Eastern expedition, particularly those aspects bearing on geography, ethnography and natural history (Pédech, 1984). Although their writings are virtually all lost, they have been incorporated in later texts, where the element of the marvellous is certainly present. For instance, Nearchos, Alexandros' navigator, described a 'primitive' people with hairy bodies and long nails which they used as rudimentary tools; in the later tradition they become a people of giants with saw-shaped hands and feet. We find the Homeric Abioi again (from *Iliad* 13. 5–6) in the deputation which was sent to Alexandros on the banks of the Iaxartos in 328 BC (Arrian, IV.1.1) – one of the many instances where Kallisthenes tried to assimilate Alexandros' expedition to the heroic exploits recounted in the Homeric epics (Pédech, 1984: 41). Other examples suggest that the reports of Alexandros' team were considerably elaborated in the later, Latin texts, though large parts of the Alexandros legends and romances may date from shortly after Alexandros' death.[9] There are large differences between the various versions, with the most wonders occurring in the Latin text of a lost Greek version of the Alexandros romance known as the *Historia de Preliis* (interpolated version I[2]).

Besides the Alexandros legends, three letters exist which purport to have been written in this connection: the *Letter of Alexandros to Aristoteles*[10] on the campaign against king Poros and the wonders of India; the *Letter of Pharasmanes to the Emperor Hadrianus*; and the *Letter of Fermes* (a corruption of Pharasmanes) *to the Emperor Traianus*.[11] These three fictitious letters contributed a number of races to the list of Oriental wonders, such as the bearded and other races of wild women mentioned in the *Letter to Hadrianus*, as well as making new additions to the bestiary of the imagination, and served as an important link in the transmission of these races to the Latin West: races known from Greek sources but which were not mentioned in these texts had little chance of passing into the later European tradition.

At least one monstrous human race was added to the list by one of the members of Alexandros' team, however. A certain Baiton referred to a people whose feet were reversed so that the toes pointed backwards, who were exceptionally swift-footed and who wandered with herds of animals. Wild Men with their heels in front and the soles and toes of their feet behind are mentioned by another of the post-Herodotean ethnologists, Megasthenes, who was sent as an emissary to the Indian court of Chandragupta early in the fourth century BC. He did travel in India, but the accounts of Indian customs which he recorded did not fail to contain fabulous elements either. Besides the strange beasts that he described, he referred to a number of the familiar and less familiar monstrous races, such as the pygmies (whom he located in India); the Astomoi, a people without a mouth who lived on the smells of roasted meat, crops and flowers; the Amyktyres, a people without noses but with two orifices for breathing that were set above their mouth, whose upper lip protrudes further than the lower one, and who are omnivorous, though they eat their meat raw; a race with ears stretching down to their feet, in which they sleep; a long-legged people (Makroskeleis); a swift-footed people (Okypodes); a goat-footed people; and the Monommatoi, a one-eyed race with dog's ears, hair standing on end and shaggy chests. He also provided descriptions of different forms of Brahmanism, whose simplicity was to appeal to later generations, especially to those writers within the Judaeo-Christian tradition.[12]

Contemporary with the Greek expansion into the Orient is the rise of a literature combining Hellenistic political reflection with much older traditions on the Golden Age. In the concluding chapters (55–60) of the second book by Diodoros of Sicily, he recounts the voyage of a certain Iamboulos and his companion to the seven islands of the Heliopolitans, a people located in the regions of India (cf. Gernet, 1968: 139-153). These people have hairless bodies, they are very tall (four cubits), they live to the age of 150 years, they are almost never ill, they have their women in common, they know the arts of cooking and they are extremely versatile in the reproduction of all kinds of sounds, including bird song. Many of these features will reappear as characteristics of the New World Indians in the letters of Amerigo Vespucci (see Chapter Four).

To turn from Greek to Roman sources, Friedman refers to the monstrous human races as 'Plinian' after the Roman author whose catalogue of them was so widely diffused throughout the Latin Middle Ages (1981: 5). Their appeal is evident in some of the titles given to Plinius' work as a book of the marvels of the world (Céard, 1977: 60). An annotated version of Plinius' *Historia Naturalis* had its place in Columbus' book collection. The Elder Plinius, who was killed during the eruption of Vesuvius in AD 79, was not the only Roman to describe such races, which entered the Roman world from the Greek one from the third century BC onwards. We are given a glimpse of this process in a passage in the *Attic Nights (IX.4)* of Aulus Gellius, where this author from the second century AD relates that he had found a Greek book full of marvellous tales on a book-stall in Brundisium. On internal evidence, both Gellius and Plinius seem to have drawn on a (lost) Greek original, perhaps itself deriving from the poem of Aristeas mentioned earlier (Bolton, 1962).

Most of the races are listed in the early books of Plinius' *Historia Naturalis*, where he quotes his sources and adds that he is largely following the Greeks. The subject of Books Three to Six of the *Historia Naturalis* is the geography of the ancient world. Plinius' account, not surprisingly, is Mediterranean-centred. In Book Three, dealing with Europe from Spain to Italy, there are no monstrous races. The closest that Plinius comes to such a people is when he mentions an Alpine tribe, the Capillati ('long-haired' or 'hairy') (3.5.47 and 3.20.135), which may have connotations of the European Wild Man imagery. The same is true of the geography of Greece presented in Book Four, where the Dardani of North-western Greece, a 'savage tribe' *(feram gentem,* 4.1.3), and the inhabitants of Makedonian Apollonia on Mount Athos, the Macrobi (4.10.37), are the only people which tend, though only slightly, towards deviations from the norms of European civilisation.

Once Plinius begins to move away from the centres of Roman civilisation, however, the monstrous human races begin to make their appearance. To the north and the Black Sea region, we find a Skythian settlement in Thrake, Gerania, where the enemies of the cranes, the pygmies, were believed to have settled at one time (4.11.44). Following a line moving steadily inland and northwards, we encounter nomads, anthropophagi, Sauromatae, Essedones, Arimaspi and, beyond the Ripaean mountains, the Hyperborei who live to extreme old age and are famous for legendary marvels (4.12.88). And once Plinius has reached the northern coasts of Skythia, we come across the following island people: the Oeonae, a people living on a diet of birds' eggs and oats; the Hippopodes, a human race with horses' feet; and the Phanesii,[13] whose bodies are naked except for what is covered by their very long ears (4.13.95).

Book Five, the description of Africa, displays a similar structure. Once the account passes from the relatively well-known coastal regions to the desert of the interior, the imagination is given free rein and we are introduced to the Atlantes, who have no names or dreams; the Trogodytae, cave-dwellers who squeak like bats and live on snakes; the promiscuous Garamantes; the Augilae, who worship only infernal powers; the Gamphasantes, who are naked, peace-loving and have no contact with foreigners; the Blemmyae, who have no head and whose mouth and eyes are on their chests; the Satyri, whose only human attribute is their shape; the Aegipani ('Goat-Pans'); and the Himantopodes ('Strap-feet'), who crawl like snakes and who appear in an Oriental context in the Alexandros romance (5.8.45–46).

The account of India in Book Six also presents us with pygmies (near Mount Indus, 6.22.70), fish-eaters (Ichthyophagi, 6.25.95) and turtle-eaters (6.28.109). It is Ethiopia, however, which occupies pride of place as the location of human monstrous races. Plinius suggests that this may be due to the excessive heat, and proceeds to list, besides pygmies (6.35.188), tribes of people without noses, others with no upper lip, and others without tongues (6.35.187). The members of one tribe without nose or mouth have a single opening through which they breathe and drink by means of straws (6.35.188). In this district there are also people who live very long, the Macrobii; elephant-eaters; Gymnetes, who never wear clothes; and a nomad tribe which lives on the milk of cynocephali. These cynocephali appear to be animals (cf. 7.2.31), although the Cynocephali were also one of the monstrous human races. The Ethiopian coast tribes include the Nicicathae and Nisitae, names which are supposed to mean 'men with three eyes' or 'men with four eyes', alluding to the keen sight of these maritime Ethiopians as archers (6.35.194); and the Carthaginian military leader Hanno is reported to have visited an island off the coast of Mauretania where the women's bodies were covered with hair and where the men were swift-footed (6.36.200).

More remote still are the Ethiopians who are consigned by Plinius to the realms of the fabulous: the people of the one-eyed king; the Agriophagi, who live on the meat of wild animals; the omnivorous Pamphagi; the Anthropophagi; the dog-headed Cynamolgi ('dog-milkers'); the four-footed Artabatitae, who rove about like wild animals; and the locust-eaters (6.35.195).

The popularity of Plinius in the sixteenth century, however, was due above all to the list of monstrous races in Book Seven, and separate editions of this book were published (Céard, 1977: 12).[14] The human monstrous races in Book Seven are listed in order to show the ingenuity of Nature, and Plinius' account is followed by remarkable human individuals, such as exceptional and monstrous births. Some of the monstrous races presented here have already been mentioned in the marvels of Skythia, Africa and the Orient in Books Four to Six, but Plinius adds to them a number of others culled from the Greek sources, such as the inhabitants of Abarimon in the Himalayas, where a swift-footed people who live in the forests have their feet turned backwards (7.2.11). Once again it is India and parts of Ethiopia which have the lion's share of marvels (7.2.21): the Gymnosophistas who stare at the sun all day; the Indian people with their feet turned backwards who live on Mount Nulus; the dog-headed mountain people who dress in animal skins and bark like dogs; the swift-footed Sciapodes or Monocoli with their enormous single foot; cave-dwelling Trogodytae; neckless Blemmyae with their eyes in their shoulders; Satyri; the Choromandae, a forest tribe with hairy bodies and dog-like teeth; the people without nose (Sciritae) or mouth (Astomi); giants and pygmies; and long-lived Macrobii (7.2.21–32).

Plinius' account is structured in a similar way to that of Herodotos. In both writers, the monstrous human races are a part of a system of roughly concentric circles with their centre in the region of Italy or Greece. The further one progresses from the centre, the wilder the inhabitants become.[15] At the same time, regional specificity becomes relatively unimportant. It is the similarity between extremes of wildness in Ethiopia, Skythia or India which links them together, rather than their situation in relation to other, less wild peoples of their own region.

There are a few additions to this list within the European tradition after Plinius. We should mention the geographical work *De Chorographia* of a contemporary, Pomponius Mela, who mentions a number of the Plinian races.[16] In the early third century AD we also have the compilation of Solinus, *Collectanea*

Rerum Memorabilium, a work that utilised Plinius, Pomponius and other sources and was widely read in the Middle Ages. Solinus tends to elaborate and dramatise his sources, and like Aulus Gellius, he preserves a relative autonomy with respect to Plinius (cf. Mommsen, 1895: xv–xvi). Moreover, there appears to have been a cycle of illustrations to Solinus dating from late antiquity, including representations of monstrous human races (D.J.A. Ross, 1963: 78).

A 'Mandeville of the Dark Ages', as Ross calls it (ibid: 79) is the geographical description of the world attributed to one Aethicus Ister (a work which has been connected with Virgil, the eighth-century Irish Bishop of Salzburg), in which several traditions relating to Alexandros are reported, including the legend of Gog and Magog.

Some of the races are mentioned by the fifth century authors Macrobius and Martianus Capella, whose works were extremely influential in the Middle Ages.[17] Augustinus of Hippo lists a number of monstrous races in Book 16 of *De Civitate Dei*, where he argues that all men throughout the world who worship the same god are members of the universal city, which does not exclude the unusual races of men, although Augustinus only tentatively traces their descent from Adam. Augustinus asked his friend Paulus Orosius, a Spanish priest, to write a brief universal history, and the resulting work, *Historiarum adversum paganos libri septem*, was frequently used as a standard textbook in the Middle Ages, finding its way into an Old English version made by King Alfred in the late ninth century.

The tradition contained in these Latin texts is continued in the *Etymologiae* of Isidorus, bishop of Sevilla (ca. 570–636) and the anonymous *Liber Monstrorum*. Book 11 of the *Etymologiae sive origines* by Isidorus deals with both individual portents and monstrous races. In fact, Isidorus tends to treat them as analogous, though without explaining how this is so. Isidorus adds the satyrs to the list, taking them from Jerome's *Life of Paul the Hermit*. He also distinguishes two kinds of Blemmyes: those without a head, whose eyes and mouth are situated on their chest, and those without a neck whose eyes are in their shoulders. He deviates from Plinius in his account of the Macrobii: while they were understood to be long-living by Plinius, Isidorus explains the word in terms of a long *stature*, thereby confusing or conflating them with giants. As we shall see, this conflation recurs in depictions and descriptions of the inhabitants of the New World, where some of its inhabitants are credited with both long life and gigantic proportions.

The *Liber Monstrorum* is of uncertain date, provenance and authorship. Friedman (1981: 149f.) gives a date in the eighth century and sees in it both a reflection of Celtic Irish learning, notions and attitudes and familiarity with the Alexandros cycle.[18] The work has been associated with Aldhelm of Malmsbury and his circle. At any rate, the codex of the work from St Gallen, which also contains a Macrobian zone map and the *Etymologiae* of Isidorus, can be dated on paleographical grounds to the ninth century, thereby providing a *terminus ante quem* for the composition of the work (Knock, 1978). The *Liber Monstrorum* adds to the Plinian catalogue a number of Greek and Roman monsters, most of which come from the Roman poet Vergilius. They are given a hostile treatment in the work, foreshadowing the tone of later works like the rhyming *Etymologiae* of Isidorus from the eleventh century, which intensifies an aversion to the monstrous races which was already latent in the original *Etymologiae*.

Another source from late antiquity is the *Navigatio Sancti Brendani Abbatis*, a Latin work dated variously between the ninth and tenth centuries, and known from later Germanic and Dutch versions (*Van Sente Brandane*) from around 1150. St. Brendan himself was an Irish monk from the sixth century. In the German and Dutch versions, he threw a book into the fire in which he had read of wonders which he could not believe. His disbelief became the motive for a voyage of atonement, in the course of which he was confronted with marvellous places and people to convince him of God's power in creating wonders. For instance, he encounters an island that turns out to be an enormous fish; a mermaid; a siren; various devils; a man the size of a thumb who lives on a leaf in the sea and is engaged in counting the number of drops of water in the ocean; and the Walscheranden of Multum Bona Terra, a population of fallen angels who have pigs' heads. The Latin version of his voyage is somewhat different: there he travels to an enchanted island where time runs at a different tempo. This island gave rise to the belief in the blessed island(s) of Brendan, which make their appearance on the Hereford map of ca. 1290 and on the Erbstorfer world map, and later on the maps made by Ortelius and Mercator. Fernando, the son of Christopher Columbus, reports that the Brendan Islands were known to his father. In fact, Columbus senior claimed to have met sailors from Madeira in 1484 who wanted a ship to look for an island that appeared every year on the horizon (Colón, 1984: 19).[19]

From the late Middle Ages the main sources for the monsters include Honorius Augustodunensis, whose *De Imagine Mundi* drew heavily on Solinus and Isidorus; Jacob of Vitry, author of a three-volume work on the history of Jerusalem, whose composition is conventionally dated around 1220, and of which the first part, *Historia Orientalis*, was widely circulated and translated; Thomas of Cantimpré (1186–1263), who was influenced by Jacob of Vitry and who between 1228 and 1244 composed a work with a similar devotional purpose, *De Natura Rerum*, the third book of which is devoted to *monstruosi homines*; Bartholomaeus Anglicus, who produced an encyclopedic *De proprietatibus rerum* in the thirteenth century; Vincent of Beauvais (1190–1264), who drew heavily on his predecessors for the compilation of his *Speculum*, which in turn was a major source for Mandeville; and Gervais of Tilbury, whose *Otia imperialia*, dedicated to Kaiser Otto IV, was edited in 1707 by Leibniz.[20] There is a short list of some of them in the *Architrenius* of Jean de Hanville, dating from 1184, where they indicate the variety which nature is capable of producing and serve positive symbolic functions (Klaus, 1985).

Besides such encyclopedic works, romance and travellers' tales influenced one another, as they were to do again in the eighteenth century (Osterhammel, 1989: 14–15). For example, a manuscript dating from ca. 1400 (Bodley 264) includes an Alexandros romance and the travels of Marco Polo.[21] In the case of the cosmography of the French cardinal Pierre d'Ailly (1352–1420), whose *Tractatus de imagine mundi* was known to Columbus, the travellers' tales of the thirteenth and fourteenth centuries are ignored, and d'Ailly prefers to draw on fable and legend for his material. At this point we thus return to where we began: the travels of Marco Polo and those of 'Sir John Mandeville' from the fourteenth century.

Finally, we should mention another genre: the special treatment of the monstrous races within universal chronicles of history. This can first be documented for the *World Chronicle* of Antoninus of Florence (first published in Venice in 1474–1479). This work largely follows Augustinus, but now the monstrous races are introduced into the history of the world rather than as ethnographical curiosities. Among its successors we can single out the Nuremberg *Weltchronik* of Hartmann Schedel (1493), which follows Plinius, the *Cosmographia* (768–784) of Pseudo-Aethicus Ister and Filippo Foresti's *Supplementum Chronicarum* (Venice, 1483). In Schedel's work, the Plinian races are a part of God's plan: by introducing such diversity into the world, God was only demonstrating an awareness of their aesthetic value of contrasts. A later work, Sebastian Franck's *Chronika, Zeitbuch und Geschichtsbibel* (1531) follows Schedel, on which in turn Sebastian Münster's *Cosmographia* (1544; and 46 editions up to 1650) was based.[22] These more recent works are valuable because in addition to the texts they carry a number of woodcut illustrations. Those for Schedel's *Weltchronik* were executed by Dürer's tutor, Wohlgemut. These woodcuts were also used in Münster's work, as well as in the *Prodigiorum ac ostentorum chronicon* (1557) of Conrad Wolffhart, better known under the pseudonym of Lycosthenes. We can close this series with Ulisse Androvandi's *Monstrorum Historia* (1642), in which the individual monsters are represented in forms borrowed from the traditional monstrous races. This shift from race to individual is symptomatic, for while Androvandi is prepared to give credence to accounts of singular births, he tends to deny the existence of the monstrous races or to prefers to see them as imaginative exaggerations of real phenomena.

At this point we can close the (by no means complete) list of sources for the monstrous human races in the Greco-Roman tradition and that of the Middle Ages. Rather than piling up even more unfamiliar names, it will be more useful to follow the vagaries of one particular monstrous race through the sources to give an indication of the intricacies of this tradition. For this purpose, the dog-headed race of Cynocephali may serve as an example.

Marco Polo, writing at the start of the fourteenth century, tends to fare better than 'Sir John Mandeville' among modern critics for his keenness of perception, although Mandeville's work is more comprehensive than either that of Polo or that of Oderic of Pordenone. However, when Polo presents a description of the inhabitants of the Andamans it is equally fabulous and picturesque, to our imaginations, as that of Mandeville with which we began:

Andaman is a very big island. The people have no king. They are idolaters and live like wild beasts. Now let me tell you of a race of men worth describing in our book. You may take it for a fact that all the men of this island have heads like dogs, and teeth and eyes like dogs; for I assure you that the whole aspect of their faces is that of big mastiffs. They are a very cruel race: whenever they can get hold of a man who is not one of their kind, they devour him.

(Polo, 1958: 258.)

Mandeville also describes a dog-like race, although his description is much more favourable:

Thence one travels by sea to another land, called Natumeran [Nicobar islands]. It is a large and fair island, whose circuit is nearly a thousand miles. Men and women of that isle have heads like dogs, and they are called Cynocephales. These people, despite their shape, are fully reasonable and intelligent. They worship an ox as a god. [...] If they capture any man in battle, they eat him. The King of that land is a great and mighty lord, rich, and very devout according to his creed.

(Mandeville, 1983: 134)

As Wittkower (1977: 81) pointed out, Mandeville is here following Friar Odoric, who was the first to connect the Cynocephali with Marco Polo's remark on Indian Yogi who worship the ox and wear a small ox of brass or bronze on the forehead as a sort of emblem. An illustration to a German edition of Mandeville depicts a dog-headed figure which carries a model ox on top of its head (ibid: 73).

We can already see that the geographical specificity of these accounts leaves a lot to be desired. In fact, the location is hardly important: both the Nicobar and the Andaman Islands must have been equally exotic, unfamiliar and unattainable to the vast majority of the readers of Polo's and Mandeville's texts. But while the situation itself is relatively unimportant, they both attest the existence of a dog-headed people, Cynocephales. Now, this dog-headed people has a distinguished ancestry. In fact, we can trace it further back to the earliest Greek texts known to us. As we have seen, the Boiotian poet Hesiodos spoke of a half-dog people, and the Athenian dramatist Aischylos also mentioned a dog-headed people, on the testimony of Strabon (1.2.35). In fact, as Wittkower noted (1977: 197 n.29), dog-headed creatures are reported for Asia, China, Java, Siberia, Egypt and America, as well as for Europe. In China, for instance, a kingdom of dog-headed men is recorded; they have long hair, bark like dogs, and live on human flesh (de Mély, 1897: 359). We shall, however, confine our attention to Europe for the time being. In a description of the places to the west of the river Triton in Libya, Herodotos lists enormous serpents, lions, elephants, bears, hooded cobras, horned asses, kynokephaloi, akephaloi with their eyes on their shoulders, wild men and women and a number of other monstrosities (4.191). It seems clear that the kynokephaloi and akephaloi are to be thought of as human at this point, although in other sources kynokephaloi are sometimes conceived as animals.[23] In Megasthenes, at any rate, the kynokephaloi are clearly a human race. They number more than 120,000 people living in the mountains of India. They wear animal skins, instead of speaking they bark like dogs, and use their nails as hunting weapons (Plinius, HN. 7.2.23). Perhaps related to these are the Choromandae, a forest tribe of India which screeches instead of speaking and which has canine teeth (Plinius, HN. 7.2.24).

In a little-known Hellenistic poem, 'Apollon' by Simias (third century BC),[24] the poet speaks of a race of kynokephaloi. They have a dog's head above their shoulders and 'understand the articulate voice of other mortals', like the Indians of whom Ktesias says 'they understand what is said to them, but they are unable to converse themselves, but make signs' (in Photios, Bibl., p. 476.21).

In the Alexandros romance (3.28) the kynokephaloi live near a river called the Atlas close to other Plinian races. In the Letter of Alexandros, his men find a wood full of enormous Kynokephaloi, who try to provoke them and flee, shooting arrows (Boer, 1973: 32–33).

To pass to the later sources, Isidorus notes that the Cynocephali are dog-headed and that they bark (*Etymologiae* 11.3.15). The *Liber Monstrorum*, in accordance with its tendency to heighten the dramatic effect, attributes to the Cynocephali a diet of raw meat in addition to their dog-heads and bark (1.16), and in Marco Polo's account they are cannibals, a feature also found on a number of illustrations of Cynocephali in medieval bestiaries (Friedman, 1981: 11). The confusion may have arisen from the fact that Plinius sets the dog-headed Cynamolgi immediately after the Anthropophagi in his list of Ethiopian mons-trous races (6.35.195). By a process of 'contamination', the diet of the Cynamolgi thereby shifts from dogs' milk to human flesh. Besides these dog-headed Ethiopians, we find a northern geographical location in a number of sources.[25]

In the pictorial tradition there are dog-headed men on the famous twelfth-century tympanum in Vézélay in a grouping whose prototype seems to have been Greek, if not Babylonian (Wittkower, 1977: 200 n.106), and which recurs in the cosmography of Kazwini, 'the Arabic Plinius of the thirteenth century', as well as in the thirteenth-century Hereford map (ibid: 54). In medieval treatments of missionary activity, the dog-headed race often represents the eastern races (Friedman, 1981: 59ff.). It can stand for Islam, as in the Armenian gospel book illustrated by T'oros Roslin in 1262 (ibid: 66), the Jews, as in the work of Hugh of St Cher, and the Saracens, as in a world map of 1430 depicting the Saracen Ethiopian king with his dog-headed people. The Cynocephali enter German epic in the twelfth century as soldiers of the pagan king of Funde (Lecouteux, 1982, I: 81).

Besides these examples of dog-headed races, there are examples of individual cynocephali too. They are connected with the saints Mercurius and Christopher. In an eastern version, St Christopher began life as a cynocephalus before his conversion, and in the Irish *Libar Breac* Christopher is dog-headed (as he is in an Old English Martyrology). As for St Mercurius, his grandfather was eaten by cannibal cynocephali in the neighbourhood of Rome. They were prevented from eating his father through the intervention of an angel. Mercurius' father converted them, and they helped Mercurius in battle against the pagans, reverting to their previous form when required.

The Apostles Andrew and Bartholomew are said to have come across a dog-headed monster (in the Ethiopic *Contendings of the Apostles*). It is worth quoting the description of this monster in full:[26]

> Now his appearance was exceedingly terrible. He was four cubits in height, and his face was like unto the face of a great dog, and his eyes were like unto lamps of fire which burnt brightly, and his teeth were like unto the tusks of a wild boar, or the teeth of a lion, and the nails of his hands were like unto curved reaping hooks, and the nails of his toes were like unto the claws of a lion, and the hair of his head came down over his arms like unto the mane of a lion, and his whole appearance was awful and terrifying.

The rest of the story resembles that of St Christopher.[27] We also find isolated examples of individual cynocephali outside the hagiographies too. Dog-headed individuals crop up in the compilations of prodigious births,[28] and Jakob Mennel's *Tractatus de Signis, Prodigiis...* (Vienna, 1503) shows a dog-headed monster brought before Louis the Pious in 814 (Wittkower, 1977: 65). Vincent de Beauvais, writing at the time of St Louis, recounts the same story, adding a report of the monster's huge penis and the sexual threat it posed for young girls and women (Roy, 1975: 77).

From this brief survey of the sources we see a well-documented European tradition on the existence of the Plinian races, a tradition which was not impervious to influences from the Orient[29] and which was to find no difficulty in situating them in the New World too after the discovery.

The geographical situation of the races lent itself to such borrowings because it is itself extremely instable. Wittkower discusses them as 'Marvels of the East' and records a number which were known from the Mahabharata and other Indian epics. Similar monstrous races are found in China, though the traditions vary on their exact location there (de Mély, 1897), and the monstrous races recorded in the sixteenth-century Turkish *Piri Re'îs* have been assumed to derive from a pre-Christian Chinese source. The favoured localities in the European sources are Ethiopia[30] and India,[31] though from Homeros onwards the two are often confused.[32] Another geographical location for them is the unknown north, which we already find in the (lost) *Arimaspeia* of Aristeas. In Hesiodos, the Arimaspoi are confused with the Hyperboreans, and later Greek authors simply equate the two. A northern or oriental location are often both feasible: Plinius follows Megasthenes in situating a race of men with their feet turned backwards on a mountain in India (7.2.22), while on the authority of Baiton he locates a similar race in Skythia (7.2.11).

While Mandeville locates most of the Plinian races on the Andaman Islands (1983: 137), he sets the Cynocephales, as we have seen, on another island,

Natumeran (ibid: 134), while Marco Polo puts his dog-headed race on the Andaman Island (1958: 258). There is an almost total indifference to geographical specificity in the encyclopedic works. Münster, for example, repeats illustrations from different texts, and the monstrous races of India reappear in Africa. 'Lycosthenes' similarly uses identical woodcuts to illustrate marvellous events that are widely separated in space and time. The Panotii, a race mentioned by Isidorus, with ears reaching to their feet which they use to fly, are familiar from references in the Chinese literature to heads which fly by means of their long ears (de Mély, 1897: 358), as well as from the references in the Indian epics to people who cover themselves with their ears. Ktesias also situates them in India, but Sebastian Franck transfers them to Sicily in his *Chronika*. Sometimes the situation of a race is displaced because of widening geographical horizons - for example, the 'emigration' of monstrous human races from South to North America on later maps of the continent – but more generally the regions are simply interchangeable. The Blessed Isles which Diodoros situated somewhere near India, perhaps in what is now Sri Lanka, are found in a variety of situations, and the land of the Hyperboreans, which etymologically belongs in the North, is sometimes transferred .to the West and conflated with the Garden of the Hesperides (Gernet, 1968: 144 n.31).

What all these locations have in common is the fact that they represent extremities:

> In Mercator's maps, there is a centrifugal movement from the name-laden Europe to the periphery where legends and drawings characterise vast territories without history... Brazil, the interior of Africa, or Iceland, likewise contain in the Atlas the medieval projections of monsters, marvels and anomalies associated with the far corners of the Earth.
>
> (Rabasa, 1985: 9–10; cf. Helms, 1988: 211ff.)

Such regions were thought of as being conducive to the birth of monsters. Hence Thomas of Cantimpré inclined to the view that hybrids were not born from intercourse between humans and animals, but that they originated in the remote areas of the Orient, supporting this claim with a reference to the horned and goat-footed figure that appeared to Anthony the hermit. Moreover, excessive heat was thought to play strange tricks of nature, so that desert regions were particularly conducive to the generation of monstrous races, a belief to be found in ancient Egypt as well as in the European Middle Ages.[33]

Similar to the lack of geographical specificity is a lack of specificity in the names of the monstrous races. The Greek for 'one-legged' is *monokolos*. Latin readers read this as *monoculus* ('one-eyed') and thereby confused the one-eyed Kyklopes with the one-legged Sciopodes. The switch from dog-milking to anthropophagy in the case of the dog-headed races, it was suggested, may have arisen from a similar textual sloppiness.

Sometimes the confusion is simply orthographic: should we write *Sciopodes* or *Sciapodes?* Both occur in the manuscripts. More complex are those cases where it is not clear exactly what the right name should be. When Aristeas of Prokonnesos refers to 'web-footed' men (Steganopodes), is he referring to the parasol-like feet of the Sciopodes? After all, we do find Sciapodes with two webbed feet in *Herzog Ernst*, and a Sciapod with one webbed foot in an illustration to the Old French version of Thomas of Cantimpré, though not in the text itself (Lecouteux, 1982, I: 268–269). Or should we treat the Steganopodes as a separate monstrous race?

In one of the manuscripts of the Latin Letter of Alexandros to Aristoteles, hairy men and women are described, whom the Indians call *faunos*. They are amphibian and live on a diet of raw fish. When Alexandros' men tried to approach them, they plunged into the sea. The editor of the text supports the word *faunos* here, but other manuscripts have Ichthyophagi ('fish-eaters'), a reading which is supported by Gunderson (1980: 57). It seems impossible to decide whether we should adopt the more familiar Ichthyophagi, or see in *faunos* the vestige of a separate race which resists assimilation. Another such case is that of the Sannali recorded by Pomponius Mela (*Chorographia* 3.56). The description of them matches that of the long-eared Phanesii mentioned by Plinius and Solinus, or the Enotokoitai mentioned by Megasthenes, while the name given them by Isidorus, Panotii ('all-ears'), is simply a description of their most distinguishing characteristic. Perhaps the term Sannali bears the trace of an indigenous name for this people. At any rate, such separate races tend to disappear in the work of philology, which often eradicates the unfamiliar or the *hapax legomenon* to replace it with a more familiar equivalent[34] – a process which itself mirrors the European tendency to accept the new only if it can be assimilated to the old and the familiar.

Such problems of nomenclature raise the question of the definition of the races themselves. It might not seem so far-fetched to include the Choromandae, a race with dog-like teeth, or the dog-eared, one-eyed Monommatoi mentioned by Megasthenes, among the dog-headed people, though Isidorus mentions the Cynodontes, a race of men with two rows of teeth, as a separate race. It might even be admissible to relate them to the 'inverted' Cynocephali of Thomas of Cantimpré, whose animal sexuality is expressed by their being 'men toward the head and mad dogs below the loins' (3.47-54). But there are other candidates for inclusion which seem to deviate even more from the central definition of a dog-headed people. In the illustrations to Schedel's *Liber Chronicorum*, the upper torsos of both a man and a dog are both fastened at the waist to a single body, while the Latin text (*habens faciem hominis retro canis*) refers to a being with the face of a man at the front and of a dog at the back. In the travels of St Brendan, the Irish monk comes to the castle of the Walscheranden on Mount Syone. The Walscheranden were previously angels who had neglected to rise to the assistance of God against the revolt of Lucifer. As a punishment for their swinish inactivity, they were given pigs' heads. However, they are animal-like in more ways too: they have the teeth of wolves, the hands and torso of men, the feet of dogs and the long necks of cranes. Half of their body is hairy like a dog because of their doglike behaviour in heaven.

These walking bestiaries recall the composite figure of Abominable, the dog-headed cannibal converted by the Apostles Andrew and Bartholomew, or the Giant Herdsman of Chrétien de Troyes' *Ywein*, but the mass of extra attributes renders them intractable as regards classification within the races. Similar uncertainties and variations in fact surround most of the names from the Plinian catalogue. Sciopodes tend to be one-legged, but in an illustration of Ethiopia by Jan Collaert for Stradanus' *Venationes Ferarum, Avium, Piscium* two-legged Sciopodes are shown. On the other hand, where our sources refer to one-legged monsters, we cannot always be sure that they had enormous feet.

In order to interpret the Plinian races, it is first necessary to attempt some form of classification, despite the proviso given above. The various traits of the Greek and Roman accounts have been grouped by Friedman under the headings of food and dietary practices; the possession of articulate language; the forming of villages and cities; the practice of the arts of urban life – law, social intercourse, worship, art, philosophy; and the existence of industry (1981: 26–36). These traits are cultural traits. The scheme by which Herodotos classified the 'savage' peoples at the extremities of the known world lays down most of these features already. He distinguishes between vegetarians, those who live on raw fish and raw meat, those who practise a restricted anthropophagy, and those who are downright cannibals. In congruity with this spectrum is a geographical scheme according to which the furthermost regions are the most 'savage'. Sexually, he displays similar gradations from the *droits de seigneur* of the king, the *droits de seigneur* of all the guests at a wedding, the promiscuity of women to an unbridled sexuality and generalised promiscuity. These scales also accommodate gradations in the degree of agricultural development, religious development, the use of tools and precious metals, and political organisation (Rossellini and Saïd, 1978). Though Herodotos does not do so, we might easily accommodate language within this scheme: a lack of articulation at the dietary, sexual or other levels might be supposed to indicate a lack of linguistic articulation.

If we try to accommodate the Plinian races to these categories, we can note the stress on dietary practices for the Anthropophagi, Pamphagi, Agriophagi, Cynamolgi, Oeonae, locust eaters, turtle eaters, fish eaters, Astomi or apple-smellers and straw-drinkers. The lack of articulate language arises in the case of monstrous races like the speechless men, the Kynokephaloi who can only bark in some accounts, the bat-like cave-dwellers of the African interior who live on snake meat, the Atlantes who have no names, as well as those like the Astomi and straw-drinkers who obviously lack speech altogether. The Donestre, on the other hand, pretend to speak the language of any traveller they meet. Some of the races have weapons (Kynokephaloi, maritime Ethiopian archers) or hunt with dogs (bearded women). As for religion, the Augilae of Africa have an infernal religion, while the Bragmanni have a developed religion or philosophy. As for sexual customs, the wife-givers give their wives to any traveller who stops among them.

The 'inverted' Kynokephaloi of Thomas of Cantimpré and the dog-headed creature brought before the court of Louis are sexually importunate, and the monstrous races depicted on the (no longer extant) frescoes from around 1500 in Råby Church, Denmark, exhibit an unmistakable sexual vitality, no doubt symbolising un-Christian vices.

All these cultural traits, however, obviously exclude any kind of relativism, for admission of relativism would deprive many of them of their monstrosity. That is, definition of the races in cultural terms is always bound to run up against problems in the definition of borderline cases and ethnocentrism. Any attempt to go beyond mere description necessarily involved questions of interpretation that created severe semantic difficulties for the first would-be ethnologists (Pagden, 1982: 13). A case in point is that of the Anthropophagi: within the classical sources, this is a relatively well-defined ethnic group, situated in a variety of geographical locations but always clearly definable in terms of the diet of human flesh. Problems arose when the Mediterranean image of the Anthropophagi was mapped on to the Amerindian peoples of the extended Caribbean who first appear as *caníbales* in Columbus' entry for 23 November 1492. The term is sometimes a purely geographical term, indicating those people who inhabited the island called Caniba. Or it may be an ethnic term, *los caníbales*. Soon, however, its dominant meaning became 'those who are hostile and eat human flesh', as the classical Mediterranean paradigm asserted its superiority within European discourse on native America (Hulme, 1986: 67–73).

The salient characteristic of many of the Plinian races which is less open to such vagaries, as de Mély pointed out almost a century ago (1897: 355-356), is their physical appearance. One obvious aspect is pigmentation. In French medieval literature, for instance, giants appear whose skin is black, while Adam of Bremen refers to a people with a green skin (Lecouteux, 1982, I: 33 and 83). But the reference to physical appearance is more than skin-deep. There are, after all, certain limits to the ways in which the physical appearance of the human body may be modified without doing extreme violence to its humanity. It may thus be possible to present a harder classification of these physical variations, and here we fall back upon Diderot for guidance. In the *Dream of D'Alembert* (1769, first published in 1830), Diderot explains fabulous creatures such as the Kyklops as a result of mutations in the bundle of threads which comprises the human organism. This bundle constitutes the original and first difference of all animal species (Diderot, 1951: 908). There are three mechanisms which Diderot names: suppression, duplication and combination. If we apply these three to the monstrous human races, we derive from them both a principle of classification and a model of internal logic.[35]

In the first case, suppression, we deal with loss: the loss of an eye (Kyklops), the lack of a head or neck (Blemmyae), the lack of a breast (Amazons), the lack of a mouth (Astomi), the lack of a nose (Sciritae, straw-drinkers), the lack of a leg or foot (Monocoli and Sciopodes).

Duplication leads to the monstrous races with four eyes (maritime Ethiopians), or the eight fingers and toes of the Pandae. More generally, in the form of excess it includes the protruding lower or upper lip of the Amyctyrae and the enormous foot of the Sciopodes, the androgini of Africa who have genitals of both sexes, the bearded ladies and hairy men and women, the excessively large giants and excessively small pygmies, the enormous ears of the Panotii, and the dangling testicles of the men of the land of Hormuz in the fifteenth-century metrical version of Mandeville's travels (1973, ll. 1869–1870):

> Of alle the men of that cuntree
> Hir ballokis hangeth binethe hir knee.

Third, we have the strange combinations that result from displacement, such as the reversed feet of the Antipodes and Abarimon, the displaced eyes of the Epiphagi and Blemmyae. More extreme cases of displacement involve the displacement of organs across species, as in the dog-headed races, the owl-eyed Albanians, the horse-footed Hippopodes, the goat-footed Pans. In combination, we have composite figures like the dog-headed Abominable or the pig-headed Walscheranden, who combine features of different animals in one being.

As we see, the three mechanisms elaborated by Diderot take us a long way in grouping the physical peculiarities of the monstrous races. It is interesting to note that the recent collection of 'strange tales in which the scientific and the romantic cry out to come together' groups the cases dealt with by doctor Oliver Sacks under the titles Losses, Excesses and Transports (Sacks, 1986). The fibres of Diderot also have the advantage of providing a structural passage from the monstrous races to the individual anomalies, a transfer which Isidorus of Sevilla had already made more inductively in his *Etymologiae*. The monstrous births recorded already in Babylonia, of babies with no mouth, no nostrils, or six toes on each foot, conform to Diderot's scheme in the same way as the monstrous races. But besides, the structural implications of these mechanisms help to explain the usefulness of the races for thinking with. For example, it might be justifiable to see the structural relationship between the enormous foot of the Sciapod, warding off the heat of the sun, on the one hand, and the enormous ears of the Panotii, in which they can wrap themselves up against the cold, on the other hand, as a form of reflection on the categories of hot and cold. The varied degrees of openness of the body evidenced by the Astomoi, Straw-Drinkers, etc. may also be seen as a form of reflection on the openness of the body to society through social intercourse and language. Through the systems of permutations, the various Plinian races constitute a veritable *combinatoire* by which variations on humanity, and thus humanity itself, can be thought. In this sense, they form an anthropology, that is, a way of using reflection on the limits of the body for the construction of its images of the other.

The discourse on the functions of the body is a discourse on the limits of self *in terms of distance from the other*. All discussion of 'body language', gesture, movement, sexuality, physiological functions, clothing and so on is at one and the same time a discourse on self and a discourse on the other, involving the process of 'negative self-definition', by which self is defined in terms of what it is not, namely, the other. Hence discussion of the anomalous features of the bodily constitution of the monstrous human races is a discourse on the other.

We are now ready for the linguistic turn. If the Plinian races constitute a discourse on the other, how does this discourse function? In the following chapters it will be suggested that the Plinian races do in fact operate like a language, and that they are structured like a language. The Antipodes and other races marked in terms of bodily articulation actually constitute the articulation of this language. The Astomi and other races marked in terms of the bodily orifices constitute a punctuation. Other races might be supposed to play a part in this semiotic process as well.

The Plinian races may thus be seen to provide a form of articulation: the articulation of self upon other, the articulation of the Old World upon the New. There is an ambiguity, however, in the way in which this articulation is brought about. On the one hand, the Plinian races offer a ready-made language. The variety of types that we have examined in this chapter provides an ample framework within which the other may be appropriated in terms of the familiar. Simply through the fact of constituting a language at all, they constrict at the same time as they construct. On the other hand, the shifting contours which these races assume give them a flexibility which functions in two ways: it enables them to extend their range to the furthest limits of the contours of the human body, but at the same time it evades any attempt to impose rigid distinctions upon the matter in hand. The very flexibility of these races gives the New World a means of slipping out of the clutches of the Old World which is violently trying to assimilate it. They partake of the wildness in which Taussig sees such a liberating force:

> Wildness challenges the unity of the symbol, the transcendental totalization binding the image to that which it represents. Wildness pries open this unity and in its place creates slippage and a grinding articulation between signifier and signified. [...] Wildness is the death space of signification.
>
> (Taussig, 1987: 219)

The crucial point here is that the Plinian races do not constitute *either* a language of domination (by the range they offer for encompassing the unfamiliar in terms of the familiar) *or* a language of revolt (by their Protean elusiveness). They are rather the field of forces in which the stratagems of subjugation and subversion are played out, resisting appropriation by either side. Perhaps the concept of contamination is what covers this aspect best. In the moment of confrontation, the resistance of the Plinian races to hard and fast definition works not so much as a language, but as a Babel, subverting the discourse which attempts to impose a single, unified framework on the recalcitrant data. This act of subversion derives its power from the fact that the means of resistance to a discourse seeking domination are lodged within that very discourse itself: 'the contamination of the language of the master by that which he attempts to subjugate and on which he has declared war' (Derrida, 1987b: 48).[36] This contamination, by which the language of the Plinian races both structures and subverts the workings of a discourse which is trying to assert its hegemony, is the subject of the following chapters.

Notes

1. It is not certain that Columbus ever read Mandeville: there are no explicit references to Mandeville in Columbus' works, nor does the book figure in his library preserved in Sevilla. On the other hand, both A. Bernaldez and Fernando Columbus assume that he was familiar with Mandeville's book. In view of the fact that knowledge of Mandeville penetrated the Iberian peninsula via a group of English merchants resident in Sevilla, it is extremely likely that Columbus was familiar with the contents of the book, whether he had ever read it or not.
2. The best general accounts of the Plinian races are: Friedman (1981); Wittkower's 'Marvels of the East: A Study in the History of Monsters' [1944] (reprinted in Wittkower 1977: 45–74); Pfister's 'Von den Wundern des Morgenlandes' [1955] (reprinted in Pfister 1976: 120–142); and Lecouteux (1982). I have drawn heavily on these sources in the following paragraphs.
3. The other beings which inhabit the Homeric world of the imaginary are excluded from the present analysis because they are not 'anthropological' enough. Either they are above the world of humans, like the goddess Kalypso, or they transgress the border between men and animals, as happens to Odysseus' companions when they are turned into swine by Kirke.
4. A papyrus fragment of Hesiodos (150 Merkelbach and West) is restorable with a reference to 'half-dogs'.
5. Usually dated in the 440s or 430s BC. The date of composition must at any rate be later than the eruption of Etna in 479 BC.
6. Also described by Pherekydes, FGH F 11. These may be the same as the swan maidens who live in darkness, familiar figures in Central Asiatic myth (Bolton, 1962; 101).
7. I am here following the account and translation of Wright (1981). The fragments are numbered according to the standard Greek-German edition of the pre-Socratic philosophers by Diels and Kranz.
8. The fragments of the first Greek ethnographers are collected in F. Jacoby's monumental *Die Fragmente der griechischen Historiker* (abbreviated as FGH).
9. While Kroll suggested a date in the third century AD, Aerts has suggested that the existence of portions of the work at a much earlier date may have been motivated by the need for Ptolemaic propaganda for the Greco-Egyptian dynasty (Aerts, 1987).
10. Aristoteles was supposed to have drawn on the information provided by Alexandros' research team in the compilation of his *On Animals*.
11. On the Alexandros tradition see especially Cary (1956), D.J.A. Ross (1963) and Pfister (1976).
12. Megasthenes is the source of the descriptions of these races in Strabon 15.1.57.
13. The reading *Panotii* to be found in some of the Plinian manuscripts is interpolated from Isidorus. Solinus also mentions the Phanesii.
14. For example, the annotated edition by W. Guglinger (Krakow, 1526), or the *Sommaire des Singularitez de Pline* by Pierre de Changy (Paris, 1542).
15. In this respect, there is a structural difference between the monstrous human races and the Wild Men and Women discussed in Chapter Two. While the former can be mapped

in terms of (ethno/ego)concentric circles, the latter are caught up in a binary structure articulated in terms of x and anti-x, utilising the mechanism of mirror inversion (cf. Gagnon, 1975: 86–87).

16. Among those listed are the Scimantopodes (Mela, 3.101). As Parroni (1976) has shown, this manuscript reading should be changed to Himantopodes: the word 'Scimantopodes' seems to be based on a confusion between Himantopodes and the Indian Sciritai mentioned by Megasthenes (in Plinius, *Historia Naturalis* 7.25).

17. Macrobius' *Commentary on the Dream of Scipio* ran into ten editions between 1472 and 1515 (Seeber, 1971: 81), a sufficient proof of its continuing popularity at the time of the discovery of America.

18. This dating would make it more or less contemporary with the Old English *Marvels of the East*, a compilation of Plinian races that was included in the Beowulf codex, containing various tales of the marvellous.

19. The island was associated with the Canary Islands throughout the Middle Ages. For later attempts to find it (the latest being in 1721), see Gil's interesting note in Colón (1984: 19 n.12).

20. Gervais borrowed many of his *mirabilia* from Augustinus, but he added the hydro-phages and the men without a head (Céard, 1977: 41).

21. For the relation between Polo and Columbus, see now Reichert (1988).

22. The English translation by Richard Eden, *A Treatise of the New India*, was published in 1555. A facsimile edition of the richly illustrated 1550 Basle German edition was published by De Haan in 1989.

23. In the Liber Floridus of Lambert of Saint Omer, the Cynocephali are described as *animantia*, a word that usually means animals, but which is itself open to ambiguity. Plinius, as we saw, referred to an Ethiopian nomad people who lived on the milk of cynocephali (6.35.190), and in another passage (7.2.31) he explicitly refers to the cynocephali as *animalia*.

24. Greek text in Powell, 1925: 109.

25. Adam of Bremen, *History of the Archbishops of Hamburg*, makes of them the children of the northern Amazons. See too Pseudo-Aethicus Ister, *Cosmographia*; the Hereford map (ca. 1290); Johannus de Plano Carpini (±1185–1252), *Historia Mongalorum* 9.12; and the world map of Andreas Walsperger (1448).

26. Note the technique of metonymic composition, which we encountered in Chapter Two in the description of the Wild Man by Chrétien de Troyes. I have discussed it in more detail in Mason, forthcoming c.

27. For a later example of a pig-headed monster as an enemy to Christendom, see the pen drawing from the mid-sixteenth century by Dirck Crabeth of *Pilgrim between Reason and a monk* (Filedt Kok et al., 1986: ill. 240c).

28. W. Rolevinck, *Fasciculus Temporum*, Köln 1474, cited in Céard, 1977: 75.

29. Note the Kynokephaloi on a seventeenth-century Persian manuscript mentioned by Pfister (1976: 121 n.4).

30. For sixteenth-century European contact with Ethiopia and its background see Knefelkamp (1989).

31. On the reception of Indian art in Europe during the Middle Ages and after, the most comprehensive study is Mitter (1977).

32. Nevertheless, there is sometimes a meaningful distinction between them. In such cases, Ethiopia is usually the land of aridity and the fight for survival, in opposition to India as the land of plenty.

33. Ancient Egypt: H.G. Fischer (1987); European Middle Ages: Le Goff (1985).

34. As we saw above, some of the Plinian manuscripts (*Historia Naturalis* 4.13.95) replace Phanesii by Panotii in deference to the work of Isidorus.

35. Lecouteux proposes a similar account of the various forms assumed by monstrosity:

enlargement or reduction; the absence or excess of certain organs; and hybridisation – the combining of elements drawn from different species within one exemplar (Lecouteux, 1982, I: 5). See further Mason, forthcoming c.

36. The context of Derrida's remark is a discussion of the resistance offered to domination by the English (language) in the polyglot work of James Joyce – a theme that is by no means irrelevant to the colonial situation of America.

Source: J.-F. Lafitau, Moeurs des sauvages amériquains,
comparées aux moeurs des premiers temps, Paris, 1724,
2 vols. Reproduced with permission of the University Library,
Amsterdam.

Chapter four

The monstrous human races of America

We have seen how the images of the Wild Man and the Wild Woman, the fool, the beggar, the peasant and the witch functioned as the negative images by which European culture defined itself as a culture at all. Similarly, the Plinian races served to define the exotic outer world in contrast to the familiar inner world of Europe. Representations of the exotic worlds and their fauna and flora were just as much a matter of interest to both the courtly and the urban cultures of the late Middle Ages as were the representations of less distant types against whom the civilising offensive was directed. It has been suggested that the imagery of these exotic races, projected on to the inhabitants of the New World, came to supplant the more traditional European images of the Wild Man; that Europe's inner Indians came to be replaced by its outer Indians. Such a view is not supported by the evidence, which points rather to a coexistence of both the traditional European negative internal images and the images of exotic human races in the portrayal of the peoples of America right from the start. It is thus worth looking at the ways in which the American Indians were portrayed as monstrous human races from the first.

The first predates Columbus' arrival in 1492. The first European observers of America were probably the Vikings. According to the conventional dating, it was in the first decade of the eleventh century that Norse expatriates from Iceland arrived via Greenland on the northern coasts of America. The 'wineland' (*Vínland*) that they discovered, though the subject of controversy, is generally located somewhere in the region of New England.

In the sagas relating to this expedition, there are two versions of the death of Thorvald Eiriksson. According to the account in the *Groenlendinga þáttr*, he met his death in a fight with *Skraelings*. This word, which is used indiscriminately in the sources to refer to both Eskimo and North American Indians, has roughly the connotations of the Greek *barbaroi* as applied to non-Greeks. In the second account of Thorvald's death, in *Þorfinn's saga*, he is shot in the groin by an *Einfoetingr*, a one-footed creature (Gordon, 1957: 54). This creature was familiar to the medieval Icelandic ethnographers of the imaginary, for it is mentioned in the geographical treatise *Heimlýsing ok Helgifroeði*, a treatise that is preserved in the same manuscript (the *Hauksbók*) as the Vínland sagas. It is located in North

Africa, which suggests reliance for its source material on the seventh-century *Etymologiae* of Bishop Isidorus of Sevilla, who notes as characteristic of the Sciopodes of Ethiopia their one-leggedness and their remarkable swiftness.[1]

Traditional philological approaches to these two versions tend to assume that the appearance of the one-footed creature is a late, learned embroidery on the other version. If, however, we apply a synchronic approach to the Scandinavian material,[2] we may posit a certain symbolic equivalence between *Skraeling* and *Einfoetingr*. In Scandinavian eyes, an Indian is an Eskimo, a barbarian and a monster.

Support for such an assumption can be found in iconography. Like other of the monsters depicted by Michael Wohlgemut in the *Nuremberg Weltchronik* (1493), the one-legged Sciopod makes an appearance in the same pose (lying under the shade of its own single foot) in Aldrovandi's *Monstrorum Historia* (1642). Unipeds (Monocoli) were also said to have been seen by Jacques Cartier in North America in the fabulous city of Saguenay. It is thus striking that the uniped appears in the same pose in Olaus Magnus' *Historia de Gentibus Septentrionalibus* (1555), but this time *as an Eskimo* (Honour, 1979: 270–271).

The salient characteristic in this first encounter of Europeans with the inhabitants of the New World is the fact that their otherness is portrayed in terms of the monstrous. This was to be a theme that was only too readily taken up by later illustrators of the inhabitants of the New World, who found no difficulty in replacing one Plinian monster by another if required: dog-headed men, men with their eyes on their chests and others were part of the Mandevillean stock of icons which could represent the peoples of America.

There is a second element in this first encounter which should also be singled out here. In the episode which immediately precedes the death of Thorvald at the hands of the *Einfoetingr*, Karlsefni and his men come upon five *Skraelings* who are asleep. Karlsefni's men reckon that these five must be outlaws, and kill them.

The encounter with the other in *Þorfinn's saga* thus has two forms. In the first, unfamiliar human beings are denied their humanity – they become monstrous. In the second, they are assimilated to the self which perceives them: since the Norsemen were outlaws (at least, the migrations via Iceland to Greenland and further are motivated in the sources by the outlawing of the perpetrators of killings), the people whom they encounter are assigned the same status – and killed.

To return to the theme of the *Einfoetingr*, this has its roots not in the social origins of the Norse discoverers but in the Plinian tradition, that presumably reached Iceland via the Irish Channel. As we have seen, this tradition assumed that in regions where the absence of colonialist penetration implied a lack of knowledge, this could be substituted by projections of monsters, marvels and anomalies associated with the far corners of the earth. The travels of Irish monks like St Brendan must have contributed to the diffusion of certain of these stereotypes, and they displayed a remarkable degree of persistence over time. When Frobisher set out for Baffin Island in 1576, he followed Columbus' example in taking a copy of 'Sir John mandevylle, englishe' (presumably the 1568 edition) with him (Sturtevant and Quinn, 1987: 115 n.7). Many of the illustrations known to have been made of the captives that he brought back to England with him have been lost, but they would undoubtedly have shed light on the vagaries of the Plinian iconographical tradition and its relation to these early European contacts with America.

Our second example of Plinian races in connection with America is taken from the *Historia de las Indias de Nueva España* written by the Dominican, Diego Durán. Although this work was completed in 1581, some generations after the Spanish conquest of America, its value lies in the quality of the sources, which are almost exclusively of native Indian origin (Baudot and Todorov, 1983: 38–42). After Motecuhzoma had received a report of the arrival of the Spaniards between 1517 and 1519 (the chronology of Durán's account is very confused), he first asked a painter to portray them according to the description given by an eyewitness, and then proceeded to summon various painters from different regions to see if their ancestors had given them a description of the beings which were destined to embark. The painters of Malincalo showed him a painting which depicted 'men with one eye in their forehead, like Cyclopes [...], others with more than one foot [...].' As for the painters of Marquesado, they had portraits of 'men, half-fish, from the waist down'[3] and of 'paintings of men, half-man and half-serpent' (Durán, 1967, II, LXX. 8–9). How much of this represents original native beliefs and how much is Durán's gloss is impossible for us to determine, but it would appear that behind the layers of pictorial and verbal translation which this *oratio obliqua* presents (a Spanish account based on a náhuatl original of a reported discussion concerning paintings carried out by members of a previous generation...), a knowledge of at least some of the Plinian races was present in the pre-Conquista Mexican court.[4]

These two examples seem to offer a challenge to the claim that 'it is only by way of his own culture that the European perceives the reality of the savage world which, in itself, remains foreign to him' (Duchet, 1971: 15). For they seem to point to the existence of traditions relating to monstrous human races on the American continent preceding the contact with Europe initiated by Columbus. In the first case, a sceptic might argue that, since the Scandinavian writers were not immune to the influence of the European traditions, subject as they were to the learning which the first missionaries brought with them, it is not inconceivable that the Icelandic *Einfoetingr* is a direct descendant of the monstrous races described by Isidorus. In the second case, we have drawn attention to the fact that the account purporting to refer to pre-Conquista events is itself dated a half century later, time enough for the story of the Plinian races to have crept into the account from European (Spanish) sources.

A third example, this time post-dating the Conquest, comes from Sir Walter Ralegh's *The Discovery of the Large, Rich and Beautiful Empire of Guiana* (1596). There he describes 'a nation of people, whose heades appeare not aboue their shoulders'; they are reported to have 'their eyes in their shoulders, and their mouths in the middle of their breasts, and that a long train of haire groweth backward between their shoulders' (Ralegh, 1970: 85). This people, whom he knows by the name of Ewaipanoma, figure among the Plinian races as the *Blemmyae*. Ralegh believes that such a people exist, though he does not claim to have been an eyewitness himself. His report relies on the fact that 'euery child in the provinces of Arromaia and Canuri affirme the same' (ibid.). Nor was Ralegh the only one to believe in the existence of such beings. Appended to his account are letters captured at sea in 1594 by George Popham from certain Spaniards, which include an account of Indians who had 'the pointes of their shoulders higher then the Crownes of their heades' (ibid: 127). Knowledge about these 'Indians with the high shoulders' derives from an interpreter who, in a pattern which soon becomes familiar in this type of account, situates these Indians *somewhere else,* on a mountain a quarter of a league away. Lawrence Keymis also mentioned them, and the accounts were accepted by George Abbot and others (Sheehan, 1980: 73).

This example admits of various interpretations. The native peoples of North and South America have an extensive body of ethno-anthropological beliefs which provide races as monstrous as those which European ethnography located in America. Magaña has thus concluded that 'at least a part of the accounts of the travellers on monstrous peoples were in fact derived from native informants' (1982b: 65). Is it possible that Ralegh is here merely reflecting genuine indigenous beliefs? His nineteenth-century commentator and adulator, Sir Robert Schomburgk, certainly thought so. Schomburgk was prepared to admit that Ralegh had a preconceived idea in favour of Amazons and other Plinian races before he left England, opinions which may well have been supported by an acquaintance with the 1568 English translation of Thevet's *Les Singularités de la France Antarctique* by Thomas Hacket. Nevertheless, Schomburgk is eager to clear Ralegh of the charge of dealing in fables and he appends a lengthy footnote to Ralegh's account of the Ewaipanoma, adducing other evidence for their existence. The evidence he quotes comes from Plinius the Elder, Ktesias, Herodotus and Sir John Mandeville.[5] But this list of names, familiar from the previous chapter, indicates that Schomburgk was just as much a prisoner of the Plinian tradition of monstrous races as Ralegh was. His 'evidence' is no proof of the existence of these peoples on the American continent. Hence when he brings up the question of how far the prototypes provided by these sources may have affected Ralegh's reading of the testimony of the natives, it is justifiable to raise the same question with respect to Schomburgk's own commentary. Given his complicity in the text of Ralegh, his assertion that such accounts were not the offspring of Ralegh's imagination, but that he was relating 'the common belief of the natives, not only at the period of his visit but up to this day [1848]' (Ralegh, 1970: 85) should be taken with more than a grain of salt.

Moreover, the claims made by Schomburgk and Ralegh run up against the serious problem of how far the European voyagers genuinely understood what their informants tried to tell them. In the case of Columbus, whose interpreter,

Luis de Torres, spoke Hebrew, Aramaic and some Arabic (Colón, 1984: 50), he confesses himself:

> I do not understand the language, and the people of these lands do not understand me, neither I nor my companions understand them; and as for these Indians whom I have with me, I often understand one thing as its reverse.
>
> (Colón, 1984: 67)

On a number of other occasions Columbus expresses his uncertainty about whether he has understood his informants properly. He uses a number of devices to help him in his task. Often assonance is enough to convince him that he is in the legendary East: he hears the Great Khan in *Cubanacan*, and alters the name of the island Yamaye to form Yanahica because it accords better with a place name from Marco Polo's travels (cf. Gil, 1984: XLII). To take another example of assonance, when Columbus hears the name Cibao, a region on the island of Haiti where there were gold mines, he assimilates it to Cipango, a rich island believed to lie at a distance from the coast of China, supporting his assumption by the belief that Cuba was not an island but a continent. He has no difficulty in claiming to understand that 'Caniba' must mean the subjects of the Great Khan (Colón, 1984: 78). Despite the fact that he understands very little, if any, of what is being said to him, he experiences no difficulties in understanding that the whole island is at his disposal (ibid: 86). When it is a question of gold he is also miraculously good at translation (ibid: 48–49, with the marginalia of de Las Casas). An indication of how successful the attempts at communication were can be gauged from a comical incident in late November during the first voyage. Three Christians left the boats to tell the Indians in their own language, 'which they knew a little', not to be afraid: the Indians fled for their lives (ibid: 66).

Similar doubts arise about the mutual intelligibility between Hans Staden and his Tupinamba captors, which render his descriptions of the intentions of his (so he claims) anthropophagous hosts rather doubtful. In the following century, the 'rescue' of John Smith, one of the leaders of the colony of Virginia, through the intercession of Pocahantas is interpreted by him as a timely intervention before his brains could be pounded out, though there is no guarantee that the aggressive intentions that Smith imputes to his Indian captors are an adequate reflection of reality (Hulme, 1985). At the simple level of the language barrier, it may be plausible to suppose that 'the supposed "communication" between European and native was in effect a European monologue' (Hulme, 1978: 119).[6] And of course, this lack of a two-way flow of information is not just a question of linguistic incompetence: it is symptomatic of a strategy which produces its own persuasive definitions in blissful (and wilful) ignorance of anything that might disturb them. Or, as Peter Hulme expresses it:

> [...] the radical dualism of the European response to the native Caribbean – fierce cannibal and noble savage – has such obvious continuities with the

classical Mediterranean paradigm that it is tempting to see the whole intricate web of colonial discourse as weaving itself in its own separate space entirely unaffected by any observation of or interchange with native Caribbean cultures.

(Hulme, 1986: 47)

Given this problem of communication at a very material level, we might opt for a different interpretation of the Ewaipanoma. The resemblances between European and Amerindian ethno-anthropology *might* be due to direct interchange, but they may simply be the result of the workings of a similar ethnological imagination. This leaves us free to assume that native beliefs about monstrous races are indeed genuine. The existence of European beliefs about monstrous races thus has its counterpart in the ethno-anthropological notions entertained by the peoples of the Americas on *their* exotic neighbours. As the third example shows, there may even be coincidence between European and native notions, but we are not justified in seeing this coincidence as more than fortuitous. In such cases of correspondence between European and native beliefs, given the doubts regarding the possibility of genuine communication between the Europeans and their informants, the correspondence must be regarded as insignificant, a case of 'difference degree zero'.

In such cases, it is not so much the degree of overlap between the Plinian and other ethno-anthropological systems that is interesting, but their differences: why do certain Plinian figures recur in widely separate contexts while others do not? In studying the modalities of the European perception of the other, we should not forget that this other has its own modalities of perception too.

In the following section, the focus is on those Plinian races which make their appearance in the first decades after the discovery of the New World. Besides the texts of Columbus, Vespucci and their successors, we will take into account the iconographical tradition for the first century after the discovery.[7] For the period after the publication of the first volume of de Bry's *America* (in 1590), however, the European iconographical tradition displays a complex filiation of different images which are generally dependent to a greater or lesser extent on the work of de Bry, making broad comparisons of the type in which we are now engaged hazardous and unreliable for the later period.[8]

A number of the Plinian races crop up in the writings of Columbus. Although in his letter to Luis de Santangel of 1493 reporting on the first voyage Columbus writes that he has not found monstrous men in the islands, contrary to what many believed, he makes an exception of the island of the Caribs, however, which he assumes to be inhabited by savages who live on human flesh. He adds that they have contact with the women of Matininó, who live on an island where there are no men (Colón, 1984: 144–145). Moreover, he mentions in the same letter a region 'where the people with tails are born', and receives reports of an island where the people have no hair (ibid: 143, 145). In the narrative of his first voyage he mentions that he saw three sirens, although they were not as beautiful as he had been led to expect (ibid: 111), and he also receives reports of an island where everything is gold (ibid: 87). Curious to know more about the island of Bohío on which the anthropophagi are supposed to be situated, he learns from his Indian informants that its inhabitants include men with one eye and men with dogs' heads, who are anthropophagous and who drink the blood and castrate anyone who falls into their hands (ibid: 51). This information, it should be added, is acquired *during the absence of Columbus' regular interpreters*! Columbus has his reservations, as he is aware of the possibility that these reports have been invented to keep strangers (including the Spaniards) away from the island (ibid: 62, 65). He is rather inclined to believe that the island is inhabited by the subjects of the Great Khan. During the third voyage, the structure of the narrative is the same: the second-hand account of anthropophagous men continues to situate them *elsewhere* (ibid: 211). However, by the time of the fourth voyage Columbus has lost some of the more idealistic notions that he had entertained before, and he is now convinced of the existence of anthropophagi: he sees the proof of their cannibalism written in their faces (ibid: 326).

Columbus was not the only one to refer to the dog-headed Kynokephaloi (Colón, 1984: 51). Keymis also mentioned a maritime tribe with heads like dogs' heads who speak a Carib dialect. Pedro Mexia claimed to have seen a dozen cynocephali during the festivities held in honour of Henri II, which thus constituted proof that Plinius and Aulus Gellius had not been simply making their stories up, and explained their features as the result of human artifice. And Jane, one of the chroniclers of Cavendish's expedition, wrote in 1592 that the faces of the men he met resembled those of dogs, although their voices recalled the roaring of a bull rather than the barking of a dog (Bolens-Duvernay, 1988: 162–163). As for the early iconographical tradition, Colin (1987: 19–20) provides two examples of the identification of American Indian tribes with the traditionally oriental Kynokephaloi. The first is from Lorenz Fries' *Uslegung der Carta Marina*, first published by Grüninger in 1525. This compilation of essays includes descriptions of remote places and peoples, among which are the cannibals:

> The cannibals are a ferocious and loathsome people, dog-headed, so that one shudders looking at them. And they inhabit an island which Christoffel Dauber of Jamia [sic] discovered some years ago. [...] The cannibals go about naked, except that they adorn themselves with parrot feathers of many colours. [...] This people likes nothing better to eat than human flesh, and therefore they go to the surrounding islands frequently during the year to catch people.
>
> (cited in Colin, 1987: 19)

In the illustration a dog-headed creature is cutting up a human leg, while a dog-headed female reaches out for the meat. Another Kynokephalos looks on while gnawing at an arm, and a fourth approaches leading a trussed victim tied to what is presumably a llama. This strange beast fits Pigafetta's description of a creature with the 'head and ears the size of a mule, and the neck and body of the fashion of a camel, the legs of a deer and the tail that of a horse' (Honour, 1979: 271f.).

The second New World Kynokephalos comes from a now lost German book containing descriptions of the nations of the world. Dated to the early sixteenth century, it has survived in an Italian translation of 1623 entitled *Aggivnta alla quarta parte delle Indie de Sig. Giovanni Botero*. The creature with a dog's head and horse-like legs depicted in a woodcut from this work is located in the region of Santa Cruz, where it lives from stealing and has a diet of human flesh like the people in Brazil. A third example can be added to the list from the middle of the sixteenth century: the woodcuts illustrating the remote races in Lycosthenes' *Prodigorum ac ostentorum chronicon* include one depicting a dog-headed inhabitant of America. The text makes of them barking, anthropophagous thieves, like the previous example. If we extend the range to include North America, we can also note the dog-headed and boar-headed figures engaged in a fight that are depicted on a map in the *Cosmographie Universelle* of Guillaume le Testu (1555).[9]

Columbus' men with tails derive from a tradition recorded by Pausanias on the Satyr[10] islands in the Mediterranean. The natives were said to be very noisy and to have tails as long as horses' tails. They were believed to rape the women of any ship that approached, and to be quite indiscriminating in what bodily orifices they penetrated (Pausanias I.23.7). The Satyr islands appear on a map in the *Isolario* by Benedetto Bordone (Venice, 1528), with as their legendary neighbours the magnetic rocks and the island of Amazons, and are also mentioned by Thevet (1983: 141). Despite Voltaire's belief (*Les Singularités de la nature*, 1766) that the *homo caudatus* was the product of a warm climate, we find men with tails in the cold North: Lescarbot represented the Canadian natives sitting on their tails like apes. Even in the nineteenth century, the German naturalists Spix and von Martius recorded the belief in tailed men among Indians they met, though they did not specify which tribes these were.

Greek and Roman tradition also mentioned the existence of people who lived in caves, the Troglodytes. In the Vespucci woodcuts depicting the fate of a Spanish sailor at the hands of anthropophagous Indian women, we see the buttocks of a human figure disappearing inside a cave, despite the presence of dwellings in other woodcuts and their mention in the text of Vespucci (Kohl, 1987: 79). This example may be due to the influence of the iconography which often depicted rock crevices as the natural habitat of the Wild Man and the Wild Woman.

Another of the marvels of the East is the race of *Amyctyrae*, who use their protruding upper or lower lip to shield themselves from the sun. They appear along with *canibali* as early as 1532 on the decorations after Hans Holbein the Younger made for the Grynaeus map.[11]

Although Pigafetta refused to believe the tales about the race of men with enormous ears, the Panotii, Cortés was ordered by Diego Velázquez to search for this race, and Richard Harcourt mentioned a tribe with long ears on the banks of the river Maroni in Surinam in his *Relation of a Voyage in Guiana* (1613). In an account published in the commentaries of Cabeza de Vaca in 1555, one of his captains described the island of paradise of the Orejones, a people with enormous ears who lived close to the 'lake of El Dorado' (Mahn-Lot, 1987: 414). Indians with long ears are also mentioned by J. de Laet and C. de Rochefort as well as by eighteenth-century travellers (Magaña, 1982b: 76).

Related in some accounts to the *Panotii* are the *Antipodes*, a race with their feet turned backwards (to be discussed in Chapter Six). As *curupirá* they are first recorded by José de Anchieta in 1560. They are dwarfs, they have red hair, and in some accounts they have exceptionally long ears too (da Câmara Cascudo, 1954: 220–221).[12]

Another of the Plinian races is the *Macrobii*: exceptionally long life spans are attributed to various peoples, such as 140 years to the Indian race of Cyrni (Plinius, *NH* VII. 27). In the letters of Amerigo Vespucci, the New World Indians are attributed a lifespan of 150 years, a good resistance to disease, hairless bodies and sexual promiscuity (Vespucci, 1984: 104).[13] In his *Nueva coronica i buen gobierno*, Guaman Poma de Ayala attributes a similar longevity of 150 years or more to the Indians, and Jean de Léry speaks of 100 to 120 lunar years.[14]

As we saw in the previous chapter, the Macrobii were sometimes interpreted as large in stature rather than long-living, i.e. as giants. Vespucci reported a visit to an island of giants during his voyage to the New World in 1499–1500. He and his men are received by a group of giant women, whom Vespucci likens to the Amazon queen, Penthesilea. His plans to abduct two or three of the younger girls and take them back to Spain are thwarted, however, by the arrival of the giant women's male counterparts, at which point the Europeans abandon their hopes of rape and make for their boat (Vespucci, 1984: 66 and 158-159). On the woodcut map to Petrus Apianus' *Cosmographia* (1553) South America is assigned to cannibals and giants. Giants are particularly associated with Patagonia, recurring on, for instance, a copper plate to Linschoten's *Itinerario* (1596) as well as in the illustration by de Bry to the arrival of Magellan in the strait that was to bear his name.[15] The first mention of them in Patagonia is on the Walsperger map of 1448, where they are described as being the enemies of dragons (Dreyer-Eimbcke, 1982: 124–125). Mammoth bones were an object of admiration in the cabinets of Europe as mementos of giants (Schnapper, 1986)[16] and belief in giants persisted into the eighteenth century[17] in Buffon's *Histoire Naturelle* and in Byron's image of the gigantic stature of a Patagonian chief (Adams, 1980; Boon, 1982: 27ff.).

Though Columbus failed to find giants in the New World, he did claim to have found both anthropophagi and Amazons. They are linked together by his informants, who tell him that the anthropophagous Caribs have intercourse once a year with the women of Matininó (Colón, 1984: 115). There had been interest in Amazons in Spain at least since the thirteenth century (Irizarry, 1983), and the plurality of locations assigned to them in antiquity must have made it easier to accommodate their existence in the New World without too much difficulty. Thevet, for instance, simply refers to three sorts of Amazons: the African, the Skythian and the American (Thevet, 1983: 164). Columbus' willingness to accept their existence on the island of Matininó was in line with the European tradition in which the Amazons possessed metal resources and were especially aggressive and militaristic, although they disappear from Columbus' later account. It is worth noting that there is considerable evidence for the existence of native Indian beliefs concerning a tribe of women without men, recorded by Fray Ramón Pané in 1494, though in the native accounts the presence of riches is absent (Sued-Badillo, 1986). Perhaps it was used, like the myth of El Dorado, as a ploy by the Amerindians to lure the gold-hungry Europeans away. For example, when the German expedition in which Ulrich Schmidel participated was looking for gold, the 'king' of an Indian tribe told the foreigners to set out on a two-month trek over land to a kingdom near the island of the Amazons, where they would find the gold and silver they were looking for (Schmidel, 1597: ch. XX). The native and European traditions proceeded in relative independence from one another, and when Columbus finally did land on the island of Matininó in June 1503, he made no reference at all to the mythical component of the island.

If the Amazons stood for a rigid separation between the sexes, the Hermaphrodite testified to their union within a single body. The Hermaphrodites or Androgini of Greco-Roman tradition (cf. Lecouteux, 1982, II: 85–87) played only a limited part in what the anthropological imagination saw in the New World. Columbus did not mention them, but they do appear as 'hommes-femmes' among the Timucua of Florida, described by Laudonnière and Le Moyne, who both participated in the French expedition which landed there in 1564 (Duviols, 1982).

Nevertheless, it is not one of the races recorded by Columbus, but the Blemmyae (Ewaipanoma) described by Ralegh, that are one of the most persistent of the Plinian races in the American context. Originally they are an oriental race: they are found in the company of Blacks in an Indian context in a mid-fifteenth century manuscript of *The Antichrist* (Kohl, ed., 1982: ill. 254)[18] and in a contemporary manuscript of the Alexandros romance. In antiquity they were known as the *akephaloi* and situated by Herodotos in Libya. Isidorus distinguished between two kinds: those without a head, whose eyes and mouth were on their chest, and those without a neck, who had their eyes on their shoulders *(Etymologiae* XI.3.17). Augustinus was often quoted as an authority for them,[19] and it was on his authority that Aldrovandi was prepared to accept the possibility of their existence. Lafitau was initially sceptical about the existence of the Akephaloi, for he was quite modern in attempting to explain most of the Plinian races as the result of the tendency for members of one social group to portray members of other groups as non-human, reserving the qualities of being human for themselves (cf. Pagden, 1982: 17). In the case of the Blemmyae, though, Lafitau modified his views and attached credibility to a report that he heard of an Iroquois who claimed to have come across such a monstrous being while hunting in 1721. Lafitau included an engraving by Hondius of Blemmyae in Guyana, which had been used to illustrate translations of Ralegh's account, in his *Moeurs des sauvages amériquains, comparées aux moeurs des premiers temps* (1724). Lafitau saw such reports as evidence of the existence of two nations of Blemmyae, one in the Orient and one in America. They thus served to confirm Lafitau's thesis that America had been populated by peoples from Asia. As for the origin of the deformation, Lafitau suggested that it might be the result of a deliberate act carried out in early childhood, like the binding of young girls' feet in China. He also suggested the 'imaginist' thesis that it might be the result of the imagination of the pregnant mother running wild.[20]

If we try to isolate the most persistent of the Plinian races in the representations of the inhabitants of the New World, we can single out the Anthropophagi, Blemmyae, Amazons and Giants.[21] Why were these the most popular races in this context?

The Blemmyae owe their diffusion to the representations of them by Hulsius and Hondius to illustrate the Ewaipanoma described by Ralegh and the diffusion of this illustration in Lafitau's work. The illustration for the frontispiece of the German edition of Ralegh's account (Hulsius, 1599) shows two Blemmyae displayed in frontal and dorsal view, armed with a bow and wearing nothing but a loin-cloth. The eyes, nose and mouth are placed on the thorax, above the belt which supports the quiver. The two Blemmyae are accompanied by a Wild Woman (Amazon?) who is completely naked and is similarly armed with a bow and arrow. The poses are modelled on the long-haired Wild Man and Wild Woman from the 1505 edition of Vespucci's letters.[22] In the background is a bare landscape with two exotic animals, a hut and some trees.

A second illustration[23] shows the same frontal and dorsal view, but without a female in the foreground. The main difference lies in the background, which is now peopled by three pairs of Blemmyae. In each of the latter couples one partner is armed with a bow and arrows and the other with a spear. The same fauna appear, and primitive huts are signs of habitation. The landscape is less bare, with various plants and flowers as well as trees.

Related to this is the contemporary copperplate depicting male and female *Carios* (perhaps the Tupi-speaking Guarani) in Ulrich Schmidel's *Vera historia* (Nuremberg, 1599).[24] The Indian couple is shown in an inhabited landscape amid a variety of fauna and flora, including apples, which are used to create an Adam and Eve setting.

In a third version of the Ewaipanoma taken from a map of the Guayanas by Hondius (1599),[25] we have a symmetrical pair consisting of a frontal male Blemmyae, armed with longbow and arrows, and a female Wild Woman, armed with the same weapon. It is this less stocky version which serves as the prototype for Lafitau.

The kinship between the Vespucci Wild Man illustration, the illustration of the *Carios* and the three Ewaipanoma illustrations bears out the point made earlier: the artists experienced no discomfort in the co-existence of what we would distinguish as historical *(Carios)* and mythical *(Ewaipanoma)* races. The monstrous human races are substantially the same as more recognisable or familiar human races (cf. Magaña, 1982b: 71).

However, the existence of this iconographical set of relations does not account for the importance attached to the Blemmyae or why this Plinian race was singled out to represent the inhabitants of the New World. We join Magaña in recognising that:

This is one of the most difficult problems in ethno-anthropology. It is not enough to consider the possible sources for the creation of monstrous peoples [...]; it is also necessary to determine what is culturally specific behind such mythical creations.

(1982b: 70)

One approach to the Ewaipanoma might be a culinary/digestive one. The manner of ingestion implied by the situation of the mouth on the torso implies a direct route to the stomach, without the mediation of the digestive tube. Given the symbolic equivalence of cooking with digestion, this could be seen as an alternative to the eating of raw meat: both forms of ingestion connote a natural system of alimentation in contrast to the cultural goods of cooking and digestion (cf. Magaña, 1982b: 102–103).

Another approach is the Freudian one advocated by Kappler, who suggests that the Blemmyae could be a projection of the fear of female sexuality or the fear of castration (1980: 279). Such an interpretation might be of value in the case of the well-known terracotta figures from Priene, which depict creatures with a human face *on the stomach*.[26] However, the Ewaipanoma, it must be emphasised, have their human faces *on their chest*.[27] This does not rule out psycho-analytical interpretations, but it should make us wary of following Kappler without closer scrutiny of the iconography.

Bucher has suggested the existence of a discrepancy between the text and the illustrations. While Ralegh refers to people with high shoulders, the illustrators fill this in by drawing on the stock European tradition of exotic races and faithfully portray them as Blemmyae (Bucher, 1981: 34-36). This serves as an injunction to re-read Ralegh's remarks with care. Indeed, he refers to a people with 'their eyes in their shoulders, and their mouths in the middle of their breasts, and that a long train of haire groweth backward between their shoulders' (Ralegh, 1970: 85). The salient feature of the Ewaipanoma is thus that they are headless. Perhaps this is a *political* reference to the fact that they did not satisfy the Aristotelian criteria of men as social beings. Is this a case of the hardening of metaphors which Tylor suggested as one of the mechanisms in the production of the monstrous races (1871, I: 415)? Was the figurative expression that these people had no chief taken too literally as meaning that they were without a head?[28]

There is another way of posing the problem which avoids some of the dangers of Tylor's approach. In recent years anthropologists and historians have turned their attentions to the semantic domain of bodily expression. The history of the body is at the same time an account of how meaning can be conveyed by means of bodily metaphors, as we shall see in the following chapters. Seen from this perspective, the headless Ewaipanoma might be expected to signify by means of this lack of a head.

In this case, this signification is twofold. First, there is the social connotation of a social body without a head. Before the discovery of America, virtually all the cultures with which Europe came into contact (North and West Africa, Turkey, etc.) had forms of social organisation which were not difficult to comprehend in accordance with the model of the European monarchy (Kohl, 1987: 67). How frustrating it must have been for the first explorers not to know whether they were addressing a chief or not. In the absence of insignia, large-scale public buildings and other signs of rank or political organisation, how was Columbus to know that he had finally reached the Great Khan? When he arrived on the coast of Cuba, he passed by the small settlements that he encountered on the shore in the hope of finding great cities or towns. Eventually he dispatched an embassy inland consisting of Luis de Torres and Rodrigo de Jerez to find a king or great cities. They returned after three days of travelling, but they failed to find anything resembling a political organisation or government (*mas no cosa de regimiento*, Colón, 1984: 140).

Similarly, when faced with the apparent anarchy of the Patagonians, Thevet wrote:

> There are no men so beastly, wild and cruel as these men are, who have never savoured another obedience than that which they impose one upon another, without any royalty or principality existing among them.
>
> (Thevet, 1575, cited by Lestringant, 1987a: 37)

Ralegh, like Thevet, was in the service of a monarch and must have encountered similar problems and confusions. And if we turn to the early seventeenth century Jacobean compiler of ethnographic material, Samuel Purchas, we find a conception of East–West contact that is exclusively couched in monarchical terms: there is a supposed reciprocity between sultan, raja, mogul and king, all consolidated as an argument in favour of the primacy of proper kingships (Boon, 1982: 174).

Besides the social dimension, the headlessness of the Ewaipanoma may have sexual connotations too. The symbolic equivalence of decapitation and castration is no more a stranger to the European continent than it is to the Americas. Without lapsing into some kind of pan-sexualism, it might nevertheless be plausible to suggest that the headlessness of the Ewaipanoma might connote negativity in the sexual sphere.

This suggestion might be supported in two ways. First, there is a negative argument in its favour. On a drawing of the headless man by Cubeo Indians (Magaña, 1982b: 80), his penis is clearly depicted. It may be more than just prudishness which omits this element from the European iconography of the Blemmyae.[29]

Second, in her analysis of the illustrations to de Bry's *America*, Bucher has pointed out the parallel between the weakly marked sexuality of the Indians and their powerlessness in the face of the Europeans. As a corollary, there is a relation between the independence of the Indians and strongly marked sexual differences (Bucher, 1981: 162–163). Within such a context, the portrayal of the Indians as headless was an invitation: their lack of a socially structured monarchy invited the domination of the Europeans to provide one; their lack of a clearly marked masculinity invited the thrust of European penetration. And when the famous virginity of the English queen made it difficult to apply the colonial onomastics of a virgin land being married to its rightful master and husband, the relationship was recast as a polymorphous family affair in which Elizabeth became the father, mother and heir of Guiana (Hulme, 1985: 18). The counterpart to the emasculated males are the over-aggressive Amazon-like females, whose masculinity serves to point up its lack in their male partners (Mason, forthcoming b).

The headless Ewaipanoma thus conforms to one of the rules of the production of the exotic: the exotic is always *empty*, it is characterised by *lack,* and this incompleteness calls forth and justifies attempts to fill in this gap in icono-graphical, textual, sexual and military terms.

If we turn to another image, that of the giant, we can note its persistence from the Walsperger map to the age of the Enlightenment. The first giants sighted in the New World were those seen by Vincente Pinzon in Brazil in 1500. It was Pigafetta's account in particular - later taken up by Thevet (Lestringant, 1987a and b) - which fixed the association of giants with Patagonia. The description of the Patagonians calls up associations with other Plinian races too - the Sciapodes, the Antipodes (not surprisingly, in view of their geographical location) and the Cynocephali also lend various features to the giants of Patagonia (Bolens-Duvernay, 1988). The giant belongs to remote geographical areas, and its presence at the southernmost tip of America accords with this. Moreover, this also implies a symmetry with the far North: a parallelism is established between the savagery attributed to the northern Skythian peoples in medieval tradition and the savagery conferred by analogy on the Patagonians. The giant also belongs to remote times, to the age of giants whose existence in the Old World was not confined to scattered bones. As a symbol of a youthful and intact culture, the giant could have positive connotations, but it might also suggest a stagnant society, not yet caught up in the developmental course of history, somewhat akin to the timelessness and backwardness which were seen as characteristics of Oriental society in the nineteenth century. Such a vision, of course, fails to pay any attention to the achievements of Indian culture. It presents that culture as a clean slate on which (Western) history is to be inscribed. Like the headless Ewaipanoma, the Patagonian giants are seen as needing European civilisation.

A third race, the Amazons, can easily be accommodated into the same frame-work. The placing of political power in female hands is seen as a corollary of the lack of masculinity on the part of the males, and both sides of the imbalance are seen to call for correction by Europe. At the same time, the disruption of relations between the sexes, with its corollaries of male and female homosexuality, is unable to achieve a balance by itself. It is European intervention which will try to wipe out homosexuality, as Valboa tried to do, and restore domination of the man over the woman as a corollary to the domination of Europe over the continent of America.

This view of Amazons as characterised by the disruption of normal relations, that in turn calls for intervention to redress the balance, has long historical roots. In the Greek tradition the Amazons had been a 'photographic' negative of misogynist, phallocentric Athenian society (Hartog, 1980; Tyrrell, 1982). This role can be found both within native Amerindian discourse and within that of Europe. Let us take, for instance, the horror with which Thevet describes their treatment of prisoners. The Amazons hang their victim by one leg from the branch of a tree; if he does not die a slow death in this fashion, they finish him off with a mass of arrows. In view of the strict demarcation between the sexes, the women do not consider ingesting such a victim; instead, they burn it until it is completely turned to ashes (Thevet, 1983: 167). The inversion of normal relations – the inversion of normal relations between the sexes; the inversion of hanging (by the leg instead of by the neck); and the extreme attitude toward the flesh (excessively cooked by the reduction to ashes, a counterpart to the excessive lack of cooking in the consumption of raw meat by the anthropophagi) – all point to a dreaded image that is the reverse of male norms. The (psychological) repression of such images may be the mechanism behind the *physical* repression of beings that appear to embody them.

Finally, we turn to the anthropophagi. The anthropophagi do not appear as a separate monstrous race, because anthropophagy is regarded as the virtual everyday practice of the continent. It already appears on what Sturtevant (1976: 420) regarded as the earliest representation of native America: the Portuguese manuscript map known as Kunstmann II, dating from 1502, where we are presented with the image of a white man skewered on a spit which is turned by a kneeling, naked, curly-haired, bearded, brown-skinned man. As Pagden has written, 'the European interest in man-eating amounts almost to an obsession [...] by the end of the fifteenth century the anthropophagi had become a regular part of the topography of exotic lands' (1982: 80–81). Many of the sixteenth- and seventeenth-century allegories of America see anthropophagy as *de rigueur* in depictions of the continent, often combining it with the myth of the Amazons, although it should be noted that anthropophagy is often a secondary function, and does not play an essential role in the Amazon myths (cf. Jara, 1988: 67).

Even when belief in the existence of the Plinian races is showing signs of waning, they still crop up as the Mediterranean background against which the standards of the New World can be measured. For instance, in his commentary on the *Metamorphoses* of Ovidius, dating from the early 1620s, George Sandys used the figure of the one-eyed Kyklops Polyphemos against which to set the West Indians of his day. In this comparison the novelty of Caribbean savagery is gauged in terms of the reference to classical literature. In fact, the West Indians emerge favourably from the comparison, for while Polyphemos ate the flesh of his guests, the West Indians consume only the bodies of their enemies (cf. Hulme, 1986: 154).

Despite their instrumentality within colonial discourse, the monstrous races are more than mere pawns in the enterprise of domination. Irrespective of the aims of writers, artists and their publics, we stress the many ways in which the Plinian races are capable of *signifying*. Naturally, some of these significations may become inscribed within colonial discourse, but this is neither their source nor their *raison d'être*. It is because the body can be the source, means and object of signification that the Plinian races are so rich in the variety of articulations that they offer. It is to this variety that we now turn.

Though we have seen that there is reason to doubt the veracity of early ethnographic reports of the existence of Plinian races in South America, there is a sizeable body of data which has been collected, and which is still increasing, in which the keen interest of the South American Indian tribes in ethno-anthropology is evidenced. There is a good deal of (fortuitous) overlap between the monstrous races described in these narratives and those known in the Western tradition. In a list compiled by Magaña (1982b: 73–85) of 54 mythical tribes known from the ethnographical literature on the Indians of the Guiana region from the end of the fifteenth century, we find dwarfs (*Piriyana*), anthro-pophagous dwarfs (*Haibohe*), a warrior tribe of men with their head below their shoulders (*Kainemo*), an anthropophagous creature with its mouth in its breast and eyes in the nape of its neck (*Onone*), another tribe of men with their mouth on their breast or stomach (*Paira-undepo*), a tribe of Amazon women (*Oliyana*), a hostile race with enormous ears (*Oyariculé*), another race with ears which they use to shelter from the rain (*Panaliyana*), a race of subterranean Indians (*Popoyana*), a race of Indians who live under water (*Tunayana*), a race (also mentioned by Ralegh and other travellers) of Indians who live in the tree tops (*Warrau*), and a troglodyte race of Indians who live in the mountain caves (*Wupuyana*). Many of these races were also recorded by Magaña during field-work carried out among the Kaliña of Surinam in 1980 (see the list of 23 entries, ibid: 85–88; cf. Magaña, forthcoming).

The monstrous races of the South American imaginary, however, display a variety which goes far beyond the confines of the Plinian races. Though Ralegh was prepared to countenance the existence of the headless Ewaipanoma, it is hard to imagine that he would have fallen for people with the heads of bees, for example! Examples of the vast range of the South American ethno-anthropological imagination abound. If we can rely on Penard's account of the Arawak *Haibohe*, these anthropophagous dwarfs were amphibious. They lived in the coastal areas, at river estuaries and in the interior. Their feet were below their jaws, they had a broad mouth and long sharp jaguar-like teeth. They could not walk, but their form of motion was to spring above the tops of the trees. They attacked in groups and were very numerous. They ate their food raw. Their language consisted of a single sound: *hé*, which they emitted through the nose. They performed somersaults while gnashing their teeth, in which their strength lay (Magaña, 1982b: 73).

Reports on races like these and others collected from the Guiana region (cf.

Magaña, 1982a: 216) are to be found for other parts of the continent too. For example, among the Cayapó (Gê) of Brazil, we find the following races: men with the head, feet and croak of a frog; men who can say only *po-po*, the sound of a bird; red-headed men; cannibals who use poisoned arrows; men with extremely large penises; white men; men with piraña teeth; men with swarms of bees for a head; cannibals with dog's teeth, hands and feet, subterranean cannibals, cannibal giants, men who reach adulthood in four lunar months; men with eyes in their feet... (Magaña, 1986: 102–105). The *Ka'o'ó* dwarf of the Mataco has four eyes, and sometimes two eyes on its neck or feet (Pérez-Diez, 1988: 128). From another Gê people, the Timbirá, we can add: a country of homosexual men; and red-footed men (Magaña, 1986: 106–107).

Of course there are differences in emphasis between the South American imaginary and that of Europe. The widespread anthropophagy of the American monstrous races seems to be less prevalent in the European tradition (Magaña, 1982a: 223), and the men with enormous penises of Amerindian mythology[30] are less prominent in the mythology of the Old World. Still, the dietary, culinary, sexual, residential, social and linguistic parameters by which we attempted to classify some of the Plinian races are applicable in the case of the South American imaginary races too. In dietary terms, they may live on fish, seasonal fruits and their own excrement (*Aruto*); they may live on the faeces or buttocks of others (*Kainemo*); they may live on a diet of salt (*Waiyokule*); or they may be indiscriminate in their eating habits (*Pakirayana*). In sexual terms, the males may have oversized penises, or the females may live in isolation from the males. In residential terms, they may live in the tops of trees, underground, underwater or in hollow tree trunks; they may sleep on wooden grills, or upside down like bats. Linguistically, they may be able to utter only one sound, to bray like asses, to imitate the call of a bird. And in terms of pigmentation, we can note the shiny blue buttocks attributed to the ancestors of the Amazonian Piaroa (Overing, 1985b: 263), or the rainbow-like pigmentation of Wósak among the Pilagá Indians of central Chaco (Idoyaga Molina, 1988: 100).

The most striking feature of these South American ethno-ethnographies, however, is surely the confusion of animal, vegetable and mineral categories. We find armadillo men, stone men, bamboo men, toad men and monkey men among the Gê (Magaña, 1986: 102-105). From the Wayana of Surinam and French Guiana we can add heron men, oriole men, woodpecker men (Magaña, 1987a: 31–32), from the Tarëno caterpillar men (ibid: 140), and from the Kaliña crab men (ibid: 225). Though the Plinian races do include some confusion of species, such as dog-headed men or men with canine teeth, they do not display the enormous diversity in which the South American imaginary abounds when it comes to combinations across the boundaries between plants and minerals. To find something in any way approaching this diversity in the Old World we would have to consider the European representations of the hybrid (cf. Mason, forthcoming c), but in most cases the hybrid is an individual, not a race, and therefore falls outside the scope of ethno-ethnology proper.

This seemingly infinite variety and flexibility is the strongest argument against any attempt to reduce such imaginary races to a misperception of some empirical reality. Block Friedman, for example, suggests that under the fabulous descriptions of the Plinian races real people are to be found. He supposes that yoga positions might lie behind some of the descriptions of one-legged men, and that the men with their faces on their chests are a misperception of men bearing shields (1981: 25). Roth similarly took up the theories of Tylor to suggest that lake people came to be seen as fish, and that monkeys lay behind fantasies of hairy Wild Men (cf. Magaña, 1982b: 69). Apart from the inherent implausibility of such explanations, they clearly have a very limited field of extension. There is no way in which the hundreds of monstrous human races detailed in the ethnographies of the South American Indians could be reduced to some Lévy-Bruhlian category confusion and misperception.

All the same, these monstrous races do have some relation to observable reality. They are made up from combinations of elements that can be observed in daily life. The combinations, however, are what give them their peculiarity. Monstrosity throws certain elements into relief. It encourages thought about categories and the boundaries between them. As Victor Turner noted in his discussion of the liminal period of neophytes:

> Liminality is the realm of primitive hypothesis, where there is a certain freedom to juggle with the factors of existence [... the neophytes] are shown that ways of acting and thinking alternative to those laid down by the deities or ancestors are ultimately unworkable and may have disastrous consequences.
>
> (Turner, 1967: 106)

In a similar way, the exaggeration of natural features in the use of masks and other ritual attributes encourages the novices to ponder on the factors of their culture by displaying extremes that are to be avoided. Such a view is in accord with the classic Lévi-Straussian function attributed to mythology to elaborate combinations which, outside the non-existent world of mythology, would not be possible or advisable. It also coincides to some extent with Needham's (1978) emphasis on the value of evasive fantasies and the abrogation of restraint as a characteristic feature of our imagination. The monstrous races serve to populate the imaginary worlds which are the object of anthropological inquiry.

In Chapter Three an approach to the Plinian races was advocated in which they are able to signify and articulate in ways which go beyond the logocentric boundaries of any anthropo*logy* or ethno*logy*. Might it not be justifiable to see in the enormous range of possibilities opened up by the South American imaginary races a scope for rethinking traditional categories which is considerably wider than that offered by the European Plinian races? Moreover, this extension in scope is not achieved at the expense of attention to detail: in most cases the species which are combined in narratives dealing with these imaginary races are specifiable. The wide range of imaginary possibilities is coupled to a precision in the identification of natural phenomena.

The brief account of animal trials in Chapter Two indicated some of the ways in which such phenomena enable us to broaden the horizons of anthropology and to redefine the contours of the *anthropos* which functions as its centre by rethinking the human/animal distinction (cf. Mason, 1988; 1989a; forthcoming a). The animal, vegetable and mineral components of the South American imaginary enable us to go a step further: perhaps we might be able to remove *anthropos* from the central place altogether and have to redefine the contours of anthropology itself. After all, if in Guayanese ethnographies animal and vegetable 'peoples' play an equally if not more important role than the imaginary human races of a more conventional 'Plinian' type, the distinctions between human and animal, or between animal and vegetable, hardly seem relevant (Magaña, forthcoming; Mason, forthcoming d).

In the following two chapters, these ambitious claims for the monstrous human races will be substantiated by means of two case studies: those races that are marked in terms of their feet, and those that are marked in terms of their body orifices. So far the argument has displayed a gradual shift from considerations of the continent America to its inhabitants. In the following chapter the two themes are juxtaposed: as the land of the Antipodes, America functions within particular discourses as both land mass and as the habitat of a specific Plinian race – the beings with reversed feet known as the Antipodes. With the introduction of South American data into the discussion, the eurocentrism of the preceding chapters slowly makes way for a multiple ethnocentrism, as each people sets out to define itself by means of a negative self-definition: by means of what it is not. Some of the rules which this multiple ethnocentrism obeys will then be discussed in Chapter Seven.

Notes

1. Sciopodum gens fertur in Aethiopia singulis cruribus et celeritate mirabili (Isidorus, *Etymologiae* XI.iii.23). Strictly speaking we should distinguish between the Monocoli (one-legged beings) and the Sciapodes (beings with parasol-like feet), as not all Sciapodes are one-legged. As we saw in the previous chapter, however, the boundaries between the various Plinian races are by no means hard and fast.
2. For such an approach to Scandinavian mythology see Molenaar (1985).
3. López de Gómara mentions half-men, half-fish, and both Thevet and de Léry speak of a sea monster having the shape of a man (Magaña, 1982b: 81).
4. That there was interest in exotic animals is shown by the fact that the court had an aviary and a 'zoo', in which were housed ocelots, wolves, mountain lions and mountain cats (de Sahagún, 1956, Book 8, Chapter 14). This zoo is depicted on a 1524 map of Tenochtitlán based on a sketch from 1519–1520 (Sturtevant, 1976: 424 and references there).
5. It is interesting to note Ralegh's positive attitude toward the work of Mandeville, at a time when confidence in the reliability of Mandeville had already been considerably

shaken. By contrast, the second edition of Hakluyt's *Voyages*, which appeared in 1598, excluded Mandeville.

6. Though, as Hulme elsewhere (1986: 20) points out, this monologue is in no sense simple or homogeneous, since the European monologue itself contains discursive conflicts.

7. In 1976 William Sturtevant compiled a valuable list of 268 depictions of native America up to 1590, which represent the work of around 40 different artists – a remarkably low figure for what is almost a century. For present purposes, however, Sturtevant's list has to be supplemented, because he deliberately excluded illustrations that plainly have no basis in New World ethnography – the very illustrations which are of most interest to the present investigation. For some additions see Honour, 1975 and 1976.

8. The estimate of engravings of New World subjects in de Bry is 304 (Sturtevant, 1976: 446 n.10).

9. Reproduced on pages 94–95 of Cumming *et al.*, 1971.

10. The association of *homo caudatus* with the satyr was a common one (cf. Penel, 1982). Some authorities attribute the birth of children with tails to an 'imaginist' theory (the effect of the mother's mental processes on the foetus), while others see in it the result of acts of bestiality between human mothers and animal fathers.

11. Reproduced on pages 64–65 of W. Cumming *et al.*, 1971.

12. On the *curupirá* as the spirit of the forest, see Magaña (1988a: 200).

13. In the *Lettera a Lorenzo di Perfrancesco de' Medici del 1502 da Lisbona*, in which Vespucci recounts a voyage to the New World undertaken for Portugal from May 1501 to July 1502, he mentions having come across an old man who indicated by sign language that he was 132 years old (Vespucci, 1984: 81).

14. For seventeenth-century reports of enormous life spans for North and South American Indians, see Pagden (1982: 201 n.4). In the early seventeenth century, the planter Ambrósio F. Brandão recorded life spans of over 100 for the Brazilian Indians (Brandão, 1987: 104). Thevet credits the Patagonian giants with a life span of 150 years (1983: 134).

    For Las Casas, the longevity of the Amerindians was a sign of their sexual continence, for, following Aristoteles, he assumed excessive sexual activity to result in a shortening of the life span (Rech, 1985: 53).

15. It is not certain what the giant is doing with the arrow in his mouth. Bucher (1981) connects it with the use of sticks as emetics. Perhaps we should see no more in it than a proof of the giant's strength. Lestringant (1987b) links it with a theory of the humours, which depend on the extreme latitude of the region.

16. A giant molar weighing almost three pounds was examined by Fray Pedro de los Ríos in the 1560s as evidence for the existence of giants (Jansen, 1984: 76). Juan de Torquemada believed that mammoth bones were the bones of giants (Pagden, 1982: 216 n.138). The second-century Church father Tertullian had already claimed that gigantic bones were the proof of the existence of giants in his *De resurrectione carnis*.

17. Though not without its dissidents: John Narborough had already discredited and disproved physical gigantism among Patagonians in 1670, and de la Condamine, for one, was not convinced by the British propaganda on giants that served as a smoke-screen to cover up the mining interests which lay behind the expedition.

18. Kohl, ed., 1982: ill. 21 shows a statuette of a headless deity, variously located in the East or in Haiti.

19. Although it is in an apocryphal work, the *Sermo ad fratres in eremo*, that men and women without heads and with eyes in their breasts are mentioned.

20. In his attempt to explain the formation of such monstrous beings by the influence of the mother on the embryo, Lafitau had been anticipated by John Bulwer, whose

accurate observation of the native custom of artificial bodily changes led him to think that Ralegh's Ewaipanoma was the 'affectation of some race to drown the head in the breast' (*Anthropometamorphosis: Men Transformed: or the Artificiall Changling*, 1650, cited by Wittkower, 1977: 69). Lafitau's adoption of the imaginist thesis was to earn him the scorn of the Encyclopedists later in the century (see Kohl, 1981: 262 n.159).

21. The Amazons, anthropophagi and dog-headed races are the most persistent in Columbus' account (Hulme, 1986: 270 n.9), while the later period seems to witness an eclipse of the Kynokephaloi by the Blemmyes (with whom they were confused by Adam of Bremen).

22. The bow and arrow figure among the attributes of the European Wild Man as well as the club. It may be that the use of the bow, which can be used from a distance, carries connotations of inferiority that were a long-standing part of Indo-European culture, by which it is contrasted with the heroism of fighting at close quarters (cf. Le Goff, 1985: 157–161).

23. Reproduced in Kohl, ed., 1982: ill. 12.

24. Reproduced in Kohl, ed., 1982: ill. 3.

25. Reproduced in Mason, 1987a: 155.

26. Freud drew attention to these in an article of 1916 ('Mythologische Parallele zu einer plastischen Zwangsvorstellung', in Freud, 1940–52, Vol. X); they have been discussed in more detail by Devereux (1981).

27. In suggesting the possibility of a relation between the Priene figure and the solar deity who appears in Greco-Egyptian belief as headless (or decapitated), Delatte (1914: 240 n.2) makes clear distinctions between headless figures (*akephaloi*), figures with their heads on their chests (*Blemmyes*), and figures with their heads on their stomachs (*gastrokephaloi*).

28. The interpretation put forward here is a very tentative one. However, it might find some confirmation in South American indigenous thought. The Kaliña of Surinam, for instance, arrange their villages along the course of a river, with the chief's residence at the *head*, while further on the river has its *mouth* (E. Magaña, personal communication).

29. We might compare the decent obscuring of the penis of a sperm-whale stranded on the Dutch shore at Beverwijk in an engraving of 1602 by Jan Saenredam; in other engravings of stranded whales the awesome penis is conspicuously present (Schama, 1987: 130ff; Duerr, 1985: 9–10).

30. Examples abound in the four volumes of *Mythologiques*. The penis of Buok'a, the older brother of the Piaroa creator god, was so long that he wrapped it round his shoulders and made love from a distance (Overing, 1986b: 143).

5   A member of a mouthless Plinian race, the Astomi

Source: Conradus Lycosthenes, *Prodigiorum ac Ostentorum Chronicum...*, Basle, 1557. Reproduced with permission of the University Library, Amsterdam.

Chapter five

A monstrous idiom: articulation

When Marcel Mauss introduced the study of 'les techniques du corps' in his 1936 article of that name, he stressed that this new field of study had to be won at the expense of what had previously been grouped under the heading 'Miscellaneous' (Mauss, 1950: 365–386). Postures and gestures, fashions in swimming, national styles of marching, sexual 'positions' – these and other diverse facets of bodily action were now to be subsumed under a comparative study of bodily techniques.

Since then, considerable attention has been devoted to the body and its techniques, and not by anthropologists alone.[1] The symbolism attaching to various parts of the body forms a part of these studies. In a variety of ways, the body can impinge on different symbolic codes: the acoustic, the visual, the sexual, the culinary are some of the possibilities by which the techniques of the body can be seen to form part of a wider symbolic field. Over a period of two decades, Lévi-Strauss has approached the ways in which a typology along the lines of bodily techniques might help to throw light on the ability of mythical thought to translate certain fundamental notions in such terms. Already in the third volume of his *Mythologiques*, he stressed that:

> An entire work would be required to arrange a typology of these beings who are blocked or pierced, above or below, in front or behind, incapable of taking in anything except liquids or smoke [...], without a mouth or anus, and thus without digestive functions. On the alimentary level, they illustrate a series that has its parallels elsewhere: on the sexual level, that of beings without a penis or endowed with a long penis, without a vagina or provided with a large vagina [...]; again, in terms of relations, without eyes or joints, and thus unable to see or to move.
>
> (Lévi-Strauss 1968: 393)

Since then, Lévi-Strauss has returned to these mythical figures in an attempt to show how native Amerindian thought had already developed ample concepts of anality and orality long before the birth of psycho-analytic theory (Lévi-Strauss, 1984; 1985).

The mythical characters to which Lévi-Strauss refers, such as the dwarfs who lack an anus and who live on an aromatic diet, are by no means confined to the

American continent. As he himself notes (1968: 394), the scent inhalers can be found in Greek and Roman sources as the Astomi, and it is precisely their occurrence in widely separate times and places which provides the argument for their ability to translate certain fundamental notions.

Before discussing the Astomoi and other Plinian races which are marked with respect to the openings of the body, however, specific attention will first be paid to those beings who are marked in respect of their joints or articulations. The role of one specific Plinian 'tribe', the Antipodes, within *l'imaginaire médiévale* leads us from the Old World to the New. In following the Lévi-Straussian path from the New to the Old World in retrograde motion,[2] we return to the excessively closed or open figures with which he began and endeavour, by a methodology which still owes much to his lessons in structural analysis, to indicate some of the fundamentally *graphic* notions which these races help to articulate. These remarks should be read as a preliminary guide to the workings of the monstrous language articulated by the Plinian races.

The name Antipodes itself has a double sphere of reference. On the one hand, it can refer to Plinian beings who are marked in a special way with regard to their feet. On the other hand, it can have a cosmological significance, referring to a world that is, in some sense of the word, an anti-world. It is a curious fact that the ancient and medieval authorities quoted were able to lend more credibility to the people whose feet were turned backwards than to the people who supposedly live under the earth and walk upside down in relation to the upper hemisphere. Today it would no doubt be easier to find adherents to the view that the southern hemisphere is inhabitable and inhabited than to the view that people with inverted feet exist. In viewing both conceptions within the framework of a single system, it may be possible to come to a better understanding of the reasons for this shift in the plausibility of these imaginary ethnographies. Moreover, since the cosmological version of the Antipodes enables us to link up the theme of the imaginary worlds discussed in the first chapter with that of the imaginary human races that filled Chapters Three and Four, the Antipodes may be seen to serve an articulatory function in the argument – a function that they are admirably equipped to fulfil, as we shall presently see.

To tackle the cosmological implications of the term first, we begin at the ninth chapter of Book 16 of St Augustinus' *De Civitate Dei*, in which he deals with the question of 'whether the lower part of the earth, which is opposite to the one we inhabit, should be supposed to be inhabited by antipodas'.[3] The Bishop of Hippo's statement is quite clear: there is no rational ground for belief in a people supposed to live on the other side of the world, 'where the sun sets when it rises for us, who trace their steps opposite to ours'.[4] Not observation but induction forms the basis of his argumentation. Since all men, according to Augustinus, are descended from the first ancestor, the antipodes could have come to exist where they are fabled to be only by crossing the boundless tracts of ocean, an impossible assumption in his eyes.

It was not belief in a lower land mass, which balanced that of the upper regions of the globe, which was problematical. The Aristotelian belief in a spherical earth was widely accepted in the Middle Ages, and it was only a minority of authorities, like the sixth-century Cosmas Indicopleustes, who were adamant in denying it. In fact, this debate was to continue into the eighteenth century, when speculation on the existence of land masses in the south, the *terra australis*, involved Kant and his contemporaries in theories of the equilibrium of the earth's sphere (Kohl, 1981: 9). The spherical earth is a prerequisite for one of the popular map types in the Middle Ages, the so-called Macrobian zone map (cf. Friedman, 1981), in which the globe is, typically, divided into five zones.[5] One of these five is the inhabited temperate zone, and for reasons of symmetry a second zone is postulated, separated from the first by a belt of raging heat, which is also inhabited, and which is sometimes labelled 'Antipodum' on the maps.

The fifth century authors Macrobius and Martianus Capella made their own contributions to the debate raised by Augustinus. Macrobius, like Augustinus, claims that 'the same sun sets by them when it rises for us, and rises when it sets for us'.[6] However, Macrobius does not venture an opinion on who the inhabitants might be, and the impossibility of crossing the equator rules out any possibility of contact between those living above and below it. Another text which was to be influential on later writers, the *De Nuptiis Philologiae et Mercurii* of Martianus Capella, which is conventionally dated to the first third of the fifth century, adheres to the five-zone theory and names the inhabitants of the southern temperate zone as 'Antipodes',[7] but avoids going into details of who these antipodes were. In a text which directly echoes Augustinus, the seventh-century Bishop of Sevilla, Isidorus, follows the line of his illustrious predecessor in attributing the belief in the antipodes to the conjectures of poets.[8]

The issue came to a head a century after Isidorus when the Irish bishop of Salzburg, a certain Virgilius, was believed to have claimed that under the earth were another world (*mundus*), other peoples (*homines*) and another sun and moon, the latter no doubt referring back to the Augustinian text as well as to Macrobius. Virgilius was summoned to Rome by the Pope, Zacharias, to give an account of himself. Whatever the result of this confrontation was, it was sufficient warning for later writers to approach with circumspection any geographical theories which might challenge the biblical claim that all mankind was descended from Adam and that the gospel had been preached to the ends of the world.

In the German and Dutch versions of the journey of St Brendan, this sixth-century Irish monk throws into the fire a book in which he had read 'how under this world there is another world, where it is night as the sun shines here'.[9] His disbelief in such wonders becomes the motive of his journey, in which he is confronted with marvellous places and peoples to convince him of God's power in creating wonders. Later in the same poem, the world under the sea is audible to the stranded voyagers. This world is that of the twelfth-century court: clocks, the barking of dogs, the blast of horns, birdsong, the song of priests, the whinnying of horses and the sounds of men and women engaged in song and dance reach the ears of Brendan from out of the depths of the sea. The poet is treading on thin doctrinal ice here, since the Irish representations of a world beneath the waters on which he is drawing (cf. Edel, 1985) come dangerously close to the unorthodox (in Roman eyes) views of Virgilius of Salzburg. Wisely enough, he concludes the episode without committing himself to the precise nature of this world *sub terra*. Brendan leaves the anchor behind that he had cast into the depths and begins the return journey without it.[10]

As we saw in Chapter Three, the voyage of Brendan helps to articulate the passage from the Old to the New World in view of the role that it played in creating representations of the inhabitants of the New World. But before we switch continents, it is enough for the present to note that, if the same sun which shines upon the northern temperate zone also shines upon its southern counterpart, it is easy to suppose that the inhabitants of the latter will resemble their northern counterparts. This is what we see, for example, on a fifteenth century manuscript illumination depicting Augustinus preaching his doctrine to the inhabitants of the upper temperate zone and to their opposites *sub terra*. An Old French poet of the late thirteenth century, however, presents a different view of the inhabitants of the Antipodes. In the Clerk of Enghien's verse translation of Thomas of Cantimpré, a people are described who have the soles of their feet transposed and who are terrifyingly ugly to see. They are 'a vile, low people, and vile and evil their law and customs, for there is no accord between them, and there are battles between them every day and thus one kills the other without one crying to the other "merci"' (Friedman, 1981: 127). This shameful disregard for the rules of courtly practice contrasts sharply with the civilised antipodes of the journey of Brendan and invites reflection on the various, opposed representations of this people.

This is the point to retrace our steps to Augustinus. In the chapter of *De Civitate Dei* which precedes the discussion of the inhabitability of the Antipodes, Augustinus lists a number of monstrous races. Among them we find a people whose feet point backwards.[11] Isidorus names this people as the Antipodae and situates them in Libya, adding that they have eight toes.[12] Both authors are following the account of the fantastic human races in Book Seven of Plinius' *Historia Naturalis*. Plinius, quoting as his authority the Greek writer Megasthenes, situates on a mountain in India called the Nulo a race of men who have their feet on backwards and who have eight toes,[13] a passage that comes up again in Solinus.[14] On the authority of a certain Baiton, Plinius locates a similar race of men in Skythia called the Abarimon. Their feet are turned backwards, they are exceptionally swift and roam with the wild beasts.[15] Aulus Gellius, who knew the work of Plinius but also had access to other sources,[16] similarly places in Skythia a race of men noted for their swiftness and for their reversed feet.[17] They are also to be found in the anonymous *Liber Monstrorum*, which is dated some time before the ninth century,[18] and appear with reversed feet and eight toes on each foot as the Anticaudae in Ratramnus of Corbie.[19]

In all of these texts, the people with reversed feet belong within a catalogue of monstrous races. They are legendary races whose very existence was for Augustinus a proof of God's power and desire to revitalise man's sense of the marvellous. Often the Antipodes, as we shall continue to call them for ease of reference, are to be found in the catalogues in close proximity to races who are also marked with respect to their feet. In Plinius, the Indian Antipodes are followed by the Monocoli, a one-legged and swift race,[20] and by the Sciopodes, a race which was already familiar to the Greeks and which was in general characterised as one-legged, very swift and able to shelter from the heat of the sun by using their enormous foot as a parasol. Augustinus similarly follows his reference to the Antipodes with a description of the Sciopodes. As for Isidorus of Sevilla, he sets his Antipodes between the Sciopodes and the Hippopodes,[21] a race with horses' hooves for feet, located by Plinius in the Baltic.

We thus find two conceptions of the Antipodes. The first refers to a people situated on the opposite part of the globe, where they walk upside down. The second refers to a people situated on a distant part of the globe (though not necessarily the opposite part) whose feet point backwards. The term Antipodes can refer to both types.

We can see how easy it is within the given geographical conceptions to combine the two, since the torrid zones in which the monstrous races tended to be placed could be made to correspond to those parts of the southern temperate zone which bordered on the central belt which was rendered uninhabitable by the scorching sun. True to the Macrobian tradition, the poet of the journey of Brendan places the encounter with the subterranean world immediately after Brendan's boat has lain still for three and a half weeks in the scorching sun, that is, the central, torrid zone of the Macrobian globe. This proximity of the Antipodes to the sun's heat figures on a copy of a map made by a certain Emetrius in 975, on which a rubric identifies 'the fourth part of the globe across the ocean whose interior is unknown to us because of the sun's heat and whose extremities Antipodes are fabulously said to inhabit' (cited in Friedman, 1981: 48).

Some authors try to derive one conception from the other. The view put forward here, however, is that, whatever source criticism may tell us about the dependence of the various authorities quoted upon one another, there is a logic by which the two conceptions – the Antipodes as the inhabitants of a specific geographical location on the other side of the globe, and the Antipodes as a monstrous human race with their feet on back to front – should be placed on an equal footing. We are thus proposing a 'structural' reading of the two Antipodean types.

Out of the vast array of possibilities by which the region of the Antipodes could be supposed to be populated, there was a predilection for either a race resembling the Europeans as their upside down mirror image, or a race composed of elements taken from the Plinian compendium of monstrous human races. If we single out those races which are noteworthy in terms of their feet, we have the Abarimon, Sciopodes, Monocoli and Hippopodes which have already been mentioned, to which we could add the Himantopodes or strap-feet, an eastern race known only from later accounts; the red-footed men located near a mythical tributary of the Nile in the Alexandros legend; and the Artibiratae, who walk on all fours. From this list[22] the Sciopodes are particularly relevant for the Antipodes, since the huge foot of a reclining Sciopod also points backwards behind the head, a point that is emphasised in some illustrations.

The vocabulary of the sources referred to so far (*versus, adversus, aversus,* etc.) indicates the direction in which we should look for further light on these races. It is the mechanism of *inversion* with which we are confronted in a number of guises.

First, we can take horizontal mirror inversion. By this process, a topic is presented on the same plane but with certain features inverted. For example, a neighbouring people is described as living on the same land mass but as practising opposite customs. There may be inversion in, for example, the roles assigned to males and females respectively; or in culinary and dietary practices; or in the linguistic sphere; etc. Many of the Greek representations of their neighbours are taken to generate, by inversion, the norms of the non-Greeks inhabiting the same continent.[23] The four volumes of the *Mythologiques* of Lévi-Strauss abound in examples of this kind taken from the Americas. However, this way of generating imaginary ethnographies runs into difficulties whenever two or more imaginary ethnographies are confronted. For if the game of inversion is continued, such triads are necessarily reduced to dyads. In other words, a rudimentary opposition of the type a/b is only operative if a and b are not further broken down; if they are subdivided, the subdivisions themselves still operate in binary terms. For instance, if the Egyptians are the opposite of the Athenians, but the Skythians are also the opposite of the Athenians, what is the relation between the Egyptians and the Skythians? As Hartog (1980: 68, 268–269) points out, the rhetoric of inversion involves the exclusion of the third term. Herein lies the rhetorical force of inversion as the privileged vehicle of utopian thought. But at the same time it also marks its limit. Alterity strictly speaking is the index of the other *of a pair.*[24] Mirror inversion inevitably involves reduction to binary schemes.

A second possibility is vertical mirror inversion. This mechanism sets up an otherworld that, as an underworld, mirrors the world above. There is a fundamental ambiguity in this trope. The vertical shift creates an upside down world that is already an inversion of the world above on which it is based as a result of the vertical shift itself. Such an inverted imaginary world links up both with the widespread these of the descent into the underworld (Le Goff, 1984) and with the land of Cockaigne, that ritual reversal so dear to the anthropologists of carnival.

The horizontal and vertical possibilities both come into play in early medieval attempts to map the world in which the life after this life takes place. Already in the sixth century, Gregorius the Great (in his commentary on the book of Job) attempted a vertical systematisation in which hell is divided into lower and upper regions. The relation between the two is seen by him as analogous to the relation between heaven and the atmosphere: atmosphere (i.e. lower heaven) and limbo (i.e. upper hell) are situated close to the upper and lower surfaces of the earth respectively, while heaven and hell play their traditional role of vertically opposed poles. In other words:

heaven : hell :: atmosphere : limbo

Though the upper region of hell described by Gregorius is limbo, his exegesis contributed to the construction of a different region of the imaginary otherworld, purgatory (Le Goff, 1981: 123). On Le Goff's dating, it was only towards the end of the twelfth century that a triple division was set up of heaven, purgatory and hell, to replace the 'structuralist' quadripartite division of Gregorius (and Augustinus).[25] In the eleventh and twelfth centuries it was the 'infernalisation' or 'satanisation' of purgatory, by which it tended to drift closer to hell rather than to occupy a position equidistant between heaven and hell, which favoured a vertical interpretation in terms of descent into the underworld. After all, it was commonly understood that entry into hell could be achieved only in a vertical position (Le Goff, 1982). But there were also versions in which purgatory was sought on the same horizontal plane, whether westwards in Ireland or eastwards in Sicily (Le Goff, 1981: 273–278).

The two cases mentioned so far concern mirror inversion. The imaginary ethnography is produced by turning an image on its (horizontal or vertical) hinge, as it were, and the result of this hinge movement is inversion.

There is a category of shift which, strictly speaking, is not a case of inversion at all. This is the case in which shift results in juxtaposition without inversion. The imaginary world is 'right way up' (as in the horizontal mirror inversion) but it is placed below 'our' world (as in the vertical mirror inversion). The result is a layered cosmos. Such a solution does at least provide some sort of answer to the objections of Lactantius. In his *Divinae Institutiones* (3.24), he refused to countenance the existence of men in the antipodes on the assumption that, since the world was a globe, they would have to walk upside down in a world where trees grow down rather than up, and rain and snow fall up rather than down.

These mechanisms of inversion and shift affect not only the construction of imaginary worlds – their cosmogony and cosmology. The same mechanisms can be shown to be at work in the construction of the inhabitants of these worlds, where once again inversion is a striking feature. In the topsy-turvy Antipodean world, the people who walk upside down have inverted the relative position of head and foot. Like the reclining Sciopodes, their head is lower than their foot.[26] The reversal of direction of the feet of the Antipodes in the Plinian catalogues is thus a horizontal version of what happens in the upside down world. Herein lies the systemicity of the two types of Antipodes: the inhabitants of the upside down world and the inhabitants of the upper world whose feet are reversed are two versions of the same theme – inversion. The relation between head and foot is in the one case a question of above and below; in the other case it is a question of in front or behind.[27] At this point we rejoin the Lévi-Straussian scheme from which we started, in which above and below, before and behind played such a prominent role.[28]

In other words, we postulate within the symbolic economy an equivalence between inversion brought about by the turning of the whole object upside down and inversion brought about by turning its feet to face in the opposite direction. Furthermore, if the inhabitants of the upside down world were also to reverse the direction of their feet, a redundancy within the symbolic economy would occur: we would be faced with an uneconomic use of inversion. Such redundancies do in fact occur: a Sciopod, for example, can at the same time be an Antipode if his foot is rotated. But such redundancies are not required by the logic of the system under examination.

A further consequence of this system is that inverse and reverse may come to occupy the same place. If the retrograde motion of the backwards turned feet leads to a lost world of the past, a Golden Age, such motion can have the same utopian connotations as the more direct utopian movement of mirror inversion. At this level, the inverted world (*monde à l'envers*, the land of Cockaigne, for example) and the world to which reverse movement tends (*monde à rebours*, the Golden Age)[29] both occupy the place of a world that is desired because it is not *here*.

At this point the system can be widened. The examples considered so far are taken from antique and medieval European representations. As Wittkower pointed out, however, the Plinian races are not confined to the European imagination. At the risk of offending certain sensibilities, we shall follow the course outlined at the end of the previous chapter and proceed to compare these imaginative products with monstrous races taken from the New World, following in the steps of Cl. Lévi-Strauss and E. Magaña, who have both discussed examples of the Plinian races drawn from the American continent (e.g. Lévi-Strauss, 1985; Magaña, 1982a; 1982b).[30]

The interpretation of the Antipodes *à l'américaine* (Lévi-Strauss, 1958: 227–255) is by no means fortuitous. The New World was used as a proof of the existence of people below the equator and soon became assimilated to the Antipodes. For instance, in the title page of his *Newe Welt Und Americanische Historien* (Frankfurt, 1655), Johann Ludwig Gottfried calls it 'Historia Antipodum oder Newe Welt', and López de Gomara refers to the Indians of Chile as Antipodes, while reserving the term *Antoikoi* for the Patagonians (Bolens-Duvernay, 1988: 160). In fact, the complicity between Old and New World representations is even stronger if we recall the example of the woodcuts created to illustrate the souls of the sinners who are alternately tormented with heat and cold whom Brendan encounters during his voyage – woodcuts which were recycled to portray the inhabitants of the New World in some editions of the letter of Amerigo Vespucci on his third voyage. It is this solidarity between Old and New World conceptions which serves as the base for a comparison of otherworlds taken from the European Middle Ages with otherworlds drawn from Amerindian sources.

In the construction of imaginary worlds, we see horizontal mirror inversion at work in the myths of the Gê Indians of Brazil who place their otherworld in the east, that is, on the same horizontal plane as their own territory. They also recount a myth of an Indian who tumbled into the underworld and came to lie on the leafy top of a *buriti* palm, which implies a cosmology in which the underworld is set vertically below the upper world, though 'right way up' (Wilbert and Simoneau, 1978: 30 and 104). Such a non-mirror shift between the upper and lower worlds is made explicit in the two-world cosmology of the Mataco of Argentina, who relate that the inhabitants of the upper and lower worlds changed places because those who lived in the lower world were tired of the excrement that kept falling down on them from their upper neighbours (Wilbert and Simoneau, 1982: 46). We even find the theme of voices coming from below in another Mataco myth: originally the world was without women, but men began to dig a hole in the ground after hearing subterranean voices and out of this hole women emerged (ibid: 62–63). Besides such vertical shift, the relation between the upper and lower worlds can take the stronger form of inversion, as the subterranean world is frequently described as a topsy-turvy version of the world above, inhabited by dwarfs.[31]

As for the second type of Antipodes, those with their feet turned backwards, these are to be found in the figure of the Curupira, a type of forest demon first recorded in 1560 by José de Anchieta, who are situated in Brazil. These dwarfs have red hair and inverted feet, and in some regions they have exceptionally long ears, an attribute of another monstrous race, the Panotii ('all-ears'), recorded by Megasthenes (da Câmara Cascudo, 1954; 220–221). The Caipora, a related figure, also has long ears, as well as a hairy body, a single eye, ankles without articulations, and blue or green teeth; it has no anus (Magaña, 1988a: 200). These dwarfs are hostile to strangers and kill all they meet (Bernardes, n.d.: 133–145).[32] In the Guyanas they are known as *kurupi* (Magaña, 1982b: 84). Two tribes described by the Kogi (the *Sangareména* and the *Gulaména*) are supposed to have reversed feet (ibid.). Still in Brazil, the Shikrin (Gê) Indians attribute to an alien tribe the inversion of head and foot that we have seen to be the case with the Antipodes: the members of this tribe have eyes in their feet (Wilbert and Simoneau, 1984: 392). Among the Chortis and the Maya of San Antonio (Belize), the Sisimite are terrible giants or dwarfs who live in caves or hills and protect the plants and animals. They are recognisable by their long hair, which hangs to the ground, and by their reversed feet (Graulich, 1987: 258). Such figures have a long New World ancestry, as can be seen from a figure depicted in *Codex Laud*.[33]

In certain North American Indian myths, the subterranean dwarfs are also characterised by a faulty articulation. In a myth of the Wyandot, a member of the Iroquois linguistic family, a race of dwarfs is described who are deprived of an elbow, as a result of which they can only bend the arm at the shoulder and at the wrist (Lévi-Strauss, 1985: 129–153 for this and other examples).[34]

The lack of articulation of the limbs is by no means confined to the New World. The Old World knew such myths too, such as that recounted by Aristophanes in Platon's *Symposion*. According to a myth recounted by Eudoxos and recorded by Ploutarchos (*Isis and Osiris* 62), Zeus's limbs were stuck together so that he could not walk until Isis had cut and separated them, a text with both an acoustic (Lévi-Strauss, 1966: 346–347) and a sexual dimension (Mason, 1984: 67). It is a feature of the one-legged Sciopodes too: in Augustinus and in the *Liber Monstrorum* they have a knee which cannot be bent.[35] The Sciopod too can be marked on the sexual dimension: the Sciopod depicted on the fifteenth-century frescoes in Råby church, Denmark, is noteworthy not only for his enormous foot but also for his undisguised erection (Friedman, 1981: 204).

The sexual connotation derives from a moral theory according to which the moral order is disrupted by what may be called a 'false step'. One of the most familiar examples of such a 'false step' in the sexual sphere is the myth of Oidipous, whose ancestors are all marked with respect to their feet (Lévi-Strauss, 1958: 227–257; Vernant, 1981) and for whom moral deviance (patricide and incest) is expressed in terms of limping or of lameness. In a myth of the Kamayurá (Xingú, Central Brazil), the sexual mistakes of the females in the narrative is expressed in terms of their not walking properly, a defect which is thus both literal and metaphorical (Jara and Magaña, 1980: 13). If one is prepared to accept Freudian accounts of foot symbolism, many more such examples could be found in which an unmistakably sexual component is present (Mason, 1984: 41–45).

On the other hand, the correct way of walking can serve as a model for the order of the cosmos. In the *Book of Chumayel*, the origin of the world links the origin of man with his two-footedness. The careful measuring of the rhythm of his steps establishes the order by which the world can be enumerated (Brotherston, 1979: 182–183). The puns in the text even allow the formulation of 'paralogistic' problems of a very abstract kind, such as the impossibility of a starting position in which right and left are simultaneous.[36]

Foot symbolism also plays an important part in shamanistic ritual. The deity Tezcatlipoca ('smoking mirror'), who has a number of shaman-like attributes, such as left-handedness, is depicted with one foot replaced by a smoking mirror in the *Codex Borgia*, an allusion to the ability of the shaman to see all and to exhibit a mastery of illusion. Another figure, this time from a Mixtec codex (*Vindobonensis Mexicanus I*), who may be interpreted as an avatar of Quetzalcoatl, is depicted with interlaced legs. This detail has been brought into connection with a shamanistic affliction of the Quiché of Guatemala, in which a man who is called to be a shaman loses the control of his legs, which become intertwined serpents (Jansen, 1982: 144).

Besides such moral, sexual and cultic connotations, difficulties in locomotion may point to difficulties in communication in general on a more cognitive level (Vernant, 1979a: 30–31; Ginzburg, 1989: 206–275). We find in this connection a relation between deviations in articulation and deviations in speech. For example, for the Arapaho, the different articulation of the dwarfs is linguistic: words acquire an opposite meaning in dwarf language (Lévi-Strauss, 1985: 129–153). In the Greek myths surrounding the foundation of Kyrene in North Africa, the family of the founder, Battos, is marked by both limping and stammering

(Vernant, 1981: 237). As for the shamanistic Tezcatlipoca, the smoke emitted from the mirror that replaces his foot is often indistinguishable from a speech scroll, suggesting 'speaking mirror' as a possible gloss of his name (Brundage, 1979). The association of foot, mirror and speech is at any rate suggestive.

In view of the relations between bodily articulations and speech articulations which the above remarks indicate, we may be justified in taking the system of articulation into which the Antipodes can be inserted *literally*. Lévi-Strauss (1985: 159) has already suggested that the anal/oral code of myth can be seen as constituting a vocabulary and a grammar of communication between the various cosmic levels. In a similar vein, it is here suggested that the bodily articulations constitute a system of articulation which is not casually connected with the articulation of language. This suggestion finds support from another source too: in an ingenious study, Nancy Troike (1982) has demonstrated how standardised postures and gestures, particularly hand gestures, are used in the Mixtec codices to communicate request and acceptance, dedication to travel and sacred mission, or hostility. This communicative aspect of the pictures dominates considerations of realistic portrayal and all other considerations.[37]

In commenting on the bodies in Hieronymus Bosch's Garden of Delights, Michel de Certeau was led to see in the forms created by them a musicality of form, both glossography and calligraphy. They form a writing which is illegible (de Certeau, 1982: 96–99). There is one feature of these bodies which is of particular interest here. They are articulated at only a very limited number of points (the neck, the buttocks, the knees, etc.). This limitation results in forms which are flexible only to a limited extent.

There thus seems to be a body language which is not a metaphor – it is not that the body is articulated *like a language* – but metonymy – the body *partakes in* language. The articulations of the body *are* the articulations of language.

This is a crucial point for the understanding of the Plinian races and their importance in mediating between the Old and the New Worlds. We are assigning them a linguistic role which is expressive of the difference between the two worlds.

We can now explore this linguistic role – and its implications for the classic anthropological distinction between 'oral' and 'written' cultures – in more detail. For instance, in language articulation has a double point of reference. When applied to speech, articulation can designate the subdivision of a spoken chain into syllables. But articulation is also the subdivision of the chain of meanings into significant units (de Saussure, 1974: 10). It is thus already situated at a point at which the division between speech and writing has not yet been made, to which Derrida refers as the 'archi-écriture' (Derrida, 1967a). The absence of a speech/writing division at this point implies the absence of a mediating function. As a corollary, it implies a certain closeness between body and speech/writing, a use of the body in forms which already prefigure the articulation of the spoken word.[38] The articulations of the limbs of the body already provides a powerful means of operating the transition from the body to the exterior world by their double function of metonym and metaphor. As metaphor, the limbs (*artus*) indicate a way of conceiving articulation, a method of ordering of external totalities like the bodies. As metonym, the limbs *are already* articulation (*articuli*).

This double articulation indicates why the Plinian races are so important for the transition from nature to culture and for that from interiority to exteriority. As speculation on the human body, their enormous range of combinations provides a means of articulation which refers not only back to the body itself but also out to the external world. If language is to be seen as an attempt to mediate the relation between words and things, the inflections of the Plinian races operate as a language which is anterior to the speech/writing division. Here 'as a language' is not a metaphor but a metonym: the articulation of the Plinian races *is* the articulation of language. At this point, and at this specific level, the distinction between 'oral' and 'literate' cultures disappears, and with it the logocentrism of anthropology is seen to be but one more form of ethnocentrism.

If we follow the grammatological implications of the articulations of the body through, they are thus seen as constituting a form of syntax.[39] In this respect, they complement the functions of the bodily orifices, for the latter may be seen as constituting a system of punctuation (see Chapter Six).

It is now possible to return to the question that was raised earlier of why belief in a race with reversed feet could be countenanced, albeit with reservations, by the Augustinian tradition while belief in an upside down world could not. If the Plinian races are seen as useful for the construction of imaginary worlds, it is not surprising that interest in them should rise in periods of expansion, when they offered a flexible and familiar means of representation of the newly discovered peoples for the consumption of the Old World. In the twelfth century, a century of expansion on all fronts, the expansion in geographical knowledge was accompanied by an expansion in the knowledge of the geography of purgatory, an imaginary world that began to assume concrete form in a specific location toward the end of the century (Le Goff, 1981). The 'language' provided by the Plinian races was one way in which the new discoveries could be 'translated' and assimilated.

An upside down world, on the other hand, has far less to offer as a means of thinking the new. Indeed, its domination by the principle of inversion renders it able to do little more than to mirror what is already familiar. It simply rephrases the new in terms of the familiar old.

The difference between the variations within the Plinian races and the inversion of the world leads to differences in the flexibility by which the new can be apprehended. It should not be forgotten, however, that both means of approach, though differing in respect of flexibility, can both be put to serve the same ends: the reduction of the Other to the Same. In the discovery of the New World, the Plinian races to which the newly discovered peoples were assimilated served the function of assimilating and thereby reducing what was strange in the New World to what was strange but familiar in the Old World. Their flexibility gave them a greater capacity to cover a wide range of phenomena, but this does not entail an elimination of the violent reduction which is at work behind and within this process.

The flexibility offered by the Plinian races is counter to the attempts to impose a unifying *logos*. However, through their very lack of geographical specificity, they are ultimately bound to be expelled from views of the world in which even the margins are accounted for. They are a mere obstruction to the construction of concrete worlds which can be mapped and colonised. Within a chronological perspective which corresponds roughly to the one adopted here, Jara and Magaña (1982) mark the end of a period of acceptance of variety and the beginning of a unifying movement whose rules are what they call the rules of imperialist method. It is in the sixteenth century that they locate a failure to recognise the heterogeneity of cultures and a desire to include them within a taxonomical scale.

If, however, one of the features of the postmodern era is the disappearance of grand, unifying theory, combined with a renewed awareness of the incommensurability of cultures (Lyotard, 1979; Overing, ed., 1985), it is perhaps time to reinstate the Plinian races. In their capacity and flexibility to construct imaginary worlds, the Plinian races provide us with an instrument by which anthropology might be opened up to the other. In their resistance to the unifying *logos* of anthropology, they invite speculation on what is other to that *logos* and on the definitions of *anthropos* which lies behind any kind of anthropology. This is the reason why the Plinian races occupy a privileged position within the practice of ethno-anthropology. Their quaintness is the quaintness of the folk usages of European epistemology. And if we try to accommodate in this folk usage 'the hitherto unaccommodated cultural representations of the muted majority of the world' (Ardener, 1985: 65), it will not be enough to stretch the concepts of anthropology – they will require a more radical treatment.

The various attitudes toward the Antipodes in the periods before and after the arrival of Columbus in the Caribbean are indicative of the different ways in which they could be evaluated. In the fourteenth century we can still trace the discussion of the Macrobian world view. One of the popularising translators of Aristoteles, Nicole Oresme (1332–1382), was still following Augustinus in denying the inhabitability of the Antipodes on doctrinal grounds. Another work from the same century, however, the *Travels* of 'Sir John Mandeville', accepts the existence of Antipodes under the Antarctic Pole:

So I say truly that a man could go all round the world, above and below, and return to his own country, provided he had his health, good company, and a ship, as I said above. And all along the way he would find men, lands, islands, cities and towns, such as there are in those countries.; For you know well that those men who live right under the Antarctic Pole are foot against foot to those who live right below the Arctic Pole, just as we and those who live at our Antipodes are foot against foot. It is like that in all parts. Each part of the earth and sea has its opposite, which always balances it.

(Mandeville, 1983: 128-129)

Mandeville's argument, like that of Macrobius before him, is based on reason alone. With the discovery of the Americas, however, a change in the relations between the Antipodes as a Plinian race and as the inhabitants of an upside down world might be expected. It is thus all the more remarkable that the framework of the argument persisted unchanged for some time after the voyages of Columbus, Vespucci and Magellan. In 1522, in a lecture delivered to students of the university of Bologna, Pietro Pomponazzi, who was particularly attracted by the contradictions between philosophy and theology,[40] declared the bankruptcy of Aristotelian cosmology (Nardi, 1965: 42–43). Pomponazzi had received a letter from Antonio Pigafetta in which the latter gave proof of the fact that the regions below the equator were inhabited. How could this proof provided by the voyage of Magellan be reconciled with the Augustinian doctrine of their exclusion from salvation? Pomponazzi refused to be drawn into providing an answer, unless 'perhaps Christ had been crucified in another pole too!'[41]

Another contributor to the age-old debate, Thomas More, juggles with the theological and the philosophical views in an ironical way: while assigning credibility to the existence of the Antipodeans on rational grounds, their real existence is at the same time denied as they are relegated to Utopia (Seeber, 1971: 83).

In his re-examination of the doctrinal issues, the Jesuit José de Acosta (1540–1600) came to a different conclusion. The absolute truth that all the races of mankind must be descended from Adam remained for de Acosta an unshakeable premiss. However, there was now evidence for the fact that there *were* humans living beneath the tropics. The solution of de Acosta is that, given the unshakeable premiss and the new ethnographic evidence, the only way out of this theoretical quandary is to posit a geographical connection between Europe and the Antipodes. For de Acosta, the Indians, like all other non-Semitic peoples, were the descendants of the sons of Japhet,[42] one of the three sons of Noah. They had crossed overland, he argued, somewhere in the region of what is now the Bering Strait (cf. Pagden, 1982: 194).

The change brought about by de Acosta's method is that it presents a perspective by which to organise the different levels of cultural attainment within a single, unifying grid. It thus makes possible ethnology, the mapping of various *ethnic* groups within one *logos*.

'Mapping' recalls the aims of Mercator in his *Atlas* of offering a homogeneous image of space, whose abstract motivation replaces an organisation of space in which the various regions were the recipients of variant symbolic investments. Within the abstract perspective of the *Atlas*, the presence of the monstrous points to sedimented symbolic associations. No region is left uncharted, and the unknown (*Terra australis incognita*) is prefigured, 'invented for a hesitant total-isation of the shape of the Earth' (Rabasa, 1985: 10). By this time, then, the Antipodes had had their day.

Notes

1. The last work of Foucault (1984b), for example, is a substantial contribution to the dietary and other techniques intended to preserve the well-being of the body as practised in the early empire of Rome. For the bodily techniques of the ancient Greeks, see Foucault (1984a) and Mason (1984)
2. Lévi-Strauss himself has reversed his tracks in moving from ancient Greek concepts to New World ones in his application of the insights of M. Detienne (1972) into the Greek aromatic and culinary codes to New World vegetation (Lévi-Strauss, 1983: 263–275).
3. An inferiorem partem terrae, quae nostrae habitationi contraria est, antipodas habere credendum sit.
4. Quod vero et antipodas esse fabulantur, id est homines a contraria parte terrae, ubi sol oritur, quando occidit nobis, adversa pedibus nostris calcare vestigia: nulla ratione credendum esse.
5. The five-zone theory is first attributed to the pre-Socratic philosopher Parmenides.
6. Idem sol illis et obire dicetur nostro ortu et orietur cum nobis occidet, Macrobius, *Commentarii in Somnium Scipionis*, 5.24.
7. Martianus Capella, *De Nuptiis Philologiae et Mercurii* 6.605ff. The writer makes a further distinction between *antipodes* and *antichthones*, but, as in his first-century predecessor Pomponius Mela (*De Chorographia* 1.4), the distinction is rather confused (cf. Parroni, 1984: 180). In the sixteenth century the cosmographer Thevet still utilised this distinction: in his account (which is not free from confusion either), the Antipodes proper are those who are diametrically opposed in terms of the four points of the compass, while the Antichthones are those who are opposed according to the intermediate axes (North–West, South–West, etc.) (cf. Thevet, 1983: 144, with the editorial note *ad loc.*).
8. Isidorus, *Etymologiae* 9.2.133: Iam vero hi qui Antipodae dicuntur, eo quod contrarii esse vestigiis nostris putantur, ut quasi sub terris positi adversa pedibus nostris calcent vestigia, nulla ratione credendum est, quia nec soliditas patitur, nec centrum terrae.
9.   Hoe dat eene wereld weere
    hier onder deze eerde
    ende als 't hier dag werde
    dat daar dan nacht zij.
             (*De reis van Sinte Brandaan*, lines 38–41)
10. For other references to the world of the Antipodes in Middle Dutch literature, see Lie (1988).
11. [...] quibus plantas versas esse post crura, Augustinus, *De Civitate Dei* 16.8.
12. Isidorus, *Etymologiae* 11.3.24: Antipodes in Libya plantas versas habent post crura et octonos digitos in plantis.
13. Plinius, *Historia Naturalis* 7.2.22: in monte, cui nomen est Nulo, homines esse aversis plantis octonos digitos in singulis habentes.
14. C. Iulius Solinus, *Collectanea Rerum Memorabilium* 52.26: ad montem, qui Nulo dicitur, habitant quibus aversae plantae sunt et octoni digiti in plantis singulis.
15. Plinius, *Historia Naturalis* 7.2.11: homines aversis post crura plantis, eximiae velocitatis, passim cum feris vagantes.
16. On internal evidence Gellius has been shown to be dependent on a lost Greek source

as well as on Plinius (Bolton, 1962). A relative autonomy from Plinius has also been claimed for Solinus by Mommsen (1895: xv–xvi).

17. Aulus Gellius, *Noctes Atticae* 9.4.6: alios item esse homines apud eandem caeli plagam [Skythia] singulariae velocitatis vestigia pedum habentes retro porrecta.

18. *Liber Monstrorum* 1.29: plantae retro curvatae officio capitis contrariae videntur.

19. This ninth-century French Benedictine is the author of a letter on the Cynocephali in which he argued for their humanity (Friedman, 1981: 188ff.).

20. Plinius, *Historia Naturalis* 7.2.23: Idem hominum genus, qui Monocoli vocarentur, singulis cruribus, mirae pernicitatis ad saltum.

21. In the work of Ratramnus of Corbie, they appear as the Hippodes.

22. For details see the references in Chapter Three.

23. See, for example, Hartog (1980); Rossellini and Saïd (1978).

24. This point is further discussed at the end of the final chapter.

25. Le Goff's dating depends on his 'nominalist' approach to purgatory, in which the first appearance of the substantive *purgatorium* plays such an important role. However, in view of the appearance of 'purgatory-like' elements much earlier, it is debatable how much emphasis should be attached to this lexicological side of Le Goff's thesis.

26. In this respect too, the world of the dead often conforms to images of an inverted otherworld. Thus in Jewish exegesis it is claimed that the dead walk on their heads, as Isaac did when he left paradise, to the great astonishment of Rebecca (Schmitt, 1987: 47–48).

27. This is explicit in the *Liber Monstrorum* (1.29), where the feet turned backwards appear to be contrary to the direction of the head.

28. Nor would it be stretching the point to go beyond Lévi-Strauss to Freud: the horizontal and vertical inversions would both fall within his category of displacement.

29. For the distinction between *monde à l'envers* and *monde à rebours* see further Le Goff, 1985: 24 and 34.

30. Of course, examples can be found outside the Americas. For example, among the Chinese versions of monstrous human races discussed by F. de Mély (1897), we find a race of men with horses' hooves resembling the Hippopodes of the Greco-Roman tradition.

31. In the pictographic system of the *Walam Olum*, recorded by the Lenape Algonkin in the seventeenth century, the devices of horizontal and vertical inversion used to express the cardinal directions and the concepts 'above' and 'below' also express negation and opposition, for which parallels can be found in Iroquoian, Sioux and 'Toltec' iconography (Brotherston, 1979: 51). An inverted glyph to denote negation or opposition is also to be found on the 'slab J' from Monte Alban in the Valley of Oaxaca, dated to around 300 BC (ibid: 229).

32. Bernardes lists a number of such spirit peoples on the authority of José de Acosta. Besides the woodland *curopirá*, he mentions the *igpupiará* who live in the water, and the *baetatá* who inhabit the coastal regions and river banks. He also records mountain dwarfs (*bergmanlin*) and dwarfs from the mines (*suebérgios*).

33. Brotherston has suggested that a deity (whom he identifies as Tepeyollotli) is shown walking backwards on page 1 of the Laud screenfold 'to mislead, like the woodland monsters of South America' (1979: 106 with illustration). As Maarten Jansen has pointed out to me, it is the deity's *head* which is reversed, not his feet. All the same, this inversion poses similar problems to the inversion of the feet.

34. The Akan (Ashanti) of Ghana believe that the forests are inhabited by *mmoatia* (dwarfs) and by forest monsters and witches. A forest monster, the *sasabonsam*, is covered with long hair, has large blood-shot eyes, long legs, and feet pointing in both directions. It sits in a tree and dangles its legs to hook up unwary hunters (Busia, 1954: 195). It is significant that the contemporary Akan believe that the communication of

the woodland dwarfs is achieved by whispering (A. Stenfert Kroese, personal communication based on fieldwork). The connection that this implies between bodily articulation and speech articulation is developed in the following paragraphs.

35. Augustinus, *De Civitate Dei* 16.8: Item ferunt esse gentem, ubi singula crura in pedibus habent nec poplitem flectunt, et sunt mirabilis celeritatis.

36. For another example of the role of footsteps in cosmogony, see the Sioux liturgy on the journey of the soul after death (Brotherston, 1979: 258–259).

37. Of course, art historians have long been familiar with this aspect of bodily gestures; see for example Chapter II of M. Baxandall (1972) for instances drawn from the systems of gestures used by the Benedictines and by itinerant preachers.

38. A Guajiro example discussed in the following chapter gives us some idea of how we might conceive the *archi-écriture* in a situation before the introduction of writing has created the difference within language between speech and writing.

39. The many-armed gods of India were interpreted as figures like a grammatical phrase made up of several different words by Charles Dupuis, a leading intellectual at the time of the French Revolution (Mitter, 1977: 103).

40. Juan Ginés de Sepúlveda, the bitter opponent of Bartolomé de las Casas, claimed to have studied under Pomponazzi while attending the Spanish college at Bologna (Pagden, 1982: 109).

41. [...] nisi forte quod Christus fecit se crucifigere etiam in alio polo!

42. Jean de Léry agreed that the Amerindians were descended from one of the sons of Noah. He opted for Ham, rather than Shem or Japhet, since he believed that the descendants of Japhet, mentioned by Moses, were situated on the islands of the Mediterranean (de Léry, 1980: 196–197). More than twenty different ancestors were put forward in the scholarly disputes over the Amerindians' ancestors, including the Jews (Ryan, 1981: 533).

Source: Conradus Lycosthenes, *Prodigiorum ac Ostentorum Chronicum* ..., Basle, 1557.
Reproduced with permission of the University Library, Amsterdam.

Chapter six

A monstrous idiom: punctuation

The text, as we know it, is inextricably tied up with the notion of a body. The *corpus* of a writer, the *headings* of a text, the *chapters*, the *index* – these are all terms by which the text is treated as a body.

On the other hand, there are cases in which the body is treated as a text. At the risk of anachronism, we might be tempted to see a trace of this conception in Father Gilij's observation that:

> Among the books which I had in the Orinoco, none appeared to me more unusual or worthy of profound speculation than the Indians with whom I lived.
>
> (Gilij, 1987, II: 49)

Gilij had a predecessor who read off the character of the Amerindians from their faces: in the record of his fourth voyage, Columbus states baldly: 'I came across another people who were anthropophagous: the ugliness of their features says so' (Colón, 1984: 326). No doubt the limit case of the treatment of the human body as a text is the literal torture described in Kafka's *In the Penitential Colony*, where the textual rule that has been broken is inscribed on the body of the victim. Or take the following example:

> They are branded with iron on their face and the initials of their successive owners are printed on their skin; they are passed from one owner to another, and some bear three or four names, so that the face of these human beings who were created in God's image has, through our sins, been transformed into writing paper.

These words are extracted from a letter to the Council of the Indies by Vasco de Quiroga. Fray Toribio Motolinía, the author of an inquiry into the customs, beliefs and organisation of the Indians before the conquest, provides a similar description of these faces which have been transformed into illegible books (cited in Todorov, 1982: 143). As Todorov puts it, it is as if a figurative expression were being taken literally, or as if the signifier were to be confused with the signified. In the ensuing literal relationship, the distance required for symbolism to function is absent.[1]

The two variants (the body as text/the text as body) point towards a minimal separation of the symbol from the symbolised. The phenomenon was already discussed by Freud in his studies of hysteria, where he came up against the common practice 'when a hysteric creates a somatic expression for an emotionally-coloured idea by symbolization'. As he goes on to say, 'it is perhaps wrong to say that hysteria creates these sensations by symbolization. It may be that it does not take linguistic usage as its model at all, but that both hysteria and linguistic usage alike draw their material from a common source' (Breuer and Freud, 1974: 254–255). Although Freud's adherence to Darwin at this point is less likely to find supporters today, his insight is an important one: there is a *solidarity* between linguistic and somatic usages.

This solidarity in turn makes possible a determinate degree of reversibility between body and text. The narrowness of this relation has its consequences, which we shall now proceed to explore.

First, the relation between body and text suggests the existence of certain problems in the formulation of a notion such as that of a 'people without writing'. In a recent study of the Guajiro of Venezuela, M. Perrin (1986) has developed some of the suggestions made by Lévi-Strauss in his well-known study of the relations between writing and power (Lévi-Strauss, 1955) and has reviewed elements in Guajiro thought and practice which may have contributed to the development of their ideas on writing. As a hunting society, the Guajiro know how to 'read' the tracks of game. The power of creation of Maleiwa, the cultural hero of the Guajiro, comes from his capacity to 'read', for it is from the traces of living beings left in clay, traces which precede the existence of these beings, that Maleiwa was able to fashion them. In following the semantic path by which the Guajiro indicate the act of reading, Perrin suggests that the facial paintings used by the Guajiro in their dances might prefigure writing. Finally, the clan markings branded on livestock or tattooed on the bodies of the Indians themselves, like the mutilations inflicted on the body of Hektor in the Homeric *Iliad*, express messages destined for the readers of another world.

This Guajiro example gives us some idea of how we might conceive the *archi-écriture* in a situation before the introduction of writing has created the difference within language between speech and writing. If we return to the Lévi-Straussian discussion of writing, we find a very different attitude towards 'savage' writing. He claimed that the Nambikwara did not know how to write or draw, with the exception of certain patterns of dots and zigzags on their gourds. The notion of writing to which Lévi-Strauss is here subscribing, however, is a very reduced one. The kinds of activity described by Perrin do not differ, fundamentally, from script. Words like 'scratch', 'trace lines', etc. are not divorced from the act of writing. As Derrida has noted, the Chinese word *wen* can designate a number of activities besides writing proper (including the veins of stone and wood, the constellations, the traces left by birds and animals on the ground, etc.), but there is no concluding from this that the Chinese did not have writing. In fact, Derrida's lengthy discussion of the Lévi-Straussian text indicates how, despite the author's well-meant intentions to avoid ethnocentrism, Lévi-Strauss' distinction between people who do or do not possess writing is itself an ethnocentric distinction (Derrida, 1967a: 149–202).[2]

Following the suggestions made by these critics of the Lévi-Straussian view, we can turn to the relation between body and text to see in what ways the body is implicated in writing. To start at the end: the limit of communication is the closed text/closed body. Communication can take place only when there is an opening and a difference. When Perrin tried to separate the narratives of his informants into separate words, they did not at first understand what he meant, for such a distinction makes any sense only when the question of meaning and its origin is raised. The meaning of a whole word, taken in isolation, is secondary, depending on the act of signification which takes place within a difference.[3]

If closure excludes the possibility of communication, the obvious focus of attention in examining the ways in which the body communicates - including the semiotic function of the monstrous human races - is thus to turn to the openings of the body. As we saw in the previous chapter, Lévi-Strauss has already suggested that the anal/oral code of myth can be seen as constituting a vocabulary and a grammar of communication between the various cosmic levels (1985: 159). He has also suggested the usefulness of an investigation of the beings which inhabit mythical thought in terms of excessively blocked or pierced bodies as well as in terms of deficient or excessive articulation (1968: 393). In following up his suggestion, we propose to deal with what may be defined in broad terms as a code of communication which finds expression through the orifices of the body. As for the ethnographic material, in directing our gaze towards the orifices of the body, towards the entrances and exits, the construction of the present chapter follows the same zigzag movement that was at work in the previous chapter, as Old World and New World representations are juxtaposed and confronted.

The bodily orifices under discussion here are the ears, the nose, the mouth, the vagina and the anus. In fact, the system could be widened: the eyes, the navel and the penis may also be considered as bodily orifices, and there are even myths which assign procreative functions to the knees, the elbows and the armpits.[4] Before going any further, it may be as well to indicate in what ways the bodily orifices may be said to constitute a system.

As Lévi-Strauss has remarked, the terms for 'eat' and 'copulate' are identical in a very large number of languages (1984: 47). This already indicates a linking of the sexual and alimentary codes, and enables us to pass from the orifices of the digestive system (mouth, anus)[5] to those of the genital system (vagina and penis). This homology between the two domains is sustained by the widespread mythical theme of the *vagina dentata*, the toothed vagina.

In other ways too, the mutual interrelations of the orifices point towards a system. The philosopher Diogenes mocked those who locked away their treasures under lock and key, while leaving the doors and windows of their body open (Stobaeus, *Florilegium* I.150.6–11). He refers in this connection to the mouth, the genitals, the ears and the eyes. To take another example, when Amerigo Vespucci comments on the lack of shame among the Americans who do not cover their genitals, he notes that they are no more ashamed than the Europeans are to show their nose or mouth (Vespucci, 1984: 135).

Other relations between the orifices will emerge in the course of our examination. It is now time to move to the privileged field of the present inquiry – the Plinian races – to see what races are marked in terms of their bodily entrances and exits.

To start at the top of the body, we begin with the eyes. One of the earliest figures to be marked in this respect is the one-eyed Homeric Kyklops.[6] By a curious coincidence, the one-eyed races (in Latin: *monoculi*) are sometimes confused with the one-legged races (in Greek: *monocoli*), as if the articulations of the body could not help evoking the body's orifices. In the Rothschild Canticles, for example, a fourteenth-century Netherlandish manuscript shows a Sciopod standing on his gigantic foot, while the text runs: 'currit cum uno crure monorulus [sic] erit et vocabitur ciclops' (cited in Friedman, 1981). The Arimaspoi mentioned by Aristeas of Prokonnesos are also one-eyed, and they figure among the Asiatic races catalogued in the *Prometheus Bound* of the fifth-century dramatist Aischylos.

The early Greek travel writers, such as Skylax, Ktesias and Herodotos, also mention one-eyed races. In the monstrous human races of the Plinian catalogue, we find a wider variety of races who are peculiar with respect to their eyes. In Ethiopia he locates the maritime Ethiopians, who are exceptionally keen-sighted (*Historia Naturalis* 6.35.194), while the list of fabulous inhabitants includes a one-eyed race (ibid: 195). Plinius' Albanians are also keen-sighted; in fact, they have the eyes of owls and can see better at night. We might also add to the list the men mentioned in the Alexandros legend whose eyes shine like lanterns (Lecouteux, 1982, II: 108). Gervais of Tilbury in his *Otia Imperialia* even records the existence of men who resemble monkeys and have eight eyes, eight feet and two horns (ibid: 117). Nor should we forget the evil eye: among the Triballi and the Illyrians, according to Plinius, there are sorcerers who can bewitch with a glance from their eyes, which are remarkable in that they have two pupils in each eye (*Historia Naturalis* 7.2.16). Chinese mythology also knows the people with one eye, to which we might add the people with an eye in the back of their head (de Mély, 1897: 365–366).

Skylax also mentioned a people with huge ears, the *Otoliknoi*. Under a variety of names (*Phanesii, Panotii, Sannali*), this race crops up in the accounts of Plinius, Solinus, Pomponius Mela and Isidorus, as well as in the Indian epics (Wittkower, 1977: 52–53) and as the flying variety of Chinese mythology (de Mély, 187: 358). By contrast, some authorities mention a race of humans without ears at all (Lecouteux, 1982, II: 8–9).

Already among the monstrous births recorded in Babylonia we find births of babies with no mouth or nostrils (Wittkower, 1977: 198 n.58). Although these individual prodigies are not the same as monstrous human races, Isidorus was later to make the transition from the former to the latter. Lack of a nose characterises the *Sciritae* and the *Astomi* of India. The former, recorded by Megasthenes, are a nomad people with holes in the place of nostrils, who also have a feeble articulation: they can walk only like snakes. As for the *Astomi*, mentioned by Plinius (*Historia Naturalis* 7.2.25), they have a nose but no mouth. Their diet is one of aroma, as they live off the scent of plants and fruit.[7] In Ethiopia Plinius records a variety of races marked in terms of the facial orifices: they are flat-faced and have no nose; or they have no upper lip; or they have no tongue; or they have a single orifice which has to do duty as nose and mouth (ibid: 6.35.187–188). By contrast, the *Amyctyrae* have a protruding upper or lower lip, which they use as a parasol, like the gigantic foot of a Sciopod.

Besides these variations on the separate orifices of the head, there is variation in the location of the head itself. The *Blemmyae*, like the Ewaipanoma which Ralegh reported having seen in the Guyanas, have their eyes and mouth on their chest. In the case of the *Epiphagi*, the face has slipped down lower to the abdomen. And Greco-Egyptian religion provides us with a master of thunder whose mouth has slipped right down to the feet (Delatte, 1914: 207) as well as a deity whose eyes are on his feet (ibid: 213). In *Daniel*, a thirteenth-century German romance, there is a monster without a trunk, which has a Gorgon head and whose legs are attached to his neck (Lecouteux, 1982, I: 195). And perhaps a limit case is provided by the Chinese dragon whose face and eyes have disappeared from the body entirely (de Mély, 1897: 368).

If we pass further down the body to the sexual organs and to the anus, we can note the Indian people mentioned by the Greek satirist Loukianos who have no anus and live on moisture extracted from the air; they produce no excrement, and practise homosexual intercrural sex (Loukianos, *True Story*). The mention of homosexuality here is explicable in terms of the lack of an anus: these are 'hypervirile' men, who cannot be penetrated.[8] Mention should also be made here of a race mentioned by Plinius and Isidorus, the *androgini*, men-women with the genitals of both sexes.

These various Plinian races were passed down from antiquity to the European Middle Ages via such intermediaries as Mandeville. In his description of the inhabitants of the Andaman Islands, all of the races he mentions are marked either in terms of the bodily articulations or in terms of the bodily orifices (Mandeville, 1983: 137). As we have seen, they recur in descriptions of the inhabitants of the New World. Columbus receives a report on the one-eyed natives of the island of Bohío (Colón, 1984: 51), while *Amyctyrae* with a protruding lower lip appear on the Grynaeus map of 1532, and various travellers' accounts mention a race with enormous ears, the *Panotii* of Isidorus.

Besides these European representations of the native peoples of America, we also have representations due to the Americans themselves. In the *Codex Borgia*, the sanctuary entrances are depicted as mouths, and the teeth are steps; the exits are vaginal or oral. Brotherston (1979: 84) compares this with the sandpaintings of the Navajo, which are framed by a human body which functions as the single entrance/exit to the sanctuaries. In the *Histoyre du Méchique* (translated from a Spanish original by Thevet), Quetzalcoatl and Tezcatlipoca brought the goddess Tlalteotl down from the heavens: 'she had eyes and mouths in all her joints, which she used to bite like a wild animal'; and when the same gods have to recreate the earth after the flood, they do so by penetrating Tlalteotl in the mouth and the navel (Graulich, 1987: 59–60). In a different context, M. Perrin (1988a: 149) describes a people of aggressive dwarfs (*akalakui*) taken from a myth of the Guajiro who penetrate the anus, nostrils and all the body orifices; in another Guajiro myth they fatally attack a girl who has gone out to sow millet, penetrating her in the eyes, anus and mouth (ibid: 153).

In a Mixtec codex, *Vindobonensis Mexicanus I*, ten anonymous male/female pairs appear as descendants of Sr. 5 Wind and Sra. 9 Lizard. Among them we can single out a pair lacking ears and sexual organs; a pair lacking a mouth, eyes and nose (and anus?); and a pair lacking an upper and a lower lip. It has been suggested that these absences are meant to connote a lack of humanity: it is precisely the marking of the body as a human body that these beings miss (Jansen, 1982: 117–119).

There are two particularly important features which can be selected from these lists. First, there is a high level of mutual interchangeability between the various orifices. For instance, Ploutarchos records the belief that the weasel was impregnated in the ear and gave birth through the mouth (*Isis and Osiris* 74). Psychoanalysis only confirms the symbolic equivalences set up in ancient Greek thought between the eye and vagina (cf. Devereux, 1956), and the same is true of the equivalence between eye and penis (cf. Mason, 1984: 43–44). These exchanges are a part of the *symbolic economy* of the bodily orifices, which come together to form a system.

Second, it is significant that a number of the features involving bodily orifices impinge on the articulations of the body. The way in which these two fields tend to exercise a mutual attraction on one another will be of importance when we consider the solidarity between the two systems. For example, distinct narratives of the Tarëno (or Trio, members of the Carib linguistic family) relate the origin of agriculture to either the hero's lack of an anus or to his lack of articulations in his limbs (elbows, knees, ankles) (Magaña, 1988b: 580). A Wayana myth from the same area links bodily orifices and articulations in a similar way: a man who has promised to give his daughters in marriage to the jaguar fashions substitutes from wood, but they lack both orifices and articulations; when they fall from the hammock, they break (Magaña, 1987a: 44). Apparently the two systems are related in some way.

We can thus proceed to a closer examination of some of the New World myths in which the bodily orifices figure. Among the Barasana of Vaupés (Colombia), whose mythology has been described in the important study by S. Hugh-Jones (1979), the hero of the myths, Yurupary, was born without a mouth. He could neither eat nor speak, and had to be fed with tobacco smoke that was blown over him. He grew up very rapidly and at the age of six a mouth was cut in his face

(Hugh-Jones, 1979: 201). Warimi, who corresponds to Yurupary in other Barasana myths, had a very small mouth; he could pronounce only the words '*we we we we*' (ibid: 171).

In contrast to this excessive closedness, yet another avatar of Yurupary, *He* Anaconda, had a mouth as large as a cavern, which he used to consume the neophytes. In another Barasana myth on the birth of Yurupary, the baby was full of holes (ibid: 201, 203 n.11). And, to return to Yurupary, his excessive closedness was followed by a phase of excessive openness: he sang at full volume, disgorged children through his wide mouth, and uttered groans which could be heard all over the country (ibid: 200).

We might say that it ran in the family. Yurupary's mother was excessively closed – she had no vagina – until she was penetrated by a jaguar (ibid: 170). A neighbouring people, the Cubeo, also make use of the metaphor of openness to represent the first menstruation. It is thus a significant detail that the agent who performs this act of opening in the Cubeo myth, the moon, has such large teeth that it cannot close its mouth (ibid: 199).

The anus fits into this system too. In other versions of the myth of Yurupary, the hero ingests initiates through the mouth or through the anus (ibid: 200), and the tapir tries to suck a girl in through the anus (ibid: 141). At the same time, the anus is contrasted with the vagina: the howler monkey engages in controversy with the tapir because the *He* instrument is needed to *open* the vaginas of the women in order to create human beings. The tapir and the howler monkey can thus been seen to form an opposed pair within this system (ibid: 122): the tapir connotes anal retention, while the howler monkey, here as elsewhere (cf. Lévi-Strauss, 1984) connotes anal incontinence.

The nose can be shown to belong to the same system too. In the Barasana myth of Warimi (Hugh-Jones, 1979: M_4), the hero tries to escape from the body of Anaconda through the anus and through the mouth; when these attempts fail, he irritates Anaconda's nose and is sneezed out:

> Warimi tried to get out of Poison Anaconda's body; he went down to his anus but Poison Anaconda blocked it with his hand; he went up to his mouth but Poison Anaconda clamped it shut and gritted his teeth. Then Warimi tickled the inside of Poison Anaconda's nose; he sneezed and Warimi escaped.
>
> (Hugh-Jones, 1979: 281)

The open nostrils function in the same way as the open throat (vomiting) and the open anus (diarrhoea). This opposition of the anal and oral confirms Lévi-Strauss' claim that mythical thought 'copes with perfect ease with notions which belong to the recent discoveries of psychoanalysis in our society' (1984: 111).[9]

For the Barasana, to eat food which has not been blown over with tobacco smoke beforehand will lead to wasting away as the body is dissolved in the enlarged anus. The link between the nasal and anal cavities is demonstrated in other ways too. Thus the characteristics of a body that is excessively open – vomiting and diarrhoea – are caused by the drugs which are used to open up the initiates. The use of both the nasal and anal passages for the introduction of hallucinatory drugs into the body (cf. de Smet, 1985) also provides confirmation of the solidarity between the nasal, oral and anal passages. There are other correspondences too: Yurupary ceaselessly farts and belches, while Manioc-stick Anaconda emits uncontrollable farts and blows snuff from his mouth with a terrible blast (Hugh-Jones, 1979: 200).

If the closed body may be seen as one extreme, the oral and anal passages lead us to its opposite: the body that is full of holes. The body of Uakti, yet another avatar of Yurupary, is riddled with holes which produce a sound when the wind draws across them (ibid.). Like the *He* instruments, such a body makes it possible to set up relations of correlation and opposition between the open and the closed.

The Barasana data are not exceptional. The mythology of the River Campa also contains a variant of Uakti: the monster *kasónkati* has a hole in its knees by which it produces a dreadful whistling sound. And the tapir which attacks men with its enormous penis, filling their body openings and creating new ones, is a variant of the Barasana tapir (Weiss, 1975: 286).

Another variant in this system of body orifices is the *vagina dentata*. This is the result of the combination of the reversibility of the mouth and the anus (upper/lower) with the opposition between the anus and the vagina (frontal/dorsal). This dangerous vagina is practically universal: we find it among the Mataco of Argentina (Wilbert and Simoneau, 1982); the Tapirapé of central Brazil (Wagley, 1977: 179); the Waiwai (Fock, 1963: 47); the pre-Columbian Chavín (Roe, 1982: 278, with illustration); among the Mexica as the consuming mother (Gruzinski, 1979); and in the mythology of ancient Greece (Pellizer, 1979; Mason, 1984).

The system can be expanded further thanks to a Chinook myth (Lévi-Strauss, 1983: 241–251). The hero arrived among a group of cannibals. He pretended to eat the human flesh, but he evacuated it without having digested it by means of a hollow tube which he inserted in his body to replace the digestive tube. He was thus excessively open, in contrast to the daughter of his host who was given to him in marriage: she was excessively closed, as she had no vagina.[10]

The effect of the hollow tube is to displace the mouth vertically to a lower position, cutting out the intermediate role of the digestive tube. The same displacement took place in the case of the Epiphagi, the Plinian race with their mouths on their stomachs. There is a Barasana myth (Hugh-Jones, 1979: M7.F) involving a further displacement: formerly the penis was situated at the level of the navel; the navel is said to represent the scar left by the penis, when the latter was removed to occupy its normal, lower position.

We could go on expanding the material by drawing on other mythological systems, but it should by now be clear that the bodily orifices are involved in complex systems. The interrelationships between the orifices constitute systems which, in turn, are articulated with wider systems of relations. For example, Lévi-Strauss has already demonstrated the relation between menstruation and the moral rules of society: the physiological nature of the former bears witness to the solidarity between the social and the cosmic rhythms (1968: 182). In a similar vein, Foucault set out to explicate a political economy of the body (1975) and 'to show how the apparatuses of power are directly articulated on the body' (1976: 200).

This moral order is also illustrated by the Barasana data. Although the first menstruation is marked by an opening of the body, young girls receive systematic lessons to learn how to control themselves. The three moral vices of women are supposed to be incontinence, loquacity and curiosity. Now, these vices can be translated directly in terms of the bodily orifices. An excessive openness of the vagina points toward incontinence; an excessive openness of the mouth is a sign of loquacity; and an excessive opening of the eyes and ears is a sign of curiosity. Hence in the Yurupary myth of neighbours of the Barasana, the Tariana, the perfect woman is mute, patient and lacking in curiosity (Hugh-Jones, 1979: 130).

The moral order into which males are initiated is also articulated in terms of open and closed. The Barasana initiates have to wake up to vomit, which presents an alternative to evacuation via the digestive tube. While they eat, they must cover their mouth with their hands, and they are taught not to reveal the secret rites and to moderate their sexual activities. An excessive openness after having taken *yagé* would be fatal. Besides, openness on the part of the male initiates or of menstruating females indicates slovenliness: it is thus the well-tempered body which is a precondition of culture. The body of the Barasana shaman, whose sucking and blowing activities seem to correspond to continence and incontinence respectively (ibid: 124), is in a sense the symbol of this tension between the two extremes, according well with the mediatory function of the shaman in social life.

Terms like incontinence have a moral connotation, but at the same time they refer to the bodily orifices and thus share in the more general theme of communication. To repeat, the relation is not metaphorical, it is metonymic. This literal relation enables us to arrive at a more abstract level and to return to the question of language, its articulation, its syntax and its punctuation. A clue to the direction to be followed is also provided by the Barasana material: the laziness of initiates and menstruating females, expressed by the excessive openness of their bodies, is combatted by working in *tex*tiles (Hugh-Jones, 1979: 202). *Texture/textiles*: the characteristic structure of a text thus resembles (or is identified with) the structure by which the bodily orifices are kept in check.

The direction of the argument should now be clear: the present hypothesis is that the structure of the system of bodily orifices can be illuminated in terms of the *archi-écriture*. Derrida has defined this writing in the following terms:

Origin of the experience of space and time, this writing of difference, this tissue of the trace allows the articulation of difference between space and time and its appearance as such in the unity of an experience (of a 'self', experienced in terms of the body of 'self').

(Deridda, 1967a: 96)

This *archi-écriture* is the pure form of the concept of writing prior to its realisation in a signifying substance. It precedes speech and writing since it precedes the very division of the regions of sensibility. It makes impossible any kind of hierarchy between the registration of acoustic phenomena and visual or graphic records (ibid: 95).[11]

Now, it is precisely this distinction between the regions of sensibility which is articulated by means of the bodily orifices. Moreover, the orifices make a system of *distribution* possible. In a Barasana myth, Yurupary becomes a *paxiuba* palm which grows noisily. It was Yurupary's body. Before ascending into the sky, he said: I leave you this palm; cut it into pieces. Each piece will produce a different sound (Hugh-Jones, 1979: M_8.62). The body of another avatar of Yurupary, Uakti, was perforated and resonated when the wind drew across it (ibid: 200). We here come up against the distribution of intervals, a theme discussed by Lévi-Strauss in *L'Origine des manières de table* (1968), where he proposed to isolate different types of intervals according to their duration, which articulate the relations between relations.

These myths provide us with material examples of space and spacing. Pauses, gaps, punctuation, intervals in general are what they set into play. In speech, spacing is the temporal sequence of the sounds uttered in their difference from one another; in writing, spacing is the spatial marker separating one part of a sequence from another. Without the intervention of this spacing, articulation and meaning would become impossible. But the spacing itself is not conceived within that meaning. It is a constitutive margin, in the sense that it forms the positive condition of the positive assertion of writing, while itself remaining 'outside' this positive assertion.[12] It marks the dead time within the presence of the living present. Or in the lapidary formulation of Derrida: 'every grapheme is essentially testamentary' (1967a: 100). This opening of the relation to death within thought that is introduced by spacing might be illustrated from a myth of the River Campa: the men who were penetrated by the monstrous tapir became female *mironi*. That is, their excessive opening meant death.

Punctuation, spacing in general – signification cannot evade this cadence, this caesura. A Tukano myth might even be read as a kind of parable of this theme of the fall: a *paxiuba* palm bore an unopened bunch of fruit; a very strong wind blew upon it, opening it and causing it to resonate. This sound *came down* with the wind and opened two girls up from the abdomen downwards, causing them to bleed and thus to menstruate (Hugh-Jones, 1979: 199).

The bodily orifices now appear as a system of punctuation. Punctuation, spacing - these are ways of creating division between entities. They may thus be seen as the opposite of the copula, the link between two entities, and of copulation, with its privileged signifier, the phallus. Following Lacan, we situate the phallus on the side of *difference* (*Spaltung*), that gap created by the difference between the appetite for satisfaction and the demand for love (Lacan, 1971, II: 110). If we want a mythic parable, we might refer to a Tupi myth on the *paxiuba* palm which is transformed to become the long penis of Maira. It is cut into pieces and distributed among the women (Hugh-Jones, 1979: 202 n.9). The Lacanian difference here evokes the central theme in Derrida's work: difference (or *différance*). And this difference cannot be thought without the notion of the trace, this trace which is the difference between appearance and signification, articulating the animate on the inanimate, this trace which is not capable of description in any kind of metaphysic (Derrida, 1967a: 95). And if we look for the parable of this *différance*, perhaps we might try to trace it in the traces of the Guajiro, these traces left by creatures which pre-date the very existence of the creatures themselves.

The leap from bodily orifices to punctuation is not as wild as it may seem at first sight. After all, it is the cavities of the body through which the voice resounds:

> The body, through the voice, gives itself as the foundation of the text, which is divided up only by the play of the spacing and pauses for breath.
>
> (Le Bot, 1988: 16)[13]

Vocal exteriority is also the stimulant and the condition of possibility of its opposite in script (de Certeau, 1975: 248). Punctuation of the body, like punctuation of the text, introduces closure. It provides the means of closing off certain avenues which were previously open. It attempts to block the infinite multi-referentiality of the text. It tries to reconcile the different voices at work within the text. The humanity of the human body is marked by the limits which are set to it. But the possibility of shifting this punctuation that is always an open possibility prevents the body from turning into a corpse and staves off any form of ultimate foreclosure.

If the human body and the body of the text are ultimately defined in terms of limits, there are attempts to go beyond these limits. On the one hand, the gods can avoid the limitations of humans by a progressive 'de-incarnation' (Kirk, 1980). Hence the Homeric gods have *ichor* in their veins instead of blood (*Iliad* 5.340, 416). Similarly, the Greek gods live from the aromas which they derive from sacrifice and have no need of food (Vernant, 1979b: 61 n.1). Perhaps the theme of the denial of an anus or the production of excrement which Loukianos mentions in his *True Story* has the same intention: to suggest that such beings approach divine status in their impenetrability.

This detour via the gods brings us back to the work of M. de Certeau from which we began. The fourth- and sixth-century versions of the idiot which he presents (1982: 47–70) treat the body as a refuge from language. In escaping from the articulations of language, the idiot finds shelter in a body which refuses to make use of its facilities for language. When a nameless member of a women's convent near Panopolis, Egypt, does venture to speak, she simply repeats the words and gestures of her interlocutor; she remains herself, intact. She becomes the Other of the signifier to such an extent that she becomes a limitless nothing in which she eventually loses herself/is lost (ibid: 66).

To this excessive closedness of the gods and the idiots we may contrast excessive openness. In Amazonian mythology, as we saw, this is often seen as a typically female attribute, implying licentiousness, curiosity and gossip-mongering. It is interesting to note that in fourteenth-century French conceptions of hell, the bodily orifices are not seen as openings but as rifts and ruptures, the result of violent action carried out on the body, which is carried to excess in the infernal regions; paradise, by contrast, is connoted by the hermetically closed form of the sphere and by closed, rounded surfaces in general (Baschet, 1985). From the same century, the illustrations to Book XXI of the *City of God* by Guillebert de Mets depict devils with several mouths: on the elbows, on the knees and on the belly.[14]

After these remarks on the typology and structure of the systems of the bodily orifices, and their metonymic relation with language, it is time to see in what ways these systems interlock with the articulations of the body and of language which were discussed in the previous chapter. If we try to follow Lévi-Strauss' injunction to study the relations of relations (1968: 393), our question becomes: what is the relation between the syntactic functions of the two systems (the bodily orifices and the bodily articulations)?

There are three axes along which the bodily orifices are arranged. First, there is the high/low axis: the orifices of the head, sometimes shifted to the upper part of the torso, are contrasted with those of the lower part of the body, namely the genitals and the anus. Second, there is an inner/outer distinction, for by their very nature the orifices are both entrances and exits, mediating the interiority of the body (inner space) with the exteriority of the outer world. These orientations (high/low; inner/outer) have also been isolated by Le Goff as being the main orientations of the European Middle Ages (1985: 134; cf. Ginzburg, 1986). Third, there is the axis of before/behind (the opposition of genitals/anus). Of course, inversion may take place along two of these axes simultaneously: in Piaroa mythology, in the upside down world of pre-society, people lived in ignorance, symbolised by people having a blue eye on their buttocks. The eye has shifted from before to behind *and* from above to below (Overing, 1985b: 264).

If we retrace our steps to the system of articulations, we find both the opposition of above/below (head/foot; with its cosmological variant of upper world/Antipodes) and the opposition of before/behind ('normal' feet/reversed feet). This homology in the systems of oppositions which both the system of articulations and the system of orifices utilise explains why it is so easy to pass from one system to the other: the structural operations which they share allow a high degree of translatability. This is why the Caribbean myths outlined at the beginning of this chapter can make use of *either* the bodily articulations *or* the bodily orifices: both systems are homologous, and the difference is one of idiom.

If we want to pursue this difference of idiom further, a first approximation might be offered in terms of transitivity and intransitivity. The Kalapalo, a Carib-speaking community of the Upper Xingu Basin, make a distinction between passive or inanimate body parts (such as the feet, head, fingernails and trunk of the body), on the one hand, and active or animate organs, which include the eyes, intestines, stomach, womb, anus and genitalia, on the other (Basso, 1985: 64–65). These entities have different syntactic functions and different sound symbols. For instance, sounds produced by inanimate body parts are onomatopoeic in form and occur when they are used in action or are being acted upon by an animate being. Even though they do not participate actively as agents, they are still made memorable in narrative by the onomatopoeic sound attached to them. On the other hand, sounds produced by the animate organs of the body are called by the same term as that for the calls of living things. Unlike the latter, however, the animate organs of the body are not capable of goal-oriented action. They are capable of motion and feeling, and can emit noises independently of being acted upon, but they do not think.

We thus see how these systems of articulation and punctuation contain the elements of a theory of script. One consequence is that the difference between oral and written cultures becomes problematical. The difference becomes a technological one, relating to the role of graphism within a culture. And one implication of this is that it becomes impossible to draw any meaningful antithesis between oral and literate cultures with respect to types of rationality (cf. Parry, 1985).

Another consequence is that the opening of the body is an opening to exteriority in general, and thereby to the Other. The Plinian races, we have repeatedly pointed out, are of crucial importance for any theory of alterity. Is it more than coincidence that the foundations of European anatomy, the dissection of the human body and the revelation of its inner world, coincide with the discovery of the New World and the European interest in cannibals there (Goldmann, 1982: 160 n.17)?[15] At this point, the innermost parts of the body and the outermost parts of the world coincide.

Finally, this link between the bodies of the peoples of the New World and the act of writing has an erotic dimension. In the account of his travels in Brazil written by Jean de Léry, the naked women indicate a new relation to the world: a textual one. The act of writing produces its own surplus (through the economy of *différance*). This surplus can be defined in terms of savagery and pleasure. Pleasure is what is not written down, and the aesthetic/erotic attraction of the savage is a function of the economy of writing (de Certeau, 1975: 246).

Perhaps this emphasis on the visual erotic component in the perception of the New World is linked up with the sadism of the *Conquistadores*. In sadism, it is the surface, the skin, which operates an erotogenic zone (Freud, 1977: 84). And it is this same skin which is the object of the manifold attentions of the aggressors, on which they write their illicit desires.[16] To take just one of the countless examples: Miguel de Cueno, who accompanied Columbus on his second voyage, recounts how he captured a beautiful Carib woman and tried to rape her in his cabin. When she put up a resistance, he whipped her with a cord and then proceeded to enjoy taking one-sided pleasure with her (Todorov, 1982: 53–54). Inscribing the blank surface of the naked Amerindian bodies here goes hand in hand with colonial penetration.

It is to the monotony of this colonialist discourse and practice that the Plinian races offer a welcome contrast. The varieties of punctuation provided by the bodily orifices prevent a petrification of the body into a single, unified form and prevent the censoring of the plurivocality of the text. The introduction of spacing in writing means that it lacks unity, becoming equivocal and partially opaque. The varieties of syntax provided by the bodily articulations are so many ways of ordering and reordering in a continuous work of *bricolage* that is not peculiar to the 'savage mind'. They are all evidence of a struggle against the testamentary nature of the grapheme.

Notes

1. We could cite a Greek case of the same phenomenon: the mutilation of the Skythian subjects during the embalming of the Skythian king marked each body with the 'arms' of the Skythian royalty. The Skythians are thus reduced to body speech, and the content of their message is in fact the same at its form: namely, that they are subjects (Hartog, 1980: 161). In a different setting, the mutilation of the body may serve to render it capable of bearing tidings to the otherworld of the dead (Devereux, 1983).
2. For further discussion of the inconsistencies in the Lévi-Straussian view, see Brother-ston, 1985; Duchet, 1985: 202ff. For the relation between the deconstruction of oral/literate and that of common noun/proper noun, see further Mason (1987a: 164–169).
3. Separation between words is in fact a relatively recent phenomenon, introduced first in the British Isles in the early Middle Ages and later in the rest of Europe (Saenger, 1989).
4. A few ethnographic examples: in a Mataco myth, Tawkxwax had no wife, so he buried his penis in his arm and his arm became pregnant. He shook his arm vigorously and a baby boy fell out (Wilbert and Simoneau, 1982: 148). In the prose Edda, it is said of the giant Ymir that a man and a woman grew under his left hand and that one of his feet begat a son with the other (Molenaar, 1985: 48). In a Balinese-Javanese tradition that dates back at least to the sixteenth century, the *De Tantu Panggelaran*, Lady Uma consents to sexual intercourse with a handsome young cowherd. In his discussion of the myth, J. Boon sees three vaginal positions in the act of intercourse: the 'normal' position of the vagina, the presence of an implicit vagina between her thighs, and another implicit vagina in the cleft of her toe (Boon, 1982: 184–187). At a certain point it becomes difficult to think of any kind of break in the surface of the body which does *not* lend itself to thought processes of this kind.
5. Anus and mouth are themselves linked as the contrastive pair of an opposition. For instance, Middle Dutch literature refers to the *voormond* and the *achtermont*, i.e. the mouth and anus respectively, as two kinds of mouths, a homology that is extensively elaborated in terms of mastication (the theme of the *anus dentatus*), speech (talking/breaking wind) and other attributes in the considerable scatological literature of the period (Pleij, 1979: 120ff).
6. Wittkower (1977: 197 n.30) mentions one-eyed races from the Mahabharata and other Indian epics.

7. Jean de Léry mentions a Brazilian animal called the *Hay*, which is believed to live on air because it is never seen in the act of eating (de Léry, 1980: 133–134).
8. For the homosexual connotations of the absence of the anus, see Mason (1983). An ethnographic example is provided by the Chaga (cf. Raum, 1939).
9. For a suggestive example taken from North America, see Devereux (1980: 301–302).
10. For an inversion of these themes, see the discussion in Devereux, 1981: 166–170.
11. Perhaps we might see in the *archi-écriture* the 'common source' of the material of hysteria and linguistic usage, explaining how a verbal experssion like a 'stab in the heart' or a 'slap in the face' could be taken *literally*. As we saw earlier, Freud postulated the existence of such a common source (Breuer and Freud, 1974: 255), though he followed Darwin in situating it in the 'innervatory sensations which arise in the pharynx'.
12. H. Staten (1985: 17) schematises Derrida's concept of constitution in this way: X is constituted by non-X.
13. Many other of the texts collected in the 1988 issue of *Traverses* dedicated to *Le Génie de la ponctuation* are relevant here.
14. We might compare the anthropophagi of Kalina mythology with a mouth on the stomach, the right knee, and the left elbow (Magaña, 1982b: 87; 1985: 302).
15. In this connection, it is worth noting the anal penetration of a male victim by the anthropophagous women depicted in de Bry's illustrations to Hans Staden (Bucher, 1982).
16. What a loss is the Marquis de Sade's projected philosophical essay on the New World, which was to complete the first volume of the *Portefeuille d'un homme de lettres*! For some suggestions on the relation between de Sade and the behaviour of the *conquistadores*, see Mason (forthcoming b).

7   White Indian cannibals, the Guaymures of Brazil

Source: Arnoldus Montanus, De nieuwe en onbekende weereld, Jacob van Meurs, Amsterdam, 1671. Reproduced with permission of the University Library, Amsterdam.

Chapter seven

Eurocentrism and ethnocentrism

Writing from a mission station in 1697, the Jesuit missionary Stanislav Arlet wrote of the 'barbarians' whom providence had entrusted him to convert:

> They are savage men and differ little from animals in their way of life and conduct. Both males and females go around naked. They have no fixed abode, no laws, no form of government.
>
> (Arlet, 1781: 40)

Besides his own perception of these Peruvian Indians, Arlet also offers us *his* perception of *their* perception of *him*:

> As they had never seen horses, nor men who resembled us in complexion or clothing, the astonishment they displayed at our first encounter was a very entertaining spectacle for us [...]. They were beside themselves and did not know what to say; they could not imagine from where such monsters could have come to their forests. For, as they later declared to us, they thought that a man, his hat, his clothing and the horse he rode were one extraordinary animal consisting of all these items.
>
> (Ibid: 41–42)

This example of the encounter between Europeans and Indians is at the same time an encounter between two ideas of men and culture. For the missionary, the Indians differed little from animals because he assumed that they went around naked, had no settlements, no laws and no government – they did not conform to his ideas of a proper polity. The Indians, on the other hand, saw him as a monster or prodigy because they were able to conceive of an animal which was half-horse (an animal which they did not know) and half-man; it is not social organisation, but the place of the newcomers within an ordered cosmos, that structures the native classification (Magaña and Mason, 1986: 14).

The study of the various ways of classifying humankind within possible schemes of things or ontologies is the subject matter of the enterprise of ethno-anthropology. As our example shows, this is closely related to such fields as ethno-zoology,[1] since the boundaries between human and animal may be fluid (Mason, 1988; forthcoming a), ethno-geography (Reichel-Dolmatoff, 1986) and ethno-prehistory (Balzano, 1988). In the case of the encounter between Europeans and non-Europeans, it is worth asking ourselves to what extent the parties concerned may be supposed to be able to communicate at all, or to what extent their anthropologies permit some degree of commensurability. In the example presented above, there seems to be a radical difference between the European and Amerindian systems of classification. As we have seen in the previous chapters, the native reference to monstrous forms is not without its European counterparts. On the contrary, the European *imaginaire* has frequently had recourse to traditional representations of the non-European human races as monstrous beings. In particular, they form part of the strategy of European discourse on the New World.

What are we to make of this 'difference degree zero' which might lead the unsuspecting or the credulous to look for similarity between European and South American anthropologies? Are the Ewaipanoma which Ralegh deemed worthy of credibility the same as the Blemmyes of the European tradition? What is the difference between this difference and other differences, what is the difference of this difference? And how might we presume to be able to measure such differences anyway, given the fact that we are already partisans in the contact between Indians and Whites? Reflection on this contact is reflection on anthropology. Any uneasiness we may feel in examining this contact should be an uneasiness regarding the possibility of anthropology at all.

We start with a Yekuana myth as an entrance to the exploratory paths leading to liminality, monstrosity and difference, the triad with which this chapter is concerned. In the cosmogonic cycle of the Carib-speaking Yekuana (or Makiritare) Indians of Venezuela, the *Watunna*, the present age is the third cycle in the four cycles of creation. The invisible supreme being, Wanadi, has sent three successive emanations or avatars *(damodede)* to the earth. At the end of each cycle there comes a violent end followed by a new act of creation. The age which will come after the present one is the fourth and last cycle, a truly messianic age (de Civrieux, 1970).

The third avatar of Wanadi to come to the earth was Attawanadi, and it is his exploits which concern us here. After celebrating his marriage, Wanadi left home to create people. First he created a white race called Fañuru (the Spanish). He wanted to make houses for them but did not have the time to do so. The Fañuru were good people.

At the second stop he created an Indian settlement, Marakuhaña. At this stage in the proceedings, however, Wanadi's evil opponent, Odo'sha, stirred up trouble among the Fañuru by pointing out that they had no settlement while the Indians had. The enraged Fañuru marched on the settlement of Marakuhaña, killed the Indian inhabitants and settled there. From this point on, the Fañuru have been corrupted and under the influence of Odo'sha they change from good to bad.

The third stage in the narrative is the arrival of Wanadi at Ankosturaña, where he first built a settlement and then populated it with a white race, like Fañuru, called Iaranavi. This trading people was virtuous, to replace the corrupted Fañuru.

The fourth stage is Wanadi's long journey eastward to the coast. By thought he created a people there, 'otro pueblo, muy bueno, otro hombre blanco, muy bueno' (ibid: 78) at the point where the land came to an end. The place was called Amenadiña. The fifth and last stage in the creation of this ethno- geography – the mapping of a universe that mythic structures enable oral societies to inhabit – is the foundation of Karakaña.

The fivefold structure is closed by a ring composition: to the lack of a name for the settlement in the first stage corresponds the lack of a name for the inhabitants in the last stage. Land, river, mountain and sea all enter into the scene to indicate that the setting of the various settlements is correlated not only with existing places (San Fernando, Angostura, Georgetown, Caracas) but also with the cosmic order.

	Name	Residents	Qualities	Element
1	—	Fañuru whites	good > bad	river/land
2	Marakuhaña (San Fernando)	Indians	—	river/land
3	Ankosturaña (Angostura)	Iaranavi whites	good, traders	—
4	Amenadiña (Georgetown)	Hunrunko whites	good, iron & textiles	sea/land
5	Karakaña (Caracas)	—	—	mountain

After an opposition between good and bad Whites has been set up in the first three episodes, the last two episodes elaborate this distinction in more detail. Karakaña becomes the place of Wanadi's torment and crucifixion at the hands of the Fañuru and their missionaries (Fadre). But they fail to have any effect on Wanadi, for his *damodede* had left his body and returned to his mountain home at Kushamakari.

Amenadiña, on the other hand, has positive connotations. It is the settlement of plenty, as in another episode of the *Watunna* in which the two sons of Wanadi fly to this magical city which seems but one step removed from Wanadi's storehouses in heaven, and by comparison with which Ankosturaña pales into insignificance (ibid: 168–169).

Amenadiña's magical quality is in some way linked to its position between land and sea. While sharing in both elements, it belongs to neither. The emphasis in the text on its location 'where the earth ends' makes it *a name without a place*, corresponding in the formal structure to *the place without a name* of the first stage. We here encounter the theme of liminality,[2] to which we shall return: the threshold (*limen*) is self-effacing in the fact that it is a gap. It is what is not. While joining two worlds together (here, the world of the Yekuana and the world across the sea to which the Whites have access), it is itself of no account. The supplementary abundance which is to be seen in Amenadiña is, within the economy of the text, both a supplement and replacement for its own lack.

In another version of the myth, collected by David Guss in 1983, Wanadi crosses to the other side of the sea and creates the closest replica of heaven possible, but the glitter of this 'Foot of Heaven' at the extreme edge of the universe is pure illusion (Guss, 1986). Like Amenadiña, it is both excess and lack. In a way, this illusory excess recalls the proliferation of crosses in the work of the missionaries. Their liking for making crosses to show people how they had killed Wanadi is based on an illusion too, for as every Yekuana knows, Wanadi tricked the missionaries and did not die (de Civrieux, 1970: 79).

A second theme encountered in this part of the *Watunna* cycle is the theme of internal conflict or difference. It is conflict within the ranks of the Fañuru, instigated by Odo'sha, which leads to the first occurrence of war at Marakuhaña. In the journey of the two sons of Wanadi to Amenadiña, the first stage is the departure of one of them, Shikié'mona, to Amenadiña as the result of a quarrel with his brother, Iureke, over Iureke's wife (ibid: 171).

Third, we can note the presence of a monstrous portrayal of the unfamiliar. When the Fañuru take over Ankosturaña, they are cannibals (ibid: 85), like the jaguars in the rest of the *Watunna* cycle.

The second myth to which we turn was collected in 1979 by Ellen Basso from the Carib-speaking Kalapalo of the Upper Xingu Basin. The prominent figure of the narrative is Saganafa and the story begins with a conflict between him and his father. Saganafa's father hears that Saganafa has been having sexual relations with women and punishes him with a whipping. Saganafa's reaction is to leave home and go to his grandparents. The encounter with Whites occurs during a fishing expedition on which Saganafa accompanies his grandparents.

> It was still very early, before dawn.
> While they continued to do that others were coming toward them,
> some Christians were coming toward them.
> They saw something white on the sandbar, a lot of them,
> some distance from where they were just then.
> 'Look at all the *jabiru* storks,' he said to him,
> to his grandson,
> 'Grandfather,' Saganafa answered,
> 'At night I'm not well because of that very thing,
> not well at all.
> At night that's how I am.'
> 'I see.'
> He continued to go, shooting *wagiti*.
> Toward Tefupe.
> While he was doing that the Christians had already come there.

'Hey, Grandfather. Some Christians are here!'
They held onto their canoe, the Christians did.
'Well, where are you two going?' the Christians asked.
'We've come here for fish.'
'Well, come along with me.'
'All right!' Saganafa answered.
'Well, come with me, come be my daughter's husband.'
'I will! Grandfather, I really am going now, I'm going away.'
'Very well.'

While his grandfather passes the payment that is made for Saganafa on to his father, Saganafa and the Christians travel to the place where the sky ends.

For a long time they went on,
toward the place where the sky ended.
To where Kagifugukuegï the Monstrous Toad stayed.
'Quickly, hurry everyone!'
They all scraped some vines.
'Quickly, hurry everyone!'
Next they threw the balls of vine scraping in front of the creature
and it pounced on them.
That was how it was done.
The edge of the sky rose up,
and while it was like that
they went on.
'Quickly, hurry now, let's go,'
and they went on.

After arriving at the Christians' settlement, Saganafa marries the daughter of one of them, who bears him four sons. Saganafa works for the Christians, along with two other Kalapalo. When one of these companions is accused of being lazy, the Christians take him to the 'Christians' ancestor', a very old man who lives in the middle of a lake. This ancestor takes hold of the Kalapalo accused of laziness and kills him.

On the back of one knee the Christian's ancestor *tsïk*! cut him.
Blood came.
On the other side *tsïk*!
On the inside of one elbow, here on the inside of the other, *tsïk*!
One wrist *tsïk*!
and when he died the other took his body away.

The rest of the narrative is concerned with the flight of Saganafa and his remaining companion, and the subsequent conflict between the Kalapalo and the descendants of Saganafa, who have taken the side of the Christians against the Indians, culminating in a withdrawal of the Christians from the area (Basso, 1985: 41–54).

The story of Saganafa can be seen as reflection *on* contact between Europeans and Kalapalo. Perhaps it is also a reflection *of* this contact, but given the impossibility of separating the historical from the mythological in this (or any such) narrative (an impossibility deriving from the fact that history and mythology are one another's support), we can devote as much attention to the symbols used in the narrative as to the more readily accessible everyday features which seem to bear some resemblance to the *realia* of European accounts.

We can start with the Monstrous Toad, Kagifugukuegï, who lives at the place where the sky ends. Like Amenadiña in the *Watunna* cycle, this is both a place and a non-place: situated on the edge, it allows a passage to a world of a different order by self-effacement, as the sky which the monster holds down is temporarily released like a curtain. In another version of the myth, the toad is replaced by the Tick Monster, who is suspended in a web stretching across the trail (ibid: 57–58). The presence of the Monstrous Toad on the border prepares the arrival in the narrative of the Christian cannibal whose miraculous metal tools spring from his murderous activity. For another Venezuelan tribe, the Piaroa, it is also true that weapons and tools are 'the weapons and tools for the cannibalistic process, the means by which resources are captured and processed for eating, the means by which the predator captures and processes his prey' (Overing, 1986a: 92). Later in the narrative we are also introduced to the Fierce People, who live beyond the borders of the Christians and whose territory is impenetrable.

As in the *Watunna*, the *limen* in this Kalapalo myth marks the boundary between separate worlds and serves as a passage into the land of monsters. In the Kalapalo narrative, the world of the Europeans can be reached only after a trip which makes huge demands of endurance, as the narrative repeatedly emphasises, just as the journey to Amenadiña proved so exacting to the sons of Wanadi in the *Watunna*. Besides the themes of liminality and the monstrous, the Kalapalo myth of Saganafa also contains the theme of internal conflict. At the start, it is a conflict between father and son which provides a rift at which the Europeans can intervene. The ensuing rivalry between the Kalapalo (Saganafa) and the half-bloods (the half-Kalapalo, half-European children of Saganafa) perpetuates this conflict, which has now escalated beyond the limits of domestic conflict.

Ellen Basso refers to the *Watunna* in relation to this Kalapalo myth (Basso, 1985: 41). Can there have been contact between these two Carib-speaking groups which might account for the structural similarities?...

Leaving aside questions of (ethno)history,[3] we can instead pursue the internal logic of the themes involved. Is there some *inner* relation between the themes of liminality, monstrosity and internal conflict which might explain the homologies between structures situated at wide geographical intervals?

In a myth collected by Edmundo Magaña from the Apalai (Wayana) in 1985, a boy is mistreated by his step-father. He grows up and gives men metal tools.

Weary of being mistreated, he leaves the settlement. In revenge for the past, he joins the Whites and gives them the cultural goods which they now possess (Magaña, 1987a: 46, myth 54). In this interesting reversal, it is the Whites who receive cultural implements from the natives, not *vice versa*. But once again, the difference between Europeans and Amerindians, here marked by the possession of tools, has its origin in a generational conflict.

David Guss has drawn attention to the widespread theme in native American mythology of the relation between the origin of unwelcome strangers and some conflict occurring within the tribe itself (1986: 427 n.9). He suggests that this should be seen as a form of 'creative ethnocentrism peculiar to oral societies' by which 'the world introduced by the Europeans is simply relocated in the ongoing narrative structure [...] Verifiable contemporary events are recontextualised within an already established mythic universe' (ibid: 417–418). This perceptive comment suggests a link between the internal conflict and the external stranger. The strangeness of the stranger would thereby be reduced, and incorporation would be a process of assimilation by which the difference between inside and outside is reduced or even eradicated. This is certainly a possible scenario for European–Amerindian relations. For example, in the myth of Saganafa, the Europeans are first mistaken for a flock of *jabiru* storks – they are not even recognised as human beings. But they are soon enmeshed in the Kalapalo scheme of things. Saganafa mentions that he has dreamed of their arrival in advance: what at first seemed to be a novelty on the horizon is already something that is familiar, the first appearance of the Europeans is *déjà vu*.[4]

When Saganafa goes on to say to his grandfather: 'Grandfather, go away! I am really leaving right now for good with our grandfathers', reference to the Europeans as grandfathers indicates that they have been assimilated to the Kalapalo system of family relationships, an assimilation that has just been confirmed in practice by the payment made to the Christians for the young man. This assimilation is ironical, however. While the Kalapalo ethnocentric attitude toward the Europeans enables Christians and Indians to enter into social relations, it is the Christians who define the form and content of these social relations as servitude. The dreadful manner in which the grandfather of the Christians behaves indicates how the Kalapalo will never succeed in assimilating themselves with Christians because the latter retain a mysterious creative power, evidenced in their mastery of tools, which renders them powerful beings.

The ironical way in which the supposed symmetry of assimilation becomes a hierarchical asymmetry suggests a different approach, in which it is excess rather than symmetry which is the rule. One could speak of a contradiction between, say, Indians and Europeans if the terms in question showed a clearly defined or definable boundary. However, the suggestion put forward here is that the relation is not one of contradiction but of supplementarity. The domestic discord with which the myths under observation begin is a fundamental division that precedes the rest. The narratives begin, not from a unity which is subjected to violence from outside, but from a totality that is itself already fractured. This fracture is an initial lack which calls for a supplement to supplete it. The supplement, however, *is not of the same order*: it is excessive, it is not commensurable with the rift which it comes to fill. The relation Indian:European is not a reversible one because the terms in question are not homologous. What the rift in the Indians' existence calls forth is more than they bargained for.[5]

It is the excessiveness of the European presence which explains its monstrous forms. It is an unlimited presence which both postulates (cf. Hulme, 1985) and is postulated by a lack which it *over*compensates to a colossal degree. By phrasing the discussion in this way, we try to bring the structure outlined by Guss within a changed perspective. Instead of the symmetrical, Saussurian structures of a 'reverse anthropology' (cf. Hawkins, 1984), we resort to the radical asymmetry of the structures of alterity. For the Europeans are the Other in the eyes of the Amerindians. They are not just an (inverted) form of the familiar (though under certain conditions they may well assume this form as one of their possible forms) - they are what is unfamiliar, what is beyond the horizon, beyond even the spatial metaphor of the horizon itself. True, their relation with the Other may assume the *form* of a symmetrical relation, but we should not be fooled by appearances. The Other has more than one form at its disposal.

This horizon, this *limen*, is a part of the structure too. As we saw in the Yekuana and Kalapalo examples, the theme of liminality is inseparable from the presentation of the unfamiliar *on the other side of* a limit. But there is an ambiguity here too. What is radically other is unlimited, it knows no limit; it lies on the other side of the limit. The limit is *both* a non-place *and* a hyper-place, *both* self-effacing and an indication of a passage to another dimension. Nowhere is the awareness of this ambiguity among the native Americans better illustrated than in the description of the birth of the *uinal* in the *Book of Chumayel*.

> It was set out this way by the first sage Melchisedek, the first
> prophet, Napuctun, sacerdote, the first priest.
> This is the song of how the uinal was realised, before the world was.
> He started up from his inherent motion alone.
> His mother's mother and her mother, his mother's sister and his sister-in-
> law, they all said:
> 'How shall we say, how shall we see, that man is on the road?'
> These are the words they spoke as they moved along, where there was no
> man.
> When they arrived in the east they began to say:
> 'Who has been here? These are footprints. Get the rhythm of his step.'
> So said the Lady of the World,
> And our Father, Dios, measured his step.
> This is why the count by footstep of the whole world, xoc lah cab oc, was
> called lahca 12 Oc,
> This was the order born through 13 Oc,

When the one foot joined its counter-print to make the moment of the
eastern horizon.
Then he spoke its name when the day had no name,
as he moved along with his mother's mother and her mother, his mother's
sister and his sister-in-law.
The uinal born, the day so named, the sky and earth,
the stairway of water, earth, stone and wood, the things of sea and earth
realised.

Following the translation and commentary by Gordon Brotherston (1979: 184),
we see how the eastern horizon is that place and non-place where one foot joins
the other foot to constitute that moment and non-moment of movement and non-
movement at which today is not today (12 Oc) because it is tomorrow (13 Oc).

The concept of the *limen* is necessary to present the structure of alterity by
which certain native Amerindian accounts portray contact with Europeans.
Liminality, monstrosity and domestic conflict or difference have an inner
connection and interconnection because of their positions within the structure of
alterity.

I make no claims to novelty here. After all, Todorov's *La Conquête de
l'Amérique* (1982) set the whole discussion of the discovery and conquest of
America within the perspective of alterity, explicitly drawing on the work of
Emmanuel Levinas for much of his inspiration. Todorov, however, is concerned
in that particular work predominantly with the European vision of America,
while the remarks above seek to present a structure of alterity within the American vision of Europe.

We might well want to go on and ask whether the structure delineated above
can also be found in European myths. As has been demonstrated in the previous
chapters, monstrosity, at any rate, is a recurring element in the European portrayal of native America, both in written texts and in the iconographical tradition.

As for liminality, in the European imagination the monstrous human races can
be located in a variety of places as long as their location is *elsewhere*, over the
border. In the *Historia Naturalis* of Plinius the Elder, it is in the most remote parts
of Africa and India that he situates people without noses, upper lips or tongues,
the dog-headed Cynamolgi, the one-eyed people, the locust eaters, the turtle
eaters and so on. In medieval epic or romance they may be situated in the forest
or in the desert, both of which are places on the extreme margin (Le Goff, 1985:
71). In ethnography and cartography it is the uninhabited areas of the globe which
are their favourite haunts. Their steady relegation further out to the edge is in
correlation to the relentless thrust of European expansion which is constantly
extending its borders (Rabasa, 1985).

Besides this reference to space, European tradition also resorts to a temporal
framework. Within certain ideologies, Amerindians are seen as representing an
earlier stage in the historical development of humanity. This is evident in the

work of Lafitau, and we find the same idea in, for instance, a comment by Pierre Barrère on the Kaliña Indians of French Guiana:

These Indian houses have an air of extreme poverty, and they are a perfect image of the earliest times. One has only to see them to form an idea of the birth of the world [*naissance du monde*].

(Barrère, 1743: 146)

The Amerindian populations also make use of this temporal frame of reference. For them, differences are perhaps spatial ones – the Europeans come from elsewhere (cf. Helms, 1988) – but in the case of the Barasana, for instance, 'the progressive incursion of White People into Indian territory, an incursion described in historical narratives, is seen in temporal terms as a cumulative change which results from the failure of later shamans to keep the foreigners at bay' (Hugh-Jones, 1988: 145).

The third theme, that of conflict/difference, also informs the European accounts. Sometimes it is domestic social conflict, and the popular classes of Europe become assimilated with the natives of America in their joint deviance from the dominant culture. Hence in the structures of alterity in sixteenth-century German travel accounts analysed by Harbsmeier (1987), one rift is that between the 'civilised' and the 'non-civilised' members of the population of Europe, while a different rift separates the Christians from the non-Christians, or the present occupation of the Holy Land, an emblem of the Christian past, by the non-Christian members of the Ottoman empire. Sometimes it is a conflict among the Indians themselves which opens up a rift and invites European penetration. For the Indians of the Vaupés region of north-west Amazonia, a common ancestry was fractured when the culture hero offered people beeswax. The Indians refused to eat it, but women, spiders, snakes and Whites all ate it. Another difference between Indians and Whites is their choice of weapons. It is the threatening behaviour of the ancestor of the Whites armed with a gun, while the Indians have chosen the bow, which leads to the spatial relegation of the Whites to the East (Hugh-Jones, 1988: 144).

Might comparisons of this kind enable us to determine how far Eurocentrism is a specifically European form of ethnocentrism and how far it corresponds to other forms of ethnocentrism shared by peoples outside Europe? How far is ethnocentrism itself a European invention? How far are non-Europeans 'guilty' of the same systems of accommodation? And how far is it permissible to speak of 'reciprocal images' in discussing contact between Amerindians and Whites?

First of all, however, it should be noted that there is little reciprocity in the images of Europe and America. While anthropologists are currently showing more concern about what the Amerindians thought or think of the Whites, many of the Amerindians themselves do not seem unduly preoccupied with the Whites at all. For example, Hugh-Jones (1988) records the fact that among the Indians of the Vaupés region, only one mythological cycle concerns the arrival of the

Whites, while they are firmly rejected from the other cycles of myths in the area. Similarly, E. Magaña (forthcoming) notes that it is very rare to find Europeans in the mythology of the Kaliña of Surinam. When they do occur, they do not seem to have any extraordinary powers or special relation with the ancestors or the supernatural that marks them as in any way different from other animal or vegetable tribes or persons and groups who belong to Kaliña cosmography and ethnography.

This lack of preoccupation has its roots in a process of assimilation. As a structure of alterity, assimilation is a process by which the otherness of the other is eliminated and the other is reduced to self. Assimilation works in both directions, for it implies that, whether Indian is assimilated to European or European to Indian, it is possible in either case to reduce the other to the familiar, to self. It is an ego-centric strategy. We can see it at work, for example, in the harangue of the French missionaries on the Brazilian coast in 1612 by the warrior-priest Cettvy-ci, a Tupí-Guarani, who presents the Europeans as 'Carib foreigners', i.e. as assimilated to the Tupí-Guarani scheme of things.[6] In our Kalapalo example, we saw how Saganafa tried to assimilate himself to the other (the European Christians) by entering into a pact with them. In the mythology of the Vaupés Indians, Whites are assimilated to roles which previously belonged to jaguars and Indians who were classified as strangers by means of analogies which were 'of much the same kind as those which led the *conquistadores* to see tigers in jaguars and fir-cones in pine-apples' (Hugh-Jones, 1988: 152). Similarly, among the Cuna of Panama, Whites are assimilated to the pathogenous spirits associated with mental disease and manifested as Sky Jaguar (Severi, 1988).

In the case of the Kaliña, European intervention is assimilated to intervention by other social groups of the region and/or the inhabitants of the other parts of the cosmos. For instance, they are assimilated to a tribe of anthropophagous Indians who were brought to the region by the Dutch to exterminate the Kaliña. Priests in particular are supposed to be anthropophagous, a feature which is by no means confined to Kaliña mythology. Interestingly, these anthropophagous figures resemble the Blemmyae of the European tradition: as *pairaundepo* or *onone* they are white, have a mouth in their chest and eyes in their shoulders.[7] Since this cannibalism is in conformity with native Kaliña ideas about their neighbours, it does not create problems in itself. When problems do arise, they are more concerned with the supposed aquatic origin of the Europeans and the proper relationship to be established between inhabitants of the woods and inhabitants of the water (Magaña, forthcoming).

On the other hand, assimilation is just as much a part of the strategy of the European recognition of America. I do no more than refer to what is now the classic study by the late Michel de Certeau (1975, Chapter 5: 'L'oralité, ou l'espace de l'autre: Léry'), who has demonstrated how the structure of de Léry's work, which along with the structural linguistics of Ferdinand de Saussure was to be such a source of inspiration for Claude Lévi-Strauss (Lévi-Strauss, 1982), is that of a return to a single source of production by reducing the other to the same.

Is Marc de Civrieux acting differently when he tries to establish the value of the *Watunna* cycle by comparing it to the myths of Babylon, Egypt, Greece and of the Maya (1970: 9)?

Although assimilation *can* proceed in both directions, the asymmetry between Indians and Europeans explains a lack of balance in the economy of assimilation. For while examples abound of Indians who (perforce) adopt the values of their conquerors, there are few instances of the reverse. The solitary case of Gonzalo Guerrero, a Spanish castaway who adopted the language and religion of Yucatán (Todorov, 1982: 201) is all the more striking by its splendid isolation.

In the work of assimilation, the relationship is never one of equivalence. On the one hand, the knowledge and power of the Whites may be recognised as a transformation and concentration of the shamanic power and knowledge which were once the prerogative of the Indians. It thus may play a part in cults which hope to re-establish the position that has been lost and to correct the inequality in the relations between Amerindians and Whites.

Various strategies may be adopted to cope with the White hegemony. One is a form of resistance by encapsulation: the Whites are allowed to enter native thought and life, but only in certain restricted and circumscribed areas. For instance, as we have seen, their presence in the mythology may be confined to a limited number of myths or to a single mythological cycle. Another strategy is to devalue the alleged superiority of the Whites. Lévi-Strauss' account of the power attributed to writing is well-known, but not all Amerindians share this view. The Guajiro attribute a power to their shamans which is greater than that of the Whites, for while the latter are dependent on books, an external source of assistance, the Guajiro shaman is able to achieve the same results without any form of external dependence, but through the more difficult task which he performs with his own body (Perrin, 1988b: 132–133). The Yekuana have an equally negative view of writing. In fact, they see the advent of literacy as the sign of a diminution of power, for acceptance of writing is a denial of access to the invisible world of the supernatural (Guss, 1986: 425–426).

Besides assimilation or resistance, there are yet other paths available. In particular, it should not be assumed that native thought is completely static. Full assimilation of whatever is new, of full-scale resistance to it, both seem to imply a fixed body of ideas and practices which remain impervious to change, grinding in circles which ceaselessly repeat and reproduce themselves. Often, however, contact with the other as a White has been part of a dynamic process. The Yanomam, a subgroup of the Brazilian Yanomami, have interpreted the successive forms of contact with Whites over a time span of some 150 years in a variety of different ways. While Whites and their instruments have been treated as the sources of affliction and as pathogenous objects, this characterisation has been achieved in various modalities. Thus in an early period, the existence of Whites appears only in sporadic rumours of beings encountered on the edge of the disk of the world, bald and pale spectres who come from the 'back of heaven', the land of the dead. However, other features of these beings – their hairiness, their lack of toes (because covered by shoes), their ability to strip off their skin (i.e. clothes) and their extraordinary possessions – suggest that they are harmful spirits from the borders of the Yanomam territory. At a still later stage, the situation of contact called for a redefinition of Whites, and this time they were seen as a human group, but one which consisted of enemies who were trying to eliminate the Yanomam by means of 'warrior sorcery' (Albert, 1988).

As Albert points out (ibid: 87), the marginalisation of the phenomena of historical incorporation or the restriction of the ethnographic field in which they operate is due to an excessively literal understanding of the work of Lévi-Strauss rather than to limitations inherent in structural analysis. This is demonstrated by Severi's analysis of the role of negativity in Cuna traditional thought. On the one hand, the arrival of Whites can be assimilated to traditional beliefs about the Sky Jaguar, as we have already seen. On the other hand, however, it may lead to the attempt to introduce new modalities within ritual symbolism – in the case described by Severi, the offering of smoke from dollar bills to the vegetable spirits – which both challenge the limits of traditional thought and practices and open up the possibility of restructuring the same thought and practices in a profoundly new way (Severi, 1988).

The coexistence of different modalities of reception and resistance to the world of the Europeans can also be documented within a single work in the early seventeenth-century chronicle written by the Peruvian Indian Felipe Guaman Poma de Ayala. In the numerous illustrations to the text there are depictions of both native Andeans and of Europeans, which inevitably involves debate as to whether the *Nueva corónica* is a reflection of purely Andean values or whether it represents a case of assimilation to foreign, European culture. Adorno (1981) finds a negative and fragmented portrayal of European culture, contrasting with the presentation of the Andean model as integrated and unified. Integration of Andean with Christian elements therefore never signifies the Europeanisation of the Indian or the imitation of the foreigner's ways at the expense of his/her own. This exclusivity marks all the depictions of European and Andean contact in the work, and – symbolically – it is only in the jaws of Hell that the European and the Indian meet in a spirit of community (ibid: 104).

The last few examples serve to indicate the presence of breaks or ruptures in the flow of contact between Whites and Amerindians. These caesurae introduce the possibility of the existence of structures of such different kinds that they cannot be related to one another in terms of the same set of terms. Hence a curious paradox emerges from the comparison between Eurocentrism and Amerindian ethnocentrism. Though they appear in some cases to make use of similar elements – monstrosity, assimilation, liminality, (internal) opposition and splitting – the system of classification taken as a whole may differ so fundamentally that the very attempt to compare such structures is doomed to failure. This is the lesson of semantic anthropology - in a cosmos like that of the Kaliña of Surinam, where distinctions between human, animal or vegetable categories hardly seem to have any relevance at all, how are we to know that what is labelled 'European' today will not be assigned a different label tomorrow (cf. Overing, 1985a)? What is the point of trying to compare what is incommensurable?

Perhaps this seems an excessively pessimistic viewpoint to some. However, becoming aware of the limits of anthropology is not necessarily a negative exercise. In fact, the argument presented above seeks to show that these limits are intrinsic to this style of thought. To make the point a little more explicitly, we are here concerned with a situation in which the thinking person *thinks more than he or she thinks*. This formulation, borrowed like many of others from the work of Levinas, (cf. Levinas, 1957), indicates how an intentionality which tries to grasp what is unlimited is confronted with an idea which is greater than a concept: it exceeds the boundaries within which thought would like to confine/define it. This explains the source of the excess to which we have constantly drawn attention. This surplus is a result of the structure by which the self comes into contact with the other. It is the other which cannot be measured by the thought which tries to think it. They are *incommensurable*.

The situation recalls a problem in Kant's philosophy, where the faculty of judgement requires a medium by which it might operate transitions from one style of discourse to another. The metaphor which Lyotard has suggested for this situation is that of an *archipelago*. Within the heterogeneity, there may still be ways of effecting a passage from one 'island' to another (Lyotard, 1983: 189–193). Perhaps this is the status of the elements – liminality, monstrosity, etc. – which we have nevertheless tried to isolate. They have an 'as if' status, suggesting imperfect forms of passage which temporarily suspend to some extent the separateness of the 'islands' in question.

The metaphor of the mirror image, of the Whites as inverse images of the Amerindians, or vice versa, thus gives way to an approach which is dominated by notions of incommensurability and contamination. The worlds juxtaposed are incommensurable; at the same time, the relationship of self to other which they articulate is an untidy one in which the two terms (self/other) are not strictly or clearly demarcated.

Whether Europe is America's other, or America Europe's other, the terms are not reversible. The mechanisms of projection, assimilation, interiorisation, intro-jection and so on which we have examined imply that the other is still self, in and of self. On the other hand, the other has a constitutive function too: self acts as self to the other which finds it, discovers it, institutes or constitutes it (Derrida, 1987a: 10).

Oral/written, hot/cold, history/myth, America/Europe, self/other... it is not enough to reverse these oppositions. Like the spectre of totemism which Lévi-Strauss exorcised from anthropology, these monstrous trinkets taken from Euro-pean folk systems of belief are in a way liminal too: it is in their excess that they invite us to share in their self-effacement...

Notes

1. A term which goes back at least to 1914: see the article by Henderson and Harrington (1914). See too the bibliography by Chevallier in *Terrain* 10, avril 1988: 124–131.
2. This usage of the term is different from the way in which some anthropologists use it as a virtual synonym for 'marginal', 'ambiguous', etc. For present purposes, one of the most relevant aspects of the threshold is that it evades location: its site is at the same time a non-site. At the same time, its processual nature should be stressed: the threshold is there *to be crossed or transgressed*; it is self-effacing in the face of what lies to either side of it.
3. For the ethnohistorical background see, for example, de Civrieux, 1970; Guss, 1986: Wilbert, 1986: 447–450.
4. In suggesting that this act of incorporation involves a reduction or eradication of their otherness, I am following the philosopher Emmanuel Levinas, who has remarked: 'The neighbour [le prochain] as *other* is not preceded by a forerunner to delineate or announce his silhouette. He does not appear. What signal could he send me, which would not rob him of his exclusive alterity?' (1978: 109).
5. The economic metaphor of bargaining is deliberate, for the structure under discussion is ruled by an economy.
6. Text in Brotherston, 1979, quoting from Yves d'Evreux, *Voyage dans le nord du Brésil*, 1864.
7. In an amusing anecdote taken from M. Biard, 'Voyage au Brésil', which appeared in *La Tour du monde* in 1861, the portrait artist Biard recounts that it was possible to get models to pose for him by telling them that in the country of the Whites there were many individuals without a head, and that it was Biard's mission to collect as many heads for them as possible. (I am grateful to Edmundo Magaña for bringing this odd case of 'reciprocal' images to my attention.)

AMERICA.

Americen Americus retexit, & *Semel vocauit inde semper excitam*.

Ioan: Stradanus invent.
Theodor Galle fecit.

Source: Th. Galle, after 'America' by J. Stradanus. Reproduced with permission of the State Print Cabinet, Amsterdam.

Chapter eight

The elementary structures of alterity

Die Sache ist so, weil man es sagt
the thing is so because one says it
(Heidegger, 1972: 168)

In the foregoing discussions of other continents, other peoples and other bodies, we have rigorously avoided any approach which would attempt to reduce them to some supposedly external reality, of which they would be mere distorted images. It is here proposed to take them literally and seriously. It is now time to turn to the lessons that can be learnt from them about the structures of alterity.

These narratives and images produce an effect in the imaginary as a faculty of representation. These effects are situated at the level of the structure of the narrative, or they may be seen rather as that which structures the narrative. They both enable the narrative to be constructed as a narrative, and affect the recipients of the narrative, producing certain effects which in the present case relate to the structures of alterity. In a certain sense, these effects, produced by the narrative, might be seen as implicit codes by which the narrative is organised.

In applying these criteria to the account of Skythia by Herodotos, François Hartog isolated two major codes by which the Herodotean narrative was constructed and which produced specific effects on his audience. One of these is a code of (political) power, with the imaginary figure of the despot as one of the symbolic effects produced by the text. He also isolated a surveyor's code, a system of measurement in space and time, of classification, of inventarisation which likewise produces an effect on the audience (Hartog, 1980: 345–349). It seems to link the parts of the world together, covering up discontinuities and providing the narratives with both a centre and a unifying grid. At the same time, the Herodotean discourse imitates the world, for Herodotos' work in joining isolated narratives together within a whole mirrors and produces that world of which his discourse purports to be a representation.

If we turn to the discourses and first images of America, there are significant differences as regards the general axes by which they are structured. Naturally enough, there are differences between the different sources. Still, it is worth asking the question: is the earliest European discourse on America structured by the axes of political power and geometrical plotting which seem to characterise the Herodotean *logoi?* Or do Columbus, Vespucci and their sixteenth century successors organise their accounts according to other codes?

To start at the beginning – which is of course not a beginning but a secondary demarcation, inscribing itself in Europe's representation of the other – Columbus' first reaction on 12 October 1492 is not one of surprise at the Americans' lack of political organisation. Nor is Columbus' predominant concern one of fitting them geographically within a coherent but larger scheme of things. The point he hammers home is that they are naked: 'They were all naked as their mothers had born them, including the women' (Colón, 1984: 30). True, their nakedness does have political consequences, for in systematically linking their nakedness to their lack of weapons, Columbus sees in their inability to act in self-defence a sign that their military defeat will be easy. Nonetheless, political and geographical considerations are not his main concern.

The nakedness of the Indians conjures up a vision of Paradise for Columbus, fortified by the seductive qualities of the American fauna and flora in his eyes. The body of the other is erotised, and Columbus experiences his relationship to the Indians as one in which he plays the role of God, attracting both love and awe from his subjects. This transformation of the other into a female erotic object is strongly bound to Columbus' fantasy world, and we find it mythologised already in the work of Petrus Martyr (Saint-Lu, 1981). However, his attitude toward them changes once they shake off the role of fantasy objects and begin to act as real subjects.

The combination of economic and erotic components is implicated with the theme of nakedness too. The paradisiac connotations of nakedness invite the Spaniards to enter into the riches of Paradise; the erotic connotations invite them to penetrate the new continent that offers itself to them without resistance; and the siren-like hold which the natural world of America exerts on Columbus can be shaken off only by the process of disenchantment, by which Columbus transforms the wealth of natural beauty into a commodity (Moebus, 1982). The geographical links between places are subordinated to an overriding economic principle. Hence Columbus' lack of concern as to the geographical location of the places on the island of Cuba. What does concern him, through the assonance of Cubacan with the Great Khan, is the place of a region within the economic scheme of things. Sexual desire is itself also subordinated to this end, as Columbus comes to see in the well-proportioned bodies of the natives a source of economic profits to be derived from the slave trade.

These sexual and economic preoccupations are not confined to the narrative of Columbus. In Vespucci's ethnographic descriptions, the sexual aspect comes even more to the fore:

They marry as many wives as they please: and son cohabits with mother, brother with sister, nephew with niece, any man with the first women who comes his way. They divorce as often as they like.

(Vespucci, 1984: 100)

His account of the women is a voyeur's[1] paradise:

The women, as I have said, go about naked and seductively, but their bodies are attractive and clean enough. Nor are they as shameless [*turpis*] as one might perhaps suppose, because the fact of their being well filled out makes their shamelessness less apparent, since it is covered for the most part by their excellent body structure. We were surprised to see that none of them had sagging breasts[2] and that those who had given birth did not differ at all from virgins with respect to the shape and size of their bellies. The same is true for the other parts of the body, which I shall gloss over for decency's sake. When they had the opportunity of having intercourse with Christians they were driven on by excessive lasciviousness and threw all decency to the winds.

(Vespucci, 1984: 104)

This text is full of references to vision (the Latin words *apparet, operta, visum, videba(n)tur, distinguebantur*),[3] and Vespucci has certainly taken his fill of looking at the women's breasts and genitals and at their love-making, leaving the reader wondering what he glossed over 'for decency's sake'. He does his best to explain away his prurient gaze – after all, they paid no more heed to covering up their genitals in shame than did the Europeans in covering up their noses or mouths (ibid: 135).

The voyeuristic tone of Vespucci's account lays the emphasis on a visual code. The representation of the world is no longer seen as a question of contiguity and measurement, as in the Herodotean map. The world is now a terrain waiting to be perused, scrutinised and penetrated. The nude women, often depicted in early illustrations on the basis of the European canons which dominated the arts of the period, were both a symbol of this world that was to be appropriated and a part of it – both metaphor and metonym.

Another European traveller, Pero Vaz de Caminha, landed on the north-east coast of Brazil in the ship of Cabral in 1500. Although his account of what he saw was not published until the nineteenth century, and thus had no immediate impact on the formation of European images of the New World, it is worth noting in the present context that he shares Vespucci's voyeurism. On Tupí girls, for instance, he had the following to say:

There were among them three or four girls, very young and very pretty, with very dark hair, long over the shoulders, and their privy parts so high, so closed, and so free from hair that we felt no shame in looking at them very well.

(cited in Pedersen, 1987: 398)

Similarly, his comment that the naked males were not circumcised reveals a similar scopophiliac desire.

The same axes recur if we turn to Jean de Léry's account of his voyage to Brazil, in which an (economic) ethic of production is accompanied by an erotisation of the body of the other (de Certeau, 1975: 237). The economic dimension is reflected in de Léry's work at the level of consumption, as he weighs up the merits of all that he encounters in terms of its digestibility (Whatley, 1984).

The objects of the erotised desires of these European observers do not disturb their fantasies as long as they remain passive (for instance, Vaz de Caminha observes the naked males while they are asleep). However, Columbus and Vespucci see the object of their erotised desires turn into a monster once it acts as a subject. Hence Vespucci's famous account of the inhuman cruelty of the women who enlarge the sexual organs of their males by applying venomous insects to them, sometimes leading to a castration of the male (*eunuchi*, ibid: 100).[4] The fear of these castrating fiends also emerges from the attack by a group of women on a young man who went on land during Vespucci's third voyage. The scene is vividly portrayed in a series of three woodcuts, where the native women seduce the member of the crew while their colleagues prepare the ambush with a massive club. In a telling detail, the last we see of their unfortunate victim is his buttocks protruding from a cave, with anal connotations which suggest further sexual perversion on the part of the women.[5]

There is a particularly telling example of the split between idealised and realistic nude portrayals in the early-seventeenth-century illustrations to Guaman Poma de Ayala's *El primer nueva corónica y buen gobierno*. The realistic portrayal of the genitals of the Indians in these illustrations does not carry the connotations of the noble savage. Rather, sexuality is vulnerability and the sign of attack or degradation by the outsider. It exposes the Indians as victims to the invading foreigners. They are stripped bare for discipline or sexual penetration (Adorno, 1981: 70–77).

If we compare the mass of sexual and economic details which can be culled from the texts of Columbus, Vespucci, Petrus Martyr, Oviedo, de Léry, Thevet and others, and set it against the relative lack of interest in geographical precision or political forms, it is hard to resist the conclusion that the Herodotean axes do not hold for the sixteenth-century accounts of America, which are seen to be structured primarily in sexual and economic terms.

We can also approach the sexual and economic axes from a different angle. Columbus' meetings with the inhabitants of America might be seen as a case in which an economically necessary voyage leads to relations of sexual and economic dominance over the natives.[6] Economically, the parties involved could hardly be more opposed, locked as they are in the naked/clothed opposition. Sexually, they are in a position of absolute asymmetry. The sexual and economic code(s) accommodate(s) the figure of the excessively lascivious American female who is one of the symbolic effects produced by the text: she is sexually overactive and voracious, and economically wasteful. The ideal of the Europeans, on the other hand, takes them to be sexually moderate, and not to dissipate their energies in sexual wantonness at the expense of economic activity. This production of the image of the sexually overactive and economically wasteful Indian as a symbolic effect of the text conforms to a pattern that can be traced back to the origins of the European imaginary in the earliest Greek mythology (Mason, 1987b). In making the women of America conform to this pattern, Columbus' encounter reveals a dual experience: it is both the historically constituted form in which intercultural contact takes place and the translation of the unfamiliar New World in terms of the familiar Old World.

Such symbolic effects are not confined to the written text. In her analysis of the illustrations to de Bry's *America*, Bucher (1981) has demonstrated how the Indians might conform to a reversed version of the European images. They present a topsy-turvy world in which the roles of the sexes are reversed. On the one hand, the Amerindian males are portrayed as effeminate because of their lack of bodily hair, linked to the charge that they were homosexually inclined that is a commonplace of the sources right up to the Enlightenment. On the other hand, the Amazon-like women are excessively masculine to European eyes, and their prominence in the scenes of cannibal feasting once again reasserts their deviation from the norm in both sexual and economic terms. Such images could serve as a justification of European intervention to redress the balance, put matters right and restore a phallocentric order based on masculine men and feminine women.

So in text and image the difference by which the native peoples of America are constructed as Europe's others is a sexual and economic difference. However, there is a high degree of contamination between the bodies of the texts themselves and the worlds which they purport to describe. Columbus' text describes sexual and economic encounters; but his text itself undergoes the effects of a sexual and economic ordering principle.

To be more explicit on the relation between text and content: we are here treating the text as the site of a signifying activity which has both an economic and a sexual aspect.[7] The text is not the reflection of some 'sexual' or 'economic' entity external to it. The text itself constitutes the reality of sexuality and economy as social practices.[8]

For those who are prepared to accept the theoretical acquisition that the text as such is structured in sexual and economic terms, a curious result emerges for discourse on America. We have seen that this discourse produces effects that are broadly aligned along sexual and economic parameters. But now it seems that this discourse, as discourse, is itself sexually and economically structured. We could take the example of de Léry: when M. de Certeau writes: 'The profit "made" by the text seems to isolate a "remainder" which is also to define the savage and which does not figure in writing. The trace of this remainder is pleasure' (1975: 237), he is making the assertion that de Léry's text itself, and the account presented in it of the savage, both obey homologous sexual and economic structuring principles.

What are we to make of this complicity between discourse on America *as text* and the representations of America that are its effects? If we return to the argument of the first chapter, we can state that the reason why the representations of America do not follow the Herodotean axes, but present the peoples of the New World in terms of sexual and economic parameters, is the work of the text *as text*. The representations of America, in that case, are symbolic effects of sexually and economically structured texts, rather than the reflection of some sexually and economically structured external reality. In short, the discourses on America, as presented in texts and images, *are* America. *Die Sache ist so, weil man es sagt*. And as a corollary, we have no means at our disposal for severing the thread linking discourse to representation, no way of approaching America 'as it really is', because such a notion is devoid of significance.

If we consider the implications of this for the key figures in this book, the Plinian races, we can claim that, at this specific level, the Plinian races do not deviate from the sexual and economic parameters either. The Amazons and the hermaphrodites, the men with enormous penises or hanging testicles and the ithyphallic Cynocephali have an obvious sexual reference, and the variations on the disposition of the bodily orifices delineated in Chapter Six include the genitals as part of the system outlined there. As for the economic component, the distribution of the bodily forms of these races was shown to conform to a monstrous economics, making use of the economic principles of multiplication, reduction and displacement.

The Plinian races nevertheless occupy a special place. This is because of the system of articulation, syntax and punctuation which they embody. In this sense, discourse on the Plinian races is discourse on text. Their bodies are a form of script, and accounts of them are parts of intertextuality. Their closeness to the text implies a reduced symbolic distance as far as they are concerned, and they tend to signify in metonymic rather than metaphorical terms (which is why we played down Tylor's metaphorical interpretation in Chapter Four). The monstrous races are textually constituted, they partake of textuality, and they do not require discourse *about* them, because they are themselves directly legible. Their closeness to the text means that they offer some way of stepping out of the relationship between anthropology and its object, of the awkward rift between *anthropos* and *logos*, for as text they *are* an anthropo-logy. Discourse on the Plinian races is ethno-anthropological discourse.

The threads, or fibres, of the introductory chapter come together momentarily here. The Plinian races are the privileged form of ethno-anthropological discourse, which is why they occupy pride of place in the present work. Typically, its centre is thus ex-centric, pivoted on those races which are by definition (as we saw in Chapter Three) located at, or beyond, the boundary. For, as we saw in Chapter Seven, monstrosity and liminality search one another out. As an *archi-écriture*, the monstrous races constitute an anthropology that precedes the oral/ written distinction. And because they do not represent anything, but refer only by way of self-reference, they avoid the violence which is an inevitable part of the unifying and reductive labour of anthropology.

The existence of a particular sector of the anthropology of the imaginary constituted by figures without any empirical anchorage has already been noted by Lévi-Strauss (1968: 104). However, from the above remarks it will be clear that in the present context the lack of an empirical anchorage is not a significant feature. These beings can exist alongside more familiar ones without causing any disruption to the system. For instance, Lévi-Strauss has isolated a system in which the sloth, the howler monkey, the goatsucker and the dwarf without an anus are the four terms (1984: 109–111). Given the coherence of this system, there are no grounds for treating the dwarfs without an anus as different from the three other natural species, despite the fact that they may be assumed to be a figment of the imagination. Or if we look at the information on spirit beings collected among the Guajiro of Venezuela and Colombia by M. Perrin, we find two kinds of supernatural beings, *keeralia* and *akalakui*, which form a mutually reinforcing system in which the specific qualities attributed to one of these categories are simply the product of a mental operation seeking to define the complement of the other. Perrin sees in these creatures a contribution to Guajiro theories of sickness and misfortune, but also more than that:

> The remarkable human imagination, unconsciously subject to constraints imposed by the mind and to the constant pressure of sexual fantasy, manages to create fantastic humanoids whose reality it sets out to prove by attributing to them the ability to act pathogenically upon the human body.
>
> (Perrin, 1988a: 159)

These two examples illustrate the existence of mental operations which precede zoological data (Magaña, 1988c: 22). In their escape from the clutches of empirical 'reality', the Plinian races are definitively removed from every process of presentation by which we might summon them to appear in person. This elusiveness is a feature of a certain radical form of alterity, indicating that such figures need to be placed against the background of the structures of alterity, for the Plinian imaginary is linked to representations of the other (Magaña and Mason, 1986). But before passing to these structures, it is worth looking in more detail at some of the rhetorical figures used in the travel accounts. If the reality of America is a discursive reality, produced in discourse, the question arises of what rhetorical tropes and *topoi* are used to create an effect of reality, and how the strangeness of the other is accommodated.

The force of rhetoric

We start, again, with the *Histoire d'un voyage fait en la terre de Brésil* of Jean de Léry. In the preface to this work, he wrote that he had now revised his views in certain respects:

> Now, since I have been there, without approving of the fables to be read in the books of several who, confiding in reports that have been made for them

or otherwise, have written things which are completely false, I have retracted the opinion that I used to hold about Plinius and certain others who have described foreign countries. I have seen things as bizarre and prodigious as all those mentioned by them which were held to be incredible.

(de Léry, 1980: 47)

J' ai vu – the shift in his belief is presented as a result of what he saw with his own eyes. But besides this presentation as an item of (auto)biographical interest, *j' ai vu* also functions at the level of rhetorical persuasion, or, as F. Hartog puts it, '*je l' ai vu*, it is true, and it is true that it is marvellous' (1980: 272). Truth and alterity are combined in the assertion of first-hand observation (*autopsy*). The strangeness of the other is confirmed as true because it has been witnessed by the speaker.

The theme of voyeurism that was discussed above is here given a new twist, for etymologically the witness is the one who sees.[9] It is this sense which has priority over the others. Problems will arise when two or more observers differ in their observations of what they see; but as long as one can claim the status of main witness, it is this account which has a monopoly on claims to truth.

The main witness can base its claim to being so in terms of uniqueness. As a unique observer, it can present its account as the record of how things were. In this respect, there are certain instruments which can be used to stress this uniqueness and thereby reinforce the monopoly of such a witness. The primary point of reference must surely be the body: it is the physical presence of the observer elsewhere which is used to buttress the veracity of its tale. The eye is of course the organ of the body through which the other is perceived, and the eye thus enjoys a special status in this context. For example, Mercator calls history *Oculus Mundi*, the eye of the world, and Ortelius describes geography as 'the Eye of History' (Rabasa, 1985: 5). However, at times the whole body itself takes the place of one of its parts. For instance, Thevet records an adventure in which he was so ill that his body was stripped and carried by natives of America to the shore for burial, but that they were prevented from carrying out their plans by the intervention of a Scot, one of the bodyguards. By inserting this incident into his account of the giants of Patagonia – where it does not belong historically – Thevet uses it to authenticate his account of the twelve-foot tall giants (Lestringant, 1987b). It is in this light that we could read the *topoi* on the tribulations of voyagers by sea in general. Their sufferings produce a reality effect which is then used (without justification) to add credence to other items in their narratives.

The physicality of the body can be conveyed in other less direct ways.[10] For example, a number of travel accounts (de Léry, Thevet, Cartier) contain exotic native words (cf. Launay-Demonet, 1987). These written words serve to break up the linearity of the discourse when they occur sporadically in the text (de Certeau, 1975: 247), and this disruptive aspect draws attention to the fact that it is the exteriority of the voice which is both the motive and the precondition for its recording in writing. In other words, these native vocabularies represent an interruption or irruption, a fleeting appearance of the other, in the body of the text. At the same time, the recording of authentic, strange words creates an effect of opaqueness. The very fact that they are transliterated rather than translated means that the utterances of the other are not decoded,[11] but presented for what they are – a reality effect whose orchestration, it should be noted, lies firmly within the monopolistic control of the writer. Such words appear on paper only because they have passed through the ear of the eye-witness.

The collection of native words and language can easily be extended to a whole range of artefacts, of which words are simply a sub-category of linguistic artefacts. The arrows, fur cloak and other objects which Thevet took home to France to stock his curiosity cabinet are metonymically related to his physical body too. In this sense, the act of bearing witness by the body assumes something of a martyrdom.[12]

There is another modality by which the body of the observer underpins the narrative. This is in the use of measurement. The eye of the traveller measures the distance (in time or space) from one sight to another. They become linked to one another by virtue of belonging to the traveller's field of vision. Ultimately, records of measurement may serve future travellers to pass along the same route that the 'original' voyager has taken. Like other of the tropes under discussion here, the use of measurement also goes back to Herodotos as a means of conveying a tone of seriousness (Hartog, 1980: 347).[13] The relativity of such measurements is obvious when they are couched in terms of comparatives, a frequent feature of travel itineraries (Maçzak, 1987). To call one city twice as large as another implies some point of reference, but it implies a lot more: both the (ethnocentric, of course) selection of a point of reference, and its comparison with a new place through the intermediary of the body of the observer, who is the one to make the connection between A and B. Even when units of measurement are used, the same still holds. Hence much of the dispute over the size of the Patagonian giants depends on whether those doing the measuring are English or French, i.e. the units of measurement depend on the users.

In the travel literature, resorting to claims of autopsy appears as a *topos* in contrast to knowledge derived from books.[14] We find it as early as Mandeville's *Travels*,[15] where the convention of a *persona* who has witnessed the events he describes is sometimes comic in the result it produces. Earlier travellers' impressions could serve as the points of reference for later ones, and description could thereby take the form of re-inscription. Claims to autopsy should not always be taken at their face value. As Lestringant (1987b) has convincingly shown, Thevet's so-called first-hand accounts derive from Magellan. Sometimes deliberately, sometimes unwittingly, the claim to autopsy is intended to have the rhetorical force of conferring veracity on an account. The more amazing the account may appear, the more such rhetorical tropes will be in demand. The claim to be an eye-witness, coupled with the implication of physical presence, is at one and the same time the claim to the truth of the marvellous, and an attempt to translate its otherness by way of the body, through the senses, through measurement, or metonymically.

There is a second response to the strangeness of the other that is related to the *topos* of the first-hand eye-witness. This involves a splitting between a land and its inhabitants. Topographically, the land may not seem so strange, but the behaviour of its inhabitants with respect to their land is what is puzzling. This figure has a strong rhetorical force in that it justifies intervention to repair the rift and to restore harmony – if the natives cannot do the job properly, they will have to let others do it for them. For instance, when the Mexica came to occupy their capital of Tenochtitlán after years of wandering, they glossed over the fact that they drove the people out who were cultivating the area at that time by simply acting as if it were virgin territory. To legitimise their presence on the central plateau, they ignored the sedentary groups who had occupied the territory, falsified their own history by denying their past as hunters and gatherers, and claimed to have been agriculturalists for ages (Duverger, 1983: 226–227).[16] Within a colonial context, it implies a restatement of the conquered territory as virgin territory. British accounts of colonial expansion in North America (or in Ireland, as we saw in Chapter 2), systematically underplay the fact that the land was being cultivated by native peoples, despite the fact that Algonkin agriculture grew just about enough to feed the English as well as the Algonkin (Hulme, 1985: 26). Similarly, in the period between the first publication of Hans Staden's *Warhaftige Historia* in 1557 and the volumes of de Bry's *America* that began to appear in the 1590s, the references to Tupinamba tobacco and manioc cultivation, which are depicted in the woodcut illustrations to Staden's account, are systematically eliminated from de Bry.

The case of Virginia also shows how this rhetorical figure also involves retranslating acts of aggression as acts of self-defence. This is the general thrust of Simon Grynaeus' *Novus Orbis* (Basle, 1532), in which non-Europeans are assigned a general aggressiveness, while internal divisions within Europe are deliberately played down and violence is extruded to become the work of the Indians (Korinman, 1987: 426–427). It is also a related process by which the New World is seen as a source of natural history. In these terms, and on these terms, the fauna and flora are capable of description, translation and assimilation. It is the social behaviour of its inhabitants – what exceeds pure natural history – which remains an obstacle to comprehension.

This trope involving the insertion of a wedge between the land and its inhabitants is related to the former trope of autopsy, for the nakedness of the virgin territory invites and incites the voyeuristic eye of the European colonist to take possession of it/her. There is a relation between the (female) body that is emphasised in accounts of virgin land and the (generally male) body of the first-hand observer who penetrates the unknown to arrive at truth. In the case of autopsy, the economy of measurement was mediated through the body. The corpus of the text partook metonymically in the physical experiences of the eye-witness. In the case of the second trope, however, the *mise-en-scène* is different.

This time the observer is characterised by myopia. The body at issue is not his own body, but that of the virgin land that is to be appropriated. The short-sightedness tends to fall back on literary sources rather than to confront the existence of the evidence for native cultivation of the land. In this respect we find resonances of the voyage of Odysseus (Hulme, 1985); the *Aeneid* of Vergilius, worked into Thevet's account by his scholarly assistant;[17] or the myth of Jason and the Golden Fleece (Jacob, 1987). Indeed, one of Odysseus' Homeric epithets, *polytropos*, encapsulates many of the elements within this figure: his many wanderings, his use of turns of speech (tropes), and his turns of mind (Pucci, 1982), thereby making him a figure *par excellence* for use in tropes of this kind.[18]

In concentrating on the rhetorical force of these figures, the emphasis is on the effects produced by the travel accounts on their audience, then and today.[19] First-hand or eye-witness accounts and the figures associated with colonial appropriation are seen as ways of presenting a particular account in a particular way. They present the encounter with the other by subjecting its alterity to the modalities of rhetorical tropes.

At this stage, two questions arise: what other approaches to the other might one conceive? And in what sense are we justified in seeing America as the other at all?

To start with the latter point first, we can note that in some quarters a special role is attributed to America within a symbolic system of continental reference. One of the clearest statements of this special role for the New World is by Margolin:

> The Amerindian is not just the person whose physical appearance, customs
> – clothing, foods, social and economic life, warlike or peaceful habits –
> religion – or rather absence of religion – ecological and geographical
> framework have nothing in common with those of the Christians of Europe.
> It is the Other, whose presence was ignored by both the ancient Greco-
> Roman world and by the Bible, unlike the Asian and the African, old
> partners in war, commerce and all kinds of exchange, whose 'strangeness',
> 'barbarity or 'inferiority' admitted of degrees.
>
> (Margolin, 1987: 14)

In this sense, the continents of Asia, Africa and America are all other as far as Europe is concerned, but while the first two can at least be measured in terms of conformity to or deviation from European standards, America confronts Europe with a radical otherness (Todorov, 1982: 12). America and Europe are simply incommensurable – there are no points in common, no system of measurement, allowing them to be brought into relation with one another. They are absolutely other in one another's eyes. Moreover, the attribution to America of the status of the absolute *nec plus ultra* of alterity implies a redistribution of roles within the existing images of countries and continents. Thus the status of Ireland, for example, which had functioned as England's other, undergoes a change once a different other is found further to the West beyond the borders of Ireland. This leads to an associative form of alterity, in which the Celts are compared with barbarians, or are seen to resemble Amerindians; robbed of their absolute alterity, they assume a secondary alterity that derives from the new Other on the other side of the ocean.[20]

Other scholars would disagree with such a presentation. For example, Harbsmeier (1987) has argued that many sixteenth-century German travel accounts conform to a triangular structure which undergoes transformations, but which nevertheless subtends attempts to group the otherness of both the Holy Land and the New World. Briefly, among the ninety or so German travel accounts from the sixteenth century that he has examined (of which only six relate to the New World), Harbsmeier detects an opposition between Christians and non-Christians which structures the perception of the other by self. The self/other relation here, though, is a triangular one because the other is itself split: on the one hand, the positive aspect of the Holy Land for European Christians and its link with their sacred past; on the other hand, the negative aspect of the occupation of that soil by the peoples of the Ottoman Empire in a present that is the very opposite and antagonist of Christianity.

When the focus shifts to Europe itself, a different triangular structure emerges. This time the main structural opposition is between civilised and non-civilised. The self/other relation is a triad too: opposed to the self are, on the one hand, the uncultured peasant classes and other figures of popular culture in Europe, and on the other hand, their positive counterparts in the civilised elites of the same geographical area.

In the case of the six New World travel accounts,[21] Harbsmeier detects a shift over time from the first to the second model. At the beginning of the century, the 'Mandevillean' tradition is followed, with its primary opposition between Christian and non-Christian, while the accounts from the later part of the century relate the travels to the New World to the rules of the new cosmological vision, in terms of civilised versus uncivilised, that was being applied in Christian Europe.[22]

This attempt to trace the elementary structures of otherness is a valuable contribution. At the same time, it also raises questions about the internal limits and external boundaries of the Europe which serves as the basis of Eurocentrism (cf. Christensen, 1987: 259). It would thus repay further study to see to what extent these postulated structures will stand up to more detailed scrutiny and comparison of the texts in question. But leaving aside the question of the possible fit between 'theory' and 'facts', the wider question is that of the possibility of commensurability at all.[23] Of course, the strategy of travellers' tales is generally based on the implicit assumption that such a commensurability exists – in practical terms, the heathen of the New World are in principle capable of conversion to Christianity, and therefore of assimilation to European standards. Still, we do not need to take them at their face value.

If the issue is, in the last analysis, the question of whether the New World is radically and absolutely other, or whether it is commensurable with other civilisations or cultures, it is impossible to see how any answer to a question of this kind could be convincing. Nevertheless, the question can be rephrased in another way. It is not the aim of this work to assert that the New World *is* the absolute Other. Aside from the problem of how to verify such a claim, the point is that any pinning down of the discussion to a rigid descriptive framework is bound to lead to a static vision which focuses on the separate *relata* (self versus other) rather than on the relation between them. The crucial point is that self and other are relative terms that are themselves produced within the structures of alterity: in that other is always in excess of self, always contains a surplus with respect to self, always imposes the need to redraw the contours of self, the terms are permanently involved in a *process* of definition and redefinition.

We can see this in an example from the portrayal of East-West relations. In her account of the different treatment accorded to the movement of Islam and to that of the Scandinavian peoples after the collapse of the Roman Empire, J. Kaye (1985: 66) sees Islam, as Lévi-Strauss had done, as 'the West of the East in which the West can recognise its own mirror image'. But if that makes us 'the East of West', then Ireland must be 'the West of the East of the West'...

Following Buber (cf. Bernasconi, 1988), we here prefer to start from the working assumption that 'in the beginning is the relation', a category of being as readiness to be filled in with a relation between such terms as 'I-Thou' or 'I-it'. That is, it makes little sense to claim that America *is* the Other, but it does make some sense to treat *it as* the absolute Other. The difference is crucial: we replace an ontological statement about the New World with an ethical injunction to approach it with the deference appropriate to the other, not trying to impose our vision on it, but in a state of readiness for what it presents to us that is neither active nor passive.

We are thus already caught up in the issues raised by the first question: what approaches to the other might represent appropriate ways of approaching the New World? One point of entry here might be Todorov's typology of relations to the other, since it is explicitly drawn up with America in mind. Todorov sees three ways of grouping the relationship with the other: an axiological dimension, consisting of value judgements on the other (the noble versus the ignoble savage, 'natural man', etc.); a praxeological dimension, couched in terms of distancing oneself from or coming closer to the other (culture contact and assimilation, etc.); and an epistemological dimension, concerned with the identity of the other and its knowability. In all three dimensions, America is posited as the other to the self of Europe (Todorov, 1982: 191ff.).

In all three dimensions, the starting point is self, reaching out to a double that is not its double. The other is a projection from within self. It should be clear that such an ego-centric approach is foreign to the aims of the present study. If we are to conceive the relation in such terms at all, they will have to be reversed. This is the way in which Foucault posed the problem of the double. The double becomes an internalisation of the other; it is not a reproduction of the same, but an iteration of what is different. It is not the emanation of an ego, but the immanence of an other or a non-ego which is always other. I do not find myself in exteriority, but I find the other in me (cf. Deleuze, 1986: 105).

Not a promise, only an appeal

Already some of the central issues are beginning to appear. Are we dealing with the relation between self and other, or that between the same and the different? If we can speak of the invention of the other, is this genitive subjective or objective? In other words, does ego construct the other from within, or does the other take care of its own invention in ego (cf. Derrida, 1987a: 10)?

From this point on, the present text can hardly be expected to present a detailed thematisation. If receptivity to the other comes to the fore, we can do little more than open up to the other. The vibrating chords which set up resonances in others do so in an unending series. Diderot resonates in Derrida. At this point, we can do no more than register

> the differential vibration of several tonalities [...] which do not admit of stabilisation in the indivisible simplicity of a single missive [*envoi*], of self to self, or of a single countersignature, but invite the countersignature of the other, an affirmative [*oui*] which resonates in a completely different [*tout autre*] writing, another language, another idiosyncrasy, with another timbre.
>
> (Derrida, 1987b: 137)

Hence from this point on I do no more than juxtapose citations from others (mainly Emmanuel Levinas and Jacques Derrida), together with some *marginal* remarks which are situated *between Levinas and Derrida*.[24] In writing otherwise, the text opens itself up to the voice of the other.[25] The time has come to render what is due.

Alterity is a notion admitting a number of interpretations and structures, as is now becoming clear. So the first step is to isolate some of them. First, we could take the opposition of same/different, an approach that opens up the possibility of a semiotic approach to culture. Moreover, it links with the economic theme discussed earlier in this chapter, for the possibility of a difference between entities introduces the possibility of a surplus. We came up against it in the first chapter, when the first observers of the New World were faced with the problem of defining what was the same and not the same. The logical problem involved explains why Levinas (in a recent interview, given in 1986) refers to it as logical alterity: 'if there is a series, each term is other in relation to the rest' (Levinas, 1988: 179).

However, we are more concerned with a second kind of alterity, which Levinas calls 'the alterity of the face, which is not a difference, not a series, but strangeness - strangeness which cannot be suppressed, which means that it is my obligation that cannot be effaced' (ibid.). It is not a relation of identity and difference, but of self and other. This seems more appropriate to the case of the New World at first sight. It might even be possible to elaborate it further to elucidate some of the elementary structures of alterity. One direction is that suggested by the assimilatory enterprise of Bartolomé de las Casas or of Jean-François Lafitau: in their eagerness to put the Amerindians on a par with the members of the ancient civilisations of Europe, these authors operate in terms of a greater or lesser distance between self and other. They work in spatial terms: the other is closer or less close to self. José de Acosta does something similar, though in temporal terms: the motor of migration is used to articulate the differences in cultural attainment in historical terms.[26]

Moreover, this relationship links up with the sexual theme discussed earlier in this chapter. Distance, as Nietzsche knew (1955: 80), is what gives woman her seductive power.[27] Seduction is always seduction from afar (*in die Ferne*, cf. Mason, 1987c). The distance thus produced is the sexual skill of delaying the climactic moment and thereby raising the pleasure to a greater and greater intensity. There is a production of a surplus within this process of deferral. Incidentally, the trace of sexual and economic elements within these elementary structures of alterity should not come as a surprise. In fact, Levinas himself makes a similar association in *Totalité et Infini*. There the I exists as a separated being, maintaining its identity in relation to labour and economic activity. At the same time, I is called into question by the other in the sphere of feminine seduction.

All the same, the question remains:
But how can the same, produced as egoism, enter into relationship with an other without immediately divesting it of its alterity? What is the nature of this relationship?

(Levinas, 1979: 38)

Levinas' own response to the question, despite his strenuous denials, comes very close to negative theology or a theory of kenosis. He empties the other of every attempt to pin it down, to determine it, and thereby to deprive it of its otherness. For instance, 'the other is never preceded by any forerunner to depict or announce his silhouette. He does not appear. What sign could he send me which would not rob him of his exclusive alterity?' (Levinas, 1978: 109). This is the kind of alterity – *une certaine altérité* – which is definitively removed from any process of presentation by which we might summon him to appear in person (Derrida, 1972a: 21).

This introduces us to a third relation: that between self and the stranger, in which, 'paradoxically, it is inasmuch as he is *alienus* – stranger and other – that man is not alienated' (Levinas, 1978: 76). In spatial terms, it is that which is distant. However, it is not a point in the distance whose distance could be measured, but *the distance of distance* (cf. Derrida, 1978a: 38) conjured up by the double movement of Heidegger's *Entfernung* (Heidegger, 1972: 105ff.). If the distant could come nearer, its distance would be lost. Hence its structure is the distance continually produced between *logos* and what falls outside it. In temporal terms, the stranger is connected with the *trace*, to what will never be appropriated by the moment of a *presence*, to an an-archic structure of temporality which falls outside the unified discourse of synchronism and diachronism.

Where does this all lead us? To what Derrida calls a certain experience of the impossible: 'the experience of the other as invention of the impossible' (1987a: 27). The invention of the other, the coming of the other, is certainly not *constructed* as a subjective genitive, nor as an objective genitive. And the other is neither a subject, nor an object, nor an I, nor a consciousness, nor an unconscious (ibid: 53).

Confronted with the breakdown of presentation and re-presentation, what other avenues are left for us to explore? There is a suggestive example in the mutual confrontation of Europe and the Orient. The visits of diplomatic officials from the Ottoman Empire to France in the eighteenth century brought about the introduction of many oriental themes into European art, but the contact worked in two directions: besides the impact of the orient on France to produce orientalism, the world of Europe itself made an impression on the orientals. But there is a difference in the approach of the two sides to the other. While the European approach was one of assimilation, including the new oriental themes within the arts of Europe, the oriental approach to the confrontation with the other took a different form. During the visit of the Ottoman embassy to France in 1721, Mehmet Effendi visited Versailles. He found it impossible to describe what he saw, but when he was confronted with tapestries, his response was even more emotional: 'seeing them and putting the finger of admiration into my mouth were for me the same thing', he exclaimed (cf. Harbsmeier, 1985: 80). In this case, representation breaks down when faced with the impossible task of representing a representation. All Effendi can do is represent his gesture in an act of self-reference, the finger pointing into the mouth rendered speechless. The crucial point is this self-reference – the finger does not point *at* something; but it unites sight and gesture in a movement, by folding self back on self, which leaves the other intact.[28]

Without ignoring the fact that even a gesture has its syntax, can we see in this gesture of Effendi a response to the impossibility of constructing the other? And might we call this impossibility of construction *deconstruction* – the labour of preparing oneself for the coming of the other, knowing how to say 'come' and how to respond to the 'come' of the other (Derrida, 1987a: 53-54)?

It is to one of the most sensitive observers of the colonial scene that we owe a poignant statement of these themes. E.M. Forster was writing in *A Passage to India*, but let us – for one brief moment – substitute one continent for another:

How can the mind take hold of such a country? Generations of invaders have tried, but they remained in exile. The important towns they build are only retreats, their quarrels the malaise of men who cannot find their way home. India knows of their trouble. She knows the whole world's trouble, to its uttermost depth. She calls 'Come' through her hundred mouths, through objects ridiculous and august. But come to what? She has never defined. She is not a promise, only an appeal.

(Forster, 1924: 136)

Notes

1. The word is used deliberately: 'For Lévi-Strauss the ethnographer is first and foremost a viewer (and perhaps voyeur)' (Fabian, 1983: 67).
2. For the significance of this remark see the analysis in Chapter Two and B. Bucher (1981).
3. Though, as Fabian points out, there are other levels at which a text provides glosses on the world as *seen* apart from direct references to a visual vocabulary; for instance, in the use of the so-called 'ethnographic present', he argues, 'the present tense is a signal signifying a discourse as an observer's language' (1983: 86).
4. A report that was accepted by De Pauw and Carli, mentioned with horror by T. Porcacchi (*L'Isole più famose del Mondo*, Venice, 1572) and with amusement by G. de Gamerra (*La Corneide*, Livorno, 1781) (Gerbi, 1973: 237–238).
5. For the theme of the fantasy of anal penetration of males by females in the early iconography of America, see the details to the butchering scene carried out by the Tupinamba in de Bry's publication (cf. Bucher, 1982).
6. It might also be seen as a travesty of the encounter between the sexes in Rousseau's *Essai sur l'origine des langues* (1970: 123), which is extensively discussed in Derrida's *De la grammatologie*. In this scenario, girls and boys are in search of water for their economic activities. From the encounters which result from their proximity arises sexual pleasure as a surplus, as an non-necessary concomitant to this sexual interest. But 'necessary' and 'non-necessary' exchange places: the necessity of sexual contact entails economically non-necessary extra visits to the watering places ('imperceptibly, water becomes more "necessary"'). Economically, the parties involved are the same; sexually, they are different. And the originary difference, from which Rousseau goes on to derive the state of society, is thus a play (festival) with an economic and a sexual aspect (Derrida, 1967a: 372).
7. When Derrida asks

   > How to think *at the same time différance* as an economic detour which always seeks to rediscover pleasure in the element of the same [...] and on the other hand *différance* as a relation to the impossible presence, as an expense without reserves, as an irreparable loss of presence, irreversible consumption of energy, that is as a death urge and a relation to the completely-other which seems to disrupt every economy?
   >
   > (Derrida, 1972a: 20)

   he is referring to the fact that the play of the text has both an economic and a sexual aspect. The first arises from the temporal aspect of *différance* as a deferring, and the time of the text necessary for this deferral to take place is an economic surplus. The second arises from that aspect of *différance* which constitutes the pleasure of the text. For a more detailed exposition of these twin aspects of the text, see Silverman and Torode (1980: 311ff.).
8. The argument here rejoins Foucault's thesis that 'the history of sexuality [...] must first be conducted from the perspective of a history of discourses' (1976: 92). Foucault's history of sexuality started with an injunction to interrogate the notion that sex is

external to discourse and that only the removal of an obstacle can open up the path leading to it (ibid: 48–49).

9. From the Greek *istor*: see Benveniste, 1969, II: 173.

10. As we have already seen, the use of the ethnographic present as a standard rhetorical tool in ethnographic texts similarly implies the presence of the anthropologist's body and a transparent relation between him/her and reality, unmediated by distance or time.

11. Compare Derrida's untranslatable remark on translation: 'L'à-traduire du traductible ne peut être que l'intraduisable' (1987b: 60).

12. From the Greek *martyr* = witness.

13. A good example is provided by Dom João de Castro, who arrived in India in 1538. He was the first European known to us to have recorded the measurements of an Indian monument. His description of the edifice of the pagoda in Elephanta is full of precise measurements, which serve to add credence to his account of a temple 'of such marvellous workmanship that it seems impossible for it to have been made by human hands' (Primeiro Roteiro da Costa da India desde Goa até Dio, cited in Mitter, 1977: 326).

14. For discussions of some of the ancient *topoi* on first-hand observation, especially on Pausanias, see Jacob (1980–81) and Veyne (1983). For the dispute on the value of literary sources versus first-hand experience between Thevet and Belleforest, see Simonin (1987).

15. For instance in his account of a visit to the Vale Perilous where he saw a frightening devil's head (Mandeville, 1983: 173–174). Despite the attempt to add veracity to his tale by claiming that he was accompanied by two monks, Mandeville simply lifted the story from Odoric of Pordenone (ch. LXXIII).

16. This version derives from the account by the Jesuit Juan Tovar.

17. Thevet collaborated on the writing of *Les Singularités de la France antarctique* (1557) with Mathurin Héret, the translator of Alexandros of Aphrodisia and Dares the Phrygian. It was Héret who added the references to classical antiquity (and to his own work as a translator) to Thevet's text.

18. The Trojan war was to be used much later in the continent within *indigenista* narratives: see Hulme (1986).

19. For some very pertinent remarks on the rhetorical effect of dedications and other 'preliminaries', see Neuber, 1989.

20. I am grateful to Joep Leerssen for these remarks on Ireland.

21. They are: Nicolaus Federmann, *Indianische Historia*, related to his expedition in Venezuela in 1536–1537; the travel accounts by Hans Mayr and Balthasar Sprenger, who both took part in Almeida's expedition in 1505 (Sprenger's account was illustrated with woodcuts by Hans Burgkmair the Elder in 1508); Karsten Smeding; Ulrich Schmiedel, whose *Warhafftige Historien einer Wunderbaren Schiffart... 1534 bis 1554* was published in Nuremberg in 1602; and Hans Staden's *Warhaftig Historia* (Marburg, 1557).

22. As Harbsmeier himself points out, the work of Hans Staden defies classification within this scheme.

23. Some of the theoretical problems at issue here are raised in the comments on incommensurability by Joanna Overing (1985a: 155).

24. The title of a forthcoming study by Robert Bernasconi.

25. The problem of the relation *between* these two types of alterity is too complex to go into here. But any discussion of it cannot ignore Derrida's fundamental critique of Levinas (Derrida, 1967b: 187), where Derrida suggests that the recognition of the asymmetrical otherness of the other already presupposes the prior symmetry of the relation between ego and *alter ego*.

26. I have discussed this point in more detail in Mason, 1987c.
27. Proust knew it too: when the central character of *Le Côté de Guermantes* wants to kiss Albertine, he is dismayed by the fact that, in reducing the distance from her to place his lips on her cheek, his eyes will no longer see her and his nose will no longer smell her (Proust, 1954, II: 365).
28. Compare Wittgenstein's case of a person who 'naturally reacted to the gesture of pointing with the hand by looking in the direction of the line from finger-tip to wrist, not from wrist to finger-tip (Wittgenstein, 1958: 185).

Bibliography

Achilles, K. (1982) Indianer auf der Jagd. Der neue Kontinent in den *Venationes* des Johannes Stradanus, *Mythen der Neuen Welt: Zur Entdeckungsgeschichte Lateinamerikas*, K.-H. Kohl (ed.), Frölich & Kaufmann, Berlin: 161–172.

Adams, P.G. (1980) *Travelers and Travel Liars, 1660–1800*, Dover, New York, 2nd edn.

Adams, T.R. (1976) Some Bibliographical Observations on Questions about the Relationship between the Discovery of America and the Invention of Printing, *First Images of America*, F. Chiapelli (ed.), Vol. II, University of California Press, Berkeley: 529–536.

Adorno, R. (1981) On pictorial language and the typology of culture in a New World chronicle, *Semiotica* 36 (1/2): 51–106.

Aerts, W.J. (1987) Herodotus post Herodotum, *Lampas* 20 (3): 215–226.

Affergan, F. (1977) De la relégation à la réclusion: le bestiaire aux Antilles françaises, *Traverses* 8: 53–59.

Albert, B. (1988) La fumée du métal: histoire et représentations du contact chez les Yanomami (Brésil), *L'Homme* XXVIII (2–3): 87–119.

Ardener, E. (1985) Social anthropology and the decline of Modernism, *Reason and Morality*, J. Overing (ed.), ASA Monographs 24, Tavistock, London: 47–70.

Arens, W. (1979) *The Man-Eating Myth: Anthropology and Anthropophagy*, Oxford University Press, Oxford & New York.

Arlet, S. (1781) Lettre du Père Stanislas Arlet, de la Compagnie de Jésus, au Révérend Père Général de la même compagnie; traduite du latin sur une nouvelle mission du Pérou, *Lettres édifiantes et curieuses écrites des missions étrangers. Mémoires d'Amériques*, J.C. Merigot Le Jeune, Paris, VIII: 39–52.

Bal, M. (1984) *Narratologie*, HES, Utrecht [1977].

Balzano, S. (1988) L'ethno-préhistoire des anciens, *Les monstres dans l'imaginaire des indiens d'Amérique latine, Circé 16–19, le monstre 4*, texts collected by Edmundo Magaña, Lettres Modernes, Paris: 141–146.

Barrère, P. (1743) *Nouvelle relation de la France Equinoxiale*, Piget/Damonville & Durand, Paris.

Baschet, J. (1985) Les conceptions de l'enfer à France au XIVe siècle: imaginaire et pouvoir, *Annales ESC* jan.–fév. (1): 185–207.

Basso, E.B. (1985) *A Musical View of the Universe. Kalapalo Myth and Ritual Performances*, University of Pennsylvania Press, Philadelphia.

Baudot, G. & T. Todorov (1983) *Récits aztèques de la conquête*, texts selected and introduced by Georges Baudot and Tzvetan Todorov, du Seuil, Paris.

Baumunk, B.-D. (1982) 'Von Brasilischen fremden Völkern': die Eingeborenen-Darstellungen Albert Eckhouts, *Mythen der Neuen Welt: Zur Entdeckungsgeschichte Lateinamerikas*, K.-H. Kohl (ed.), Frölich & Kaufmann, Berlin: 188–199.

Baxandall, M. (1972) *Painting and Experience in Fifteenth Century Italy: A Primer in the*

Social History of Pictorial Style, Oxford University Press, London.

Benveniste, E. (1969) *Le vocabulaire des institutions indo-européennes*, 2 vols, Minuit, Paris.

Bernardes, M. (n.d.) *Transcriçôes da Nova Floresta*, 3rd edn., A. de Campos (ed.), Bertrand, Lisbon.

Bernasconi, R. (1988) 'Failure of Communication' as a Surplus: Dialogue and Lack of Dialogue between Buber and Levinas, *The Provocation of Levinas, Rethinking the Other*, R. Bernasconi & D. Wood (eds), Routledge, London & New York: 100–135.

Bernheimer, R. (1952) *Wild Men in the Middle Ages*, Harvard University Press, Cambridge, Mass.

Blanckenhagen, P.H. von (1987) Easy monsters, *Monsters and Demons in the Ancient and Medieval Worlds: Papers Presented in Honor of Edith Porada*, A.E. Farkas, P.O. Harper & E.B. Harrison (eds), Philipp von Zabern, Mainz: 85–94.

Blum, Cl. (1983) La folie et la mort dans l'imaginaire collectif du Moyen Age et du débat de la Renaissance (XII–XVI siècles), *Death in the Middle Ages*, H. Braet & W. Verbecke (eds), Mediaevalia Lovaniensia, s.I, Studia IX, Leuven University Press, Leuven: 258–285.

Boer, W. (1973) *Epistola Alexandri ad Aristotelem*, Beiträge zur klassischen Philologie, Band 50, Anton Hain, Meisenheim an Glan.

Boiteux, M. (1987) Voyage au Pays de Cocagne, *Voyager à la Renaissance: Actes du colloque de Tours 1983*, J. Céard & J.-Cl. Margolin (eds), Maisonneuve et Larose, Paris: 557–580.

Bolens-Duvernay, J. (1988) Les Géants Patagons ou l'espace retrouvé: les débuts de la cartographie américaniste, *L'Homme* XXVIII (2–3): 156–173.

Bolton, J.D.P. (1962) *Aristeas of Proconnesus*, Oxford University Press, Oxford.

Boogaart, E. van den (1979) Infernal Allies: The Dutch West India Company and the Tarairiu 1631–1654, *Johan Maurits van Nassau-Siegen 1604–1679: A Humanist Prince in Europe and Brazil*, E. van den Boogaart (ed.), The Johan Maurits van Nassau Stichting, The Hague: 519–538.

Boon, J.A. (1977) *The Anthropological Romance of Bali 1597–1972*, Cambridge University Press, Cambridge.

—— (1982) *Other Tribes, Other Scribes*, Cambridge University Press, London.

Bottigheimer, K.S. (1978) Kingdom and colony: Ireland in the Westward Enterprise 1536–1660, *The Westward Enterprise. English Activities in Ireland, the Atlantic, and America 1480–1650*, K.R. Andrews, N.P. Canny & P.E.H. Hair (eds), Liverpool University Press, Liverpool: 45–64.

Brandão, A.F. (1987) *Dialogues of the Great Things of Brazil*, tr. and annotated by F.A.H. Hall, W.F. Harrison & D.W. Welker, University of New Mexico Press, Albuquerque.

Breuer, J. & S. Freud (1974) *Studies on Hysteria*, Pelican Freud Library, Vol. 3, Penguin, Harmondsworth.

Brotherston, G. (1979) *Image of the New World: The American continent portrayed in native texts*, Thames & Hudson, London.

—— (1985) Towards a grammatology of America: Lévi-Strauss, Derrida, and the native New World text, *Europe and its Others*, F. Barker, P. Hulme, M. Iversen & D. Loxley, University of Essex Press, Colchester, Vol. II: 61–77.

Brundage, B.C. (1979) *The Fifth Sun: Aztec Gods, Aztec World*, University of Texas Press, Austin & London.

Bucher, B. (1981) *Icon and Conquest: A Structural Analysis of the Illustrations of de Bry's Great Voyages*, tr. Basia Miller Gulati, University of Chicago Press, Chicago & London [French edn 1977].

—— (1982) Die Phantasien der Eroberer. Zur graphischen Repräsentation des Kannibalismus in de Brys' 'America', *Mythen der Neuen Welt*, K.-H. Kohl (ed.), Frölich &

Kaufmann, Berlin: 75–91.
Busia, K.A. (1954) The Ashanti, *African Worlds*, D. Forde (ed.) Oxford University Press, Oxford: 190–210.
Câmara Cascudo, L. da (1954) *Dicionário do Folclore Brasileiro*, Instituto Nacional do Livro, Rio de Janeiro.
Carasso-Bulow, L. (1976) *The Merveilleux in Chrétien de Troyes' Romances*, Droz, Geneva.
Cárdenas Ruíz, M. (ed.) (1981) *Crónicas Francesas de los Indios Caribes*, Universidad de Puerto Rico, Puerto Rico.
Carlin, N. (1985) Ireland and natural man in 1649, *Europe and its Others*, F. Barker *et al.*, University of Essex Press, Colchester, Vol. II: 91–111.
Cary, G. (1956) *The Medieval Alexander*, Cambridge University Press, Cambridge [reprinted 1967].
Céard, J. (1977) *La Nature et les prodiges: L'Insolite au XVIe siècle, en France*, Droz, Geneva.
Certeau, M. de (1975) *L'Ecriture de l'histoire*, Gallimard, Paris.
—— (1979) Des outils pour écrire le corps, *Traverses* 14/15, avril: 3–14.
—— (1982) *La Fable mystique XVIe–XVIIe siècle*, Gallimard, Paris.
Chartier, R. (1984) Culture as Appropriation: Popular Cultural Uses in Early Modern France, *Understanding Popular Culture: Europe from the Middle Ages to the 19th Century*, S.L. Kaplan (ed.), Mouton, Berlin-Amsterdam-New York: 229–253.
Christensen, S.O.T. (1987) The image of Europe in Anglo-German travel literature, *Voyager à la Renaissance: Actes du colloque de Tours 1983*, J. Céard & J.-Cl. Margolin (eds), Maisonneuve et Larose, Paris: 257–280.
Civrieux, Marc de (1970) *Watunna: Mitología Makiritare*, Monte Avila Editores, Caracas.
Clarke, S. (1980) Inversion, misrule, and the meaning of witchcraft, *Past and Present* 87: 98–127.
Clastres, H. (1987) Religion without gods: the sixteenth-century chroniclers and the South American savages, *History and Anthropology*, Vol. 3: 61–82.
Cohen, E. (1986) Law, folklore and animal lore, *Past and Present* 110: 8–37.
Cohn, N. (1975) *Europe's Inner Demons: An Enquiry Inspired by the Great Witch-hunt*, Sussex University Press & Heinemann, London.
Colin, S. (1987) The Wild Man and the Indian in early 16th century book illustration, *Indians and Europe*, C.F. Feest (ed.), Herodot/Rader Verlag, Göttingen/Aachen: 5–36.
Colón, C. (1984) *Textos y documentos completos*, prologue and notes by Consuelo Varela, Alianza Editorial, Madrid, 2nd edn.
Corbey, R. (1989) *Wildheid en beschaving*, Ambo, Baarn.
Cumming, W.P., R.A. Skelton & D.B. Quinn (1971) *The Discovery of North America*, Elek, London.
Davis, N.Z. (1975) *Society and Culture in Early Modern France*, Stanford University Press, Stanford, California.
Delatte, A. (1914) Etudes sur la magie grecque V. Akephalos Theos, *Bulletin de Correspondance Hellénique*, XXXVIII: 189–249.
Deleuze, G. (1986) *Foucault*, Minuit, Paris.
Deluz, C. (1987) Le Livre Jehan de Mandeville, autorité géographique à la Renaissance, *Voyager à la Renaissance: Actes du colloque de Tours 1983*, J. Céard & J.-Cl. Margolin (eds), Maisonneuve et Larose, Paris: 205–220.
Derrida, J. (1967a) *De la grammatologie*, Minuit, Paris.
—— (1967b) *Ecriture et différence*, du Seuil, Paris.
—— (1972a) *Marges*, Minuit, Paris.
—— (1972b) *La Dissémination*, du Seuil, Paris.
—— (1978a) *Eperons: Les Styles de Nietzsche*, Flammarion, Paris.

—— (1978b) *La Vérité en Peinture*, Flammarion, Paris.

—— (1983) Mes chances: Au rendez-vous de quelques stéréophonies épicuriennes, *Tijdschrift voor Filosofie*, 45 (1), mars: 3–40.

—— (1987a) *Psyché: Inventions de l'autre*, Galilée, Paris.

—— (1987b) Ulysse gramophone: Deux mots pour Joyce, Galilée, Paris.

Detienne, M. (1972) *Les Jardins d'Adonis*, Gallimard, Paris.

Devereux, G (1956) A note on the feminine significance of the eyes, *Bulletin of the Philadelphia Association for Psychoanalysis* 6: 21–24.

—— (1980) *Basic Problems of Ethnopsychiatry*, University of Chicago Press, Chicago & London.

—— (1981) *Baubo: Die mythische Vulva*, Syndikat, Frankfurt am Main.

—— (1983) Les blessures d'Hektor et les messages vers l'autre monde, *L'Homme* 23 (1): 135–137.

Diderot, D. (1951) *Oeuvres*, compiled and annotated by André Billy, Gallimard, Paris.

Donnellan, K.S. (1977) Speaking of nothing, *Naming, Necessity and Natural Kinds*, S.P. Schwartz (ed.), Cornell University Press, Ithaca, NY & London: 216–244.

Dresen-Coenders, L. (1985) De heks als duivelsboel, *Tussen heks en heilige*, exhibition catalogue, Nijmeegs Museum 'Commanderie van Sint-Jan', SUN, Nijmegen: 59–82.

Dreyer-Eimbcke, O. (1982) Mythisches, Irrtümliches und Merkwürdiges im Kartenbild Lateinamerikas während der Entdeckungszeit, *Mythen der Neuen Welt: Zur Entdeckungsgeschichte Lateinamerikas*, K.-H. Kohl (ed.), Frölich & Kaufmann, Berlin: 121–125.

Duala-M'bedy, M. (1977) *Xenologie: Die Wissenschaft vom Fremden und die Verdrängung der Humanität in der Anthropologie*, Verlag Karl Alber, Freiburg & Munich.

Duchet, M. (1971) *Anthropologie et Histoire au siècle des Lumières*, Maspero, Paris.

—— (1985) *Le partage des savoirs: Discours historique et discours ethnologique*, La Découverte, Paris.

Duerr, H.P. (1985) *Dreamtime: Concerning the Boundary between Wilderness and Civilization*, tr. F. Goudman, Basil Blackwell, Oxford [1978].

Durán, D. (1967) *Historia de las Indias de Nueva España e Islas de la tierra firme*, A. Ma. Garibay K. (ed.), Editorial Porrua, Mexico.

Duverger, Chr. (1983) *L'Origine des Aztèques*, du Seuil, Paris.

Duviols, J.-P. (1982) La colonie de Florida (1562–1565) et la découverte de nouveaux 'sauvages', *Etudes sur L'Impact Culturel du Nouveau Monde* II, L'Harmattan, Paris: 31–43.

Edel, D. (1985) Antipoden, ankers en een wereld-onder-het-water, *Tussentijds: Bundel studies aangeboden aan W.P. Gerritsen ter gelegenheid van zijn vijftigste verjaardag*, A.M.J. van Buuren, H. van Dijk, O.S.H. Lie & F.P. van Oostrom (eds), H&S, Utrecht:101–114.

Egmond, F. (1987) The noble and the ignoble bandit: Changing literary representations of West-European robbers, *Ethnologia Europaea* XVII: 139–156.

Erasmus, D. (1928) *Opus epistolarum*, P.S. Allen, (ed.) Clarendon Press, Oxford.

Erdheim, M. & M. Nadig (1987) Wissenschaft, Unbewusstheit und Herrschaft, *Die wilde Seele, Zur Ethnopsychoanalyse von Georges Devereux*, H.P. Duerr (ed.), Suhrkamp, Frankfurt am Main: 163–176.

Evans, E.P. (1987) *The Criminal Prosecution and Capital Punishment of Animals* [with a foreword by Nicholas Humphrey], Faber & Faber, London [1906].

Fabian, J. 1983 *Time and the Other: How Anthropology Makes Its Object*, Columbia University Press, New York.

Feest, C.F. (1987) Indians and Europe? Editor's postscript, *Indians and Europe*, C.F. Feest (ed.), Herodot/Rader, Aachen: 609–628.

Filedt Kok, J.P. (1985) *Livelier than Life: The Master of the Amsterdam Cabinet or the Housebook Master, ca. 1470–1500*, Rijksmuseum, Amsterdam.

Filedt Kok, J.P., W. Halsema-Kubes & W. Th. Kloek (eds) (1986) *Kunst voor de beeldenstorm, Catalogus*, Staatsuitgeverij, The Hague.

Fischer, H.G. (1987) The Ancient Egyptian attitude towards the monstrous, *Monsters and Demons in the Ancient and Medieval Worlds: Papers Presented in Honor of Edith Porada*, A.E. Farkas, P.O. Harper & E.B. Harrison (eds), Philipp von Zabern, Mainz: 13–26.

Fischer, J.-L. (1985) Lafitau et l'acéphale: une preuve 'tératologique' du monogénisme, *Naissance de l'ethnologie? Anthropologie et Missions en Amérique XVIe-XVIIIe siècle*, C. Blanckaert (ed.), Du Cerf, Paris: 91–101.

Fock, N. (1963) *Waiwai: Religion and Society of an Amazonian Tribe*, Nationalmuseets Skrifter, Etnografisk Raekke 8, National Museum, Copenhagen.

Fontenelle, B. (1724) *De l'origine des fables*, Paris.

Forster, E.M. (1924) *A passage to India*, Penguin, Harmondsworth (1985).

Foucault, M. (1961) *Histoire de la folie à l'âge classique*, Plon, Paris.

—— (1966) *Les Mots et les Choses*, Gallimard, Paris.

—— (1975) *Surveillir et punir: naissance de la prison*, Gallimard, Paris.

—— (1976) *Histoire de la sexualité I: La volonté de savoir*, Gallimard, Paris.

—— (1980) *Power/Knowledge: Selected Interviews and Other Writings 1972–1977*, Colin Gordon (ed.), Pantheon Books, New York.

—— (1984a) *Histoire de la sexualité II: L'Usage des plaisirs*, Gallimard, Paris

—— (1984b) *Histoire de la sexualité III: Le Souci de soi*, Gallimard, Paris.

Freud, S. (1940–52) *Gesammelte Werke*, Fischer Verlag, Frankfurt.

—— (1977) *On Sexuality*, Penguin Freud Library, Vol. 7, Penguin, Harmondsworth.

Friedman, J. Block (1981) *The Monstrous Races in Medieval Art and Thought*, Harvard University Press, Cambridge, Mass. & London.

Gagnon, F. (1975) Le thème médiéval de l'homme sauvage dans les premières représentations des Indiens d'Amérique, *Aspects de la marginalité au Moyen Age*, G.-H. Allard (ed.), L'Aurore, Montreal: 82–99.

Gaignebet, Cl. & J. -D. Lajoux (1985) *Art profane et religion populaire au Moyen Age*, Presses Universitaires de France, Paris.

Gerbi, A. (1973) *The Dispute of the New World: The History of a Polemic, 1750–1900*, rev. and enlarged edn, tr. Jeremy Moyle, University of Pittsburgh Press, Pittsburgh.

Gernet, L. (1968) *Anthropologie de la Grèce antique*, Maspero, Paris.

Gerritsen, W.P., D. Edel & M. de Kreek (1986) *De Wereld van Sint Brandaan*, H&S, Utrecht.

Gil, J. (1984) Introducción, C. Colón, *Textos y documentos completos*, prologue and notes by Consuelo Varela, Alianza Editorial, Madrid, 2nd edn: IX–LXVIII.

Gilij, F.S. (1987) *Ensayo de historia americana*, Fuentes para la historia colonial de Venezuela, 3 vols, Biblioteca de la Academia Nacional de la Historia, Caracas [1965].

Ginzburg, C. (1980) *The Cheese and the Worms: The Cosmos of a Sixteenth-Century Miller*, tr. John & Anne Tedeschi, Routledge & Kegan Paul, London.

—— (1981) Charivari, associations juvéniles, chasse sauvage, *Le Charivari*, J. Le Goff & J.-C. Schmitt (eds), EHESS Paris/Mouton, Paris-The Hague-New York: 131–140.

—— (1983) *The Night Battles*, tr. John & Anne Tedeschi, Routledge & Kegan Paul, London.

—— (1984) The Witches' Sabbat: popular cult or inquisitorial stereotype?, *Understanding Popular Culture: Europe from the Middle Ages to the 19th Century*, S.L. Kaplan (ed.), Mouton, Berlin-Amsterdam-New York: 39–51.

—— (1986) *Miti Emblemi Spie. Morfologia e storia*, Einaudi, Turin.

—— (1989) *Storia Notturna*, Einaudi, Turin.

Goldmann, S. (1982) Der Kasten des Alt-Vater Noah, *Mythen der Neuen Welt*, K.-H. Kohl (ed.), Frölich & Kaufmann, Berlin: 155–160.

Gombrich, E. (1959) *Art and Illusion*, Phaidon, London.

Gordon, E. (1957) *An Introduction to Old Norse*, 2nd edn revised by A.R. Taylor, Oxford University Press, Oxford.

Graulich, M. (1987) Mythes et rituels du Mexique ancien préhispanique, Académie de Belgique, Brussels.

Greenblatt, S. (1976) Learning to curse: aspects of linguistic colonialism in the sixteenth century, *First Images of America*, F. Chiapelli (ed.), University of California Press, Berkeley, Vol. II: 561–580.

Gruzinski, S. (1979) La mère dévorante: alcoolisme, sexualité et déculturation chez les Mexicas (1500–1550), *Cahiers des Amériques Latines* 20, 2ème semestre: 7–36.

Gunderson, L.L. (1980) *Alexander's Letter to Aristotle about India*, Beiträge zur klassischen Philologie, Heft 110, Anton Hain, Meisenheim an Glan.

Guss, D. (1986) Keeping it oral: a Yekuana ethnology, *American Ethnologist* 13 (3), August: 413–429.

Hamell, G. (1987) Mohawks abroad: the 1764 Amsterdam etching of Sychnecta, *Indians and Europe*, C.F. Feest (ed.), Herodot/Rader, Aachen: 175–193.

Harbsmeier, M. (1985) Early travels to Europe: some remarks on the magic of writing, *Europe and its Others*, F. Barker *et al.*, University of Essex Press, Colchester, Vol. I: 72–88.

—— (1986a) Beyond anthropology, *Folk* 28: 33–59.

—— (1986b) Die Entdeckung mündlicher Kulturen. Texte deutschsprachiger Entdeck- ungsreisender des 16. bis 18. Jahrhunderts, *Sozialwissenschaftliche Inform- ationen*, Jahrgang 15, Heft 3: 5–12.

—— (1987) Elementary structures of otherness: an analysis of sixteenth-century German travel accounts, *Voyager à la Renaissance: Actes du colloque de Tours 1983*, J. Céard & J.-Cl. Margolin (eds), Maisonneuve et Larose, Paris: 337–355.

Hartog, F. (1980) *Le Miroir d'Hérodote. Essai sur la représentation de l'autre*, Gallimard, Paris.

Hawkins, J. (1984) *Inverse Images: The Meaning of Culture, Ethnicity and Family in Postcolonial Guatemala*, University of New Mexico Press, Albuquerque.

Heidegger, M. (1972) *Sein und Zeit*, Niemeyer Verlag, Tübingen.

Heinzelman, K. (1980) *The Economics of the Imagination*, University of Massachusetts Press, Amherst.

Held, J. (1987) Between bourgeois enlightenment and popular culture: Goya's festivals, old women, monsters and blind men, *History Workshop* 23: 39–58.

Helms, M.W. (1988) *Ulysses' Sail: An Ethnographic Odyssey of Power, Knowledge, and Geographical Distance*, Princeton University Press, Princeton, New Jersey.

Henderson and Harrington (1914) Ethnozoology of the Tewa Indians, *Bulletin of the Bureau of American Ethnology* 54.

Henrichs, A. (1980) Human sacrifice in Greek religion: three case studies, *Le Sacrifice dans l'antiquité, Fondation Hardt Entretiens XXVII*, Vandoeuvres-Genève: 195–235.

Hirsch, R. (1976) Printed reports on the early discoveries and their reception, *First Images of America*, F. Chiapelli (ed.), vol. II, University of California Press, Berkeley: 537–552.

Hirst, P. Q. (1985) Is it rational to reject relativism?, *Reason and Morality*, J. Overing (ed.), ASA Monographs 24, Tavistock, London & New York: 85–103.

Honour, H. (1975) *The New Golden Land: European Images of America from the Discoveries to the Present Time*, Allen Lane, London.

—— (1976) *The European Vision of America*, Cleveland Museum of Art and the National Gallery Washington, Cleveland.

—— (1979) Science and exoticism: The European artist and the non-European world before Johan Maurits, *Johan Maurits van Nassau-Siegen 1604–1679: A Humanist Prince in Europe and Brazil*, E. van den Boogaart (ed.), The Johan Maurits van Nassau Stichting, The Hague: 269–296.

Hugh-Jones, S. (1979) *The Palm and the Pleiades: Initiation and Cosmology in Northwest Amazonia*, Cambridge University Press, Cambridge.

—— (1988) The gun and the bow: Myths of white men and Indians, *L'Homme* XXVIII (2–3): 138–155.

Hulme, P. (1978) Columbus and the cannibals: A study of the reports of anthropophagy in the Journal of Christopher Columbus, *Ibero-Amerikanisches Archiv* (new series) 4: 115–139.

—— (1985) Polytropic man: tropes of sexuality and mobility in early colonial discourse, *Europe and its Others*, F. Barker *et al.*, University of Essex Press, Colchester, Vol. II: 17–32.

—— (1986) *Colonial Encounters: Europe and the Native Caribbean 1492–1979*, Methuen, London.

Hulsius, L. (1599) *Die Fuenffte Kurtze Wunderbare Beschreibung Dess Goldreichen Königreichs Guianae in America oder neuen Welt...*, Nuremberg.

Idoyaga Molina, A. (1988) La perception des autres: Anatomie et conduites anormales des personnages mythiques des Indiens Pilagá (Chaco Central), *Les monstres dans l'imaginaire des indiens d'Amérique latine, Circé 16–19, le monstre 4*, texts collected by Edmundo Magaña, Lettres Modernes, Paris: 99–106.

Irizarry, E. (1983) Echoes of the Amazon myth in medieval Spanish literature, *Women in Hispanic Literature: Icons and Fallen Idols*, B. Miller (ed.), University of California Press, Berkeley-Los Angeles-London: 53–66.

Jacob, Chr. (1980–81) Paysages hantés et jardins merveilleux: La Grèce imaginaire de Pausanias, *L'Ethnographie* CXXII^e année, LXXVI, 81–82: 35–67.

—— (1987) Le voyage de Pierre Gilles et la tradition des géographes grecs mineurs, *Voyager à la Renaissance: Actes du colloque de Tours 1983*, J. Céard & J.-Cl. Margolin (eds), Maisonneuve et Larose, Paris: 65–85.

Jansen, M. (1982) *Huisi Tacu: Estudio interpretativo de un libro mixteco antiguo: Codex Vindobonensis Mexicanus I*, 2 vols, CEDLA Incidental Publications 24, CEDLA, Amsterdam.

—— (1984) El Códice Ríos y Fray Pedro de los Ríos, *Boletín de Estudios Latino-americanos y del Caribe* 36: 69–81.

Janson, H.W. (1952) *Apes and Ape-Lore in the Middle Ages and the Renaissance*, The Warburg Institute, London.

Jara, F. (1988) Monstruosité et altérité: le mythe des Amazones des Indiens Kalina et Xikrin, *Les monstres dans l'imaginaire des indiens d'Amérique latine, Circé 16–19, le monstre 4*, texts collected by Edmundo Magaña, Lettres Modernes, Paris: 49–79.

Jara, F. & E. Magaña (1980) The jaguar against the wolf: analysis of a myth of the Kamayura Indians (Central Brazil), *Boletín de Estudios Latinoamericanos y del Caribe* 29: 3–31.

—— Rules of imperialist method, *Dialectical Anthropology* 7: 115–136.

Joppien, R. (1979) The Dutch vision of Brazil: Johan Maurits and his artists, *Johan Maurits van Nassau-Siegen 1604–1679, A Humanist Prince in Europe and Brazil*, E. van den Boogaart (ed.), The Johan Maurits van Nassau Stichting, The Hague: 297–376.

Kant, I. (1934) *Critique of Pure Reason* tr. J.M.D. Meiklejohn, Everyman, London.

Kappler, Cl. (1980) *Monstres, démons et merveilles à la fin du Moyen Age*, Payot, Paris.

Kaye, J. (1985) Islamic imperialism and the question of some ideas of 'Europe', *Europe and its Others*, F. Barker *et al.*, University of Essex Press, Colchester, Vol. I: 59–71.

Kirk, G.S. (1970) *Myth: Its Meaning and Functions in Ancient and Other Cultures*, University of California Press & Cambridge University Press, Cambridge & Berkeley.

—— (1980) Some methodological pitfalls in the study of ancient Greek sacrifice (in particular), *Le Sacrifice dans l'antiquité, Fondation Hardt Entretiens XXVII*, Vandoeuvres-Genève: 41–80.

Klaus, C. (1985) Les monstres dans l'Architrenius de Jean de Hanville, *Métamorphose et Bestiaire Fantastique au Moyen Age*, L. Harf-Lancner (ed.), Collection de l'Ecole Normale Supérieure de Jeunes Filles 28, Paris: 185–211.

Knefelkamp, U. (1989) Vom Nutzen einer Begegnung: der Bericht der ersten portugiesischen Gesandtschaft nach Äthiopien (1520–1526), *Der europäischer Beobachter aussereuropäischer Kulturen*, H.-J. König, W. Reinhard & R. Wendt (eds), Zeitschrift für Historische Forschung Beiheft 7, Duncker & Humblot, Berlin: 135–151.

Knefelkamp, U. & H.-J. König (eds) (1989) *Die Neuen Welten in alten Büchern. Entdeckung und Eroberung in frühen deutschen Schrift- und Bildzeugnissen*, Staatsbibliothek Bamberg.

Knock, A. (1978) The 'Liber Monstrorum': an unpublished manuscript and some reconsiderations, *Scriptorium* 32 (1): 19–28.

Kohl, K.-H. (1981) *Entzauberter Blick*, Medusa, Berlin.

—— (1987) *Abwehr und Verlangen*, Qumran, Frankfurt.

Kohl, K.-H. (ed.) (1982) *Mythen der Neuen Welt: Zur Entdeckungsgeschichte Lateinamerikas*, Frölich & Kaufmann, Berlin.

Korinman, S. (1987) Symon Grynaeus et le 'Novus Orbis': les pouvoirs d'une collection, *Voyager à la Renaissance. Actes du colloque de Tours 1983*, J. Céard & J.-Cl. Margolin (eds), Maisonneuve et Larose, Paris: 419–431.

Lacan, J. (1971) *Ecrits I & II*, du Seuil, Paris.

Lafitau, J.-F (1724) *Moeurs des sauvages amériquains comparées aux moeurs des premiers temps*, 2 vols, Paris.

Launay-Demonet, M.-L. (1987) Les mots sauvages: étude des listes utiles à ceux qui veulent naviguer, *Voyager à la Renaissance: Actes du colloque de Tours 1983*, J. Céard & J.-Cl. Margolin (eds), Maisonneuve et Larose, Paris: 497–508.

Le Bot, M. (1988) Un corps sans ride, *Le Génie de la Ponctuation, Traverses* 43, février: 11–17.

Le Goff, J. (1977) *Pour un autre Moyen Age*, Gallimard, Paris.

—— (1981) *La Naissance du Purgatoire*, Gallimard, Paris.

—— (1982) Saint Louis et les corps royaux, *Le Temps de la Réflexion* 3: 255–284.

—— (1984) The Learned and Popular Dimensions of Journeys in the Otherworld in the Middle Ages, *Understanding Popular Culture. Europe from the Middle Ages to the 19th Century*, S.L. Kaplan (ed.), Mouton, Berlin, Amsterdam & New York: 19–37 (reprinted in Le Goff, 1985).

—— (1985) *L'Imaginaire médiévale*, Gallimard, Paris.

Le Roy Ladurie, Emmanuel (1979) *Le Carnaval de Romans: De la Chandeleur au mercredi des cendres 1579–1580*, Gallimard, Paris.

Lecouteux, Cl. (1982) *Les Monstres dans la littérature allemande du Moyen Age*, Kümmerle Verlag, Göppingen, 3 vols.

Leerssen, J. Th. (1986) On the edge of Europe: Ireland in search of oriental roots, 1650–1850, *Comparative Criticism* 8: 91–112.

Léry, J. de (1980) *Histoire d'un voyage faict en la terre du Brésil*, Plasma, Paris [1578].

Lestringant, F. (1982) Catholiques et cannibales: le thème du cannibalisme dans le discours protestant au temps des guerres de religion, *Pratiques et Discours Alimentaires à la Renaissance*, J.-Cl. Margolin & R. Sauzet (eds), Maisonneuve et Larose, Paris: 233–245.

—— (1987a) The myth of the Indian monarchy: an aspect of the controversy between Thevet and Léry (1575–1585), *Indians and Europe*, C.F. Feest (ed.), Herodot/Rader Verlag, Göttingen/Aachen: 37–60.

—— (1987b) La flèche du Patagon ou la preuve des lointains: sur un chapitre d'André Thevet, *Voyager à la Renaissance. Actes du colloque de Tours 1983*, J. Céard & J.-Cl. Margolin (eds), Maisonneuve et Larose, Paris: 467–496.

Lévêque, P. & P. Vidal-Naquet (1973) *Clisthène l'Athénien*, Annales Littéraires de l'Université de Besançon, Vol. 65, Les Belles Lettres, Paris.

Lévi-Strauss, Cl. (1955) *Tristes Tropiques*, Plon, Paris.

—— (1958) *Anthropologie structurale*, Plon, Paris.

—— (1966) *Mythologiques II: Du miel aux cendres*, Plon, Paris.

—— (1968) *Mythologiques III: L'Origine des manières de table*, Plon, Paris.

—— (1982) Eine Idylle bei den Indianern: über Jean de Léry, *Mythen der Neuen Welt. Zur Entdeckungsgeschichte Lateinamerikas*, K.-H. Kohl (ed.), Frölich & Kaufmann, Berlin: 68–70.

—— (1983) *Le Régard éloigné*, Plon, Paris.

—— (1984) *Paroles données*, Plon, Paris.

—— (1985) *La Potière jalouse*, Plon, Paris.

Levinas, E. (1957) La philosophie et l'idée de l'Infini, *Revue de Métaphysique et de Morale* 62: 241–253.

—— (1978) *Autrement qu'être ou au-delà de l'essence*, Nijhoff, The Hague, 2nd edn.

—— (1979) *Totality and Infinity*, tr. A. Lingis, Nijhoff, The Hague, 2nd edn.

—— (1988) The paradox of morality: an interview with Emmanual Levinas, *The Provocation of Levinas. Rethinking the Other*, R. Bernasconi & D. Wood (eds), Routledge, London & New York: 168–180.

Lie, O.S.H. (1988) Antipodenleer in de middeleeuwen: botsing tussen geloof en wetenschap, *Culturen in contact*, R.E.V. Stuip & C. Vellekoop (eds), H&S, Utrecht: 167–183.

López Austin, A. (1980) *Cuerpo humano e ideología: Las concepciones de los antiguos Nahuas*, Universidad Nacional Autónoma de México, Mexico.

Lyotard, J.-F. (1979) *La condition postmoderne*, Minuit, Paris.

—— (1983) *Le Différend*, Minuit, Paris.

Maçzak, A. (1987) Renaissance travellers' power of measuring, *Voyager à la Renaissance: Actes du colloque de Tours 1983*, J. Céard & J.-Cl. Margolin (eds), Maisonneuve et Larose, Paris: 245–256.

Magaña, E. (1982a) Note on ethnoanthropological notions of the Guiana Indians, *Anthropologica* XXIV: 215–233.

—— (1982b) Hombres salvajes y razas monstruosas de los Indios Kaliña de Surinam, *Journal of Latin American Lore* 8 (1): 63–114.

—— (1985) Review of John Block Friedman, 'The Monstrous Races in Medieval Art and Thought' and Claude Kappler, 'Monstres, Démons et Merveilles à la fin du Moyen Age', *Anthropos* 80: 299–303.

—— (1986) Paisajes, hombres y animales imaginarios de algunas tribus Gê del Brasil Central, *Myth and the Imaginary in the New World*, E. Magaña & P. Mason (eds), CEDLA Latin America Studies 34, CEDLA/FORIS, Amsterdam/Dordrecht: 95–164.

—— (1987a) *Contribuciones al estudio de la mitología y astronomía de los indios de las Guayanas*, CEDLA Latin America Studies 35, CEDLA/FORIS, Amsterdam/Dordrecht.

—— (1987b) 'De la lógica en los mitos' por Juan Rivano, *Revista de Filosofía* Vol. XXIX–XXX, nov.: 115–122.

—— (1988a) *Orión y la mujer Pléyades. Simbolismo astronómico de los indios kaliña de Surinam*, CEDLA Latin America Studies 44, CEDLA/FORIS, Amsterdam/Dordrecht.

—— (1988b) El cuerpo y la cocina en la mitología wayana, tareno y kalina, *América Indígena* XLVIII (3): 571–604.

—— (1988c) Ethnographie imaginaire et pratiques culinaires, *Les monstres dans l'imaginaire des indiens d'Amérique latine, Circé 16–19, le monstre 4*, texts collected by Edmundo Magaña, Lettres Modernes, Paris: 7–47.

—— (forthcoming) La gente pecarí, el sacerdote caníbal y otras historias: los otros en el testimonio y la imaginación de las poblaciones selváticas, *Antropológica*, Caracas.

Magaña, E. & P. Mason (1986) Tales of Otherness, myths, stars and Plinian men in South America, *Myth and the Imaginary in the New World*, E. Magaña & P. Mason (eds), CEDLA Latin America Studies 34, CEDLA/FORIS, Amsterdam/Dordrecht: 7–40.

Mahn-Lot, M. (1987) Voyages d'exploration en Amérique espagnole: le mythe de 'El Dorado', *Voyager à la Renaissance: Actes du colloque de Tours 1983*, J. Céard & J.-Cl. Margolin (eds), Maisonneuve et Larose, Paris: 409–415.

Mandeville, J. (1973) *The Metrical Version of Mandeville's Travels*, M.C. Seymour (ed.), Early English Text Society, Oxford University Press, London.

—— (1983) *The Travels of Sir John Mandeville*, tr. C.W.R.D. Moseley, Penguin, Harmondsworth.

Margolin, J.-Cl. (1987) Voyager à la Renaissance, *Voyager à la Renaissance: Actes du colloque de Tours 1983*, J. Céard & J.-Cl. Margolin (eds), Maisonneuve et Larose, Paris: 9–34.

Marx, K. & Fr. Engels (1973–) *Collected Works*, Lawrence & Wishart, London.

Mason, P. (1983) The city of men, *The Future of Structuralism*, J.G. Oosten & A. de Ruijter (eds), Herodot, Göttingen: 253–281.

—— (1984) *The City of Men: Ideology, Sexual Politics and Social Formation*, Herodot & Rader, Göttingen & Aachen.

—— (1986) Imaginary worlds, counterfact and artefact, *Myth and the Imaginary in the New World*, E. Magaña & P. Mason (eds), CEDLA Latin America Studies 34, CEDLA/FORIS, Amsterdam/Dordrecht, 43–73.

—— (1987a) Notes on cormorant fishing: Europe and its others, *Ibero-Amerikanisches Archiv* (new series) 13 (2): 147–174.

—— (1987b) Third person/second sex: patterns of sexual asymmetry in the *Theogony* of Hesiodos, *Sexual Asymmetry*, J. Blok & P. Mason (eds), Gieben, Amsterdam: 147–189.

—— (1987c) Seduction from afar: Europe's inner Indians, *Anthropos* 82: 581–601.

—— (1988) The excommunication of caterpillars, *Social Science Information* 27 (2): 265–273.

—— (1989a) Review of D. Chevallier, 'L'Homme, le porc, l'abeille et le chien', *Anthrozoös* II (4): 278–280.

—— (1989b) The ethnography of the Old World mind: Indians and Europe, *Anthropos* 84 (4–6): 549–554.

—— (1989c) Betrayal and portrayal: the colonial gaze in seventeenth century Brazil, *Culture & History* 6: 37–62.

—— (forthcoming a) Una disputa entre frailes y hormigas. Un caso de excomunión y un problema de definición etno-etnológico, *Scripta Ethnologica*.

—— (forthcoming b) Continental incontinence. *Horror vacui* and the colonial supplement, *Yearbook of European Studies*.

—— (forthcoming c) Half a Calf, *Semiotica*.

—— (forthcoming d) Classical Ethnology in the Perception of the Peoples of the New World, *The Classical Tradition and the Americas*, M. Reinhold, J.R. Fears and W. Haase (eds), Walter de Gruyter, Berlin and New York.

Mauss, M. (1950) *Sociologie et Anthropologie*, Presses Universitaires de France, Paris.

Mély, F. de (1897) Le 'De Monstris' chinois et les bestiaires occidentaux, *Revue Archéo-*

logique (3rd series) XXXI: 353–373.

Milhou, A. (1981–83) De la destruction de l'Espagne à la destruction des Indes: histoire sacrée et combats idéologiques, *Etudes sur l'impact culturel du Nouveau Monde* I (1981: 25–47) and III (1983: 11–54), L'Harmattan, Paris.

Mitter, P. (1977) *Much Maligned Monsters: History of European Reactions to Indian Art*, Clarendon Press, Oxford.

Moebus, J. (1982) Uber die Bestimmung des Wilden und die Entwicklung der Verwertungsstandpunkts bei Kolumbus, *Mythen der Neuen Welt: Zur Entdeckungsgeschichte Lateinamerikas*, K.-H. Kohl (ed.), Frölich & Kaufmann, Berlin: 49–56.

Molenaar, H. (1985) Odinns Gift: Betekenis en Werking van de Skandinavische Mythologie, Ph.D. thesis, University of Leiden.

Momigliano, A. (1975) *Alien Wisdom: The Limits of Hellenization*, Cambridge University Press, Cambridge.

Mommsen, Th. (1895) *C. Iulii Solini, Collectanea Rerum Memorabilium*, iterum recensuit Th. Mommsen, Weidmann, Berlin.

Moore, R.I. (1987) *The Formation of a Persecuting Society*, Basil Blackwell, Oxford & New York.

Müller, K. (1972) *Geschichte der Antiken Ethnographie und ethnologischen Theoriebildung*, I, Franz Steiner Verlag, Wiesbaden.

Mustapha, M. (1982) Progrès de connaissances géographiques et idée de progrès chez les chroniqueurs de la découverte, de Pierre d'Anghiera à López de Gómara et José de Acosta, *Etudes sur l'Impact Culturel du Nouveau Monde* II, L'Harmattan, Paris: 9–29.

Myers, R. (1984) Island Carib Cannibalism, *Nieuwe West-Indische Gids* 58 (3–4): 147–184.

Nardi, B. (1965) *Studi su Pietro Pomponazzi*, Felice le Monnier, Florence.

Needham, R. (1978) *Primordial Characters*, University Press of Virginia, Charlottesville.

Neuber, W. (1989) Die frühen deutschen Reiseberichte aus der Neuen Welt. Fiktionalitätsverdacht und Beglaubigungsstrategien, *Der europäischer Beobachter aussereuropäischer Kulturen*, H.-J. König, W. Reinhard & R. Wendt (eds), Zeitschrift für Historische Forschung Beiheft 7, Duncker & Humblot, Berlin: 43–64.

Nietzsche, F. (1955) *Werke in Drie Bänden*, K. Slechta (ed.), Hanser, Munich.

Nieuhof, J. (1673) *An Embassy from the East-Indian Company of the United Provinces to the Grand Tartar Cham Emperor of China*, tr. John Ogilby, London [2nd edn].

Oexle, O.G. (1983) Die Gegenwart der Toten, H. Braet & W. Verbeke (eds), *Death in the Middle Ages*, Mediaevalia Lovaniensia, Series 1, Studia IX, Leuven University Press: 19–77.

O'Gorman, E. (1961) *The Invention of America: An Inquiry into the Historical Nature of the New World and the Meaning of its History*, University of Indiana Press, Bloomington.

Olschki, L. (1941) Ponce de León's fountain of youth: history of a geographical myth, *Hispanic American Historical Review* XXI (3): 361–385.

Osterhammel, J. (1989) Distanzerfahrung. Darstellungsweisen des Fremden im 18 Jahrhundert, *Der europäischer Beobachter aussereuropäischer Kulturen*, H.-J. König, W. Reinhard & R. Wendt (eds) Zeitschrift für Historische Forschung Beiheft 7, Duncker & Humblot, Berlin: 9–42.

Overing, J. (1985a) Today I shall call him 'Mummy': multiple worlds and classificatory confusion, *Reason and Morality*, J. Overing (ed.), ASA Monographs 24, Tavistock, London & New York: 152–179.

—— (1985b) There is no end of evil: the guilty innocents and their fallible god, *The Anthropology of Evil*, D. Parkin (ed.), Basil Blackwell, Oxford: 244–278.

—— (1986a) Images of cannibalism, death and domination in a 'non-violent' society, *The Anthropology of Violence*, D. Ricker (ed.), Basil Blackwell, Oxford: 86–102.

—— (1986b) Men control women? The 'Catch 22' in the analysis of gender, *International Journal of Moral and Social Studies* 1 (2): 135–156.

Overing, J. (ed.) (1985) *Reason and Morality*, ASA Monographs 24, Tavistock, London.

Pagden, A. (1982) *The Fall of Natural Man: The American Indian and the Origins of Comparative Ethnology*, Cambridge Iberian and Latin American Studies, Cambridge University Press, Cambridge.

Panofsky, E. (1962) *Studies in Iconology: Humanistic Themes in the Art of the Renaissance*, Harper, New York.

—— (1970) *Meaning in the Visual Arts*, Penguin, Harmondsworth.

Parroni, P.G. (1976) Ad Melae Chorogr. 3,103, *Rivista di Filologia*, 104: 417–419.

Parry, J. (1985) The Brahmanical tradition and the technology of the intellect, *Reason and Morality*, J. Overing (ed.), ASA Monographs 24, Tavistock, London: 200–225.

Pautrat, B. (1971) *Versions du soleil: Figures et système de Nietzsche*, du Seuil, Paris.

Pédech, P. (1984) *Historiens Compagnons d'Alexandre*, Les Belles Lettres, Paris.

Pedersen, K. (1987) European Indians and Indian Europeans: aspects of reciprocal cultural and social classification on the Brazilian East Coast in the early period of contact, *Natives and Neighbors in South America. Anthropological Essays*, H.O. Skar & F. Salomon (eds), Etnologiska Studier 38, Göteborgs Etnografiska Museum, Göteborg: 382–416.

Pellizer, E. (1979) Il fodero e la spada: metis amorosa e ginecofobia nell' episodio di Circe, Od. X. 133ss., *Quaderni Urbinati di Cultura Classica* n.s. 1, vol. 30: 67–82.

Penel, J.D. (1982) *Homo caudatus: Les hommes à queue d'Afrique Centrale: un avatar de l'imaginaire occidental*, Société d'Études Linguistiques et Anthropologiques de France, Paris.

Pennington, L.E. (1978) The Amerindian in English promotional literature 1575–1625, *The Westward Enterprise: English Activities in Ireland, the Atlantic, and America 1480–1650*, K.R. Andrews, N.P. Canny & P.E.H. Hair (eds), Liverpool University Press, Liverpool: 175–194.

Pérez-Diez, A.A. (1988) Personnages aux attributs monstrueux dans la mythologie des Indiens Mataco riverains du Chaco central (Argentine), *Les monstres dans l'imaginaire des indiens d'Amérique latine, Circé 16–19, le monstre 4*, texts collected by Edmundo Magaña, Lettres Modernes, Paris: 131–140.

Perrin, M. (1986) 'Savage' points of view on writing, *Myth and the Imaginary in the New World*, E. Magaña & P. Mason (eds), CEDLA Latin America Studies 34, CEDLA/ FORIS, Amsterdam/Dordrecht: 211–231.

—— (1988a) Ni hommes, ni esprits, *Les monstres dans l'imaginaire des indiens d'Amérique latine, Circé 16–19, le monstre 4*, texts collected by Edmundo Magaña, Lettres Modernes, Paris: 147–159.

—— (1988b) Du Mythe au quotidien, penser la nouveauté, *L'Homme* XXVIII (2–3): 120–137.

Petrus Martyr de Angleria (1966) *Opera*, Akademische Druck- und Verlagsanstalt, Graz.

Pfister, Fr. (1976) *Kleine Schriften zur Alexanderroman*, Beiträge zur klassischen Philologie 61, Anton Hain Verlag, Meisenheim an Glan.

Pleij, H. (1979) *Het gilde van de Blauwe Schuit*, Meulenhoff, Amsterdam.

—— (1988) *De sneeuwpoppen van 1511*, Meulenhoff/Kritak, Amsterdam/Leuven.

Polo, M. (1958) *The Travels*, tr. R. Latham, Penguin, Harmondsworth.

Pouchelle M.-C. (1981) Des peaux de bêtes et des fourrures: histoire médiévale d'une fascination, *Le Temps de la Réflexion* II, Gallimard, Paris: 403–438.

Pouillon, J. (1970) La fonction mythique, *Le Temps de la Réflexion* I, Gallimard, Paris: 83–98.

Powell, J. (1925) *Collectanea Alexandrina*, Oxford University Press, Oxford.

Proust, M. (1954) *A la recherche du temps perdu*, 3 vols, Bibliothèque de la Pléiade, Paris.

Pucci, P. (1982) The Proem of the Odyssey, *Arethusa, American Classical Studies in Honor of J.-P. Vernant* 15 (1–2): 39–62.

Rabasa, J. (1985) Allegories of the *Altas, Europe and its Others*, F. Barker *et al.*, University of Essex Press, Colchester, Vol. II: 1–16.

Ralegh, W. (1970) *The Discovery of the Large, Rich and Beautiful Empire of Guiana*, introduction and notes by R.H. Schomburgk, Lennox Hill, New York [reprint of 1848 edn by The Hakluyt Society, London].

Raum, F. (1939) Female initiation among the Chaga, *American Anthropologist* 41: 545–565.

Rech, B. (1985) Bartolomé de las Casas und Aristoteles, *Jahrbuch für Geschichte von Staat, Wirtschaft und Gesellschaft Lateinamerikas*, 22: 39–68.

Reichel-Dolmatoff, G. (1986) Algunos conceptos de geografía chamanística de los indios Desana de Colombia, *Myth and the Imaginary in the New World*, E. Magaña & P. Mason (eds), CEDLA Latin America Studies 34, CEDLA/FORIS, Amsterdam/Dordrecht, 1986: 75–93 [1981].

Reichert, F. (1988) Columbus und Marco Polo – Asien in Amerika. Zur Literaturgeschichte der Entdeckungen, *Zeitschrift für Historische Forschung* 15 (1): 1–63.

Roe, P. (1982) *The Cosmic Zygote: Cosmology in the Amazon Basin*, Rutgers University Press, New Brunswick, New Jersey.

Ross, D. (1923) *Aristotle*, Methuen, London.

Ross, D.J.A. (1963) *Alexander Historiatus, A Guide to Medieval Illustrated Alexander Literature*, Warburg Institute, London.

Rossellini, M. & S. Saïd (1978) Usages de femmes et autres nomoi chez les 'sauvages' d'Hérodote: essai de lecture structurale, *Annali della Scuola Normale Superiore di Pisa*, ser. III, vol. VIII, 8: 949–1005.

Rousseau, J.-J. (1970) *Essai sur l'origine des langues, où il parle de la mélodie et de l'imitation musicale*, ed., intro. and notes by Ch. Porset, A.G. Nizet, Paris.

Roy, B. (1975) En marge du monde connu: les races de monstres, *Aspects de la marginalité au Moyen age*, G.-H. Allard (ed.), L'Aurore, Montreal: 70–81.

Ryan, M.T. (1981) Assimilating New Worlds in the sixteenth and seventeenth centuries, *Comparative Studies in Society and History* 23: 519–538.

Sacks, O. (1986) *The Man who Mistook his Wife for a Hat*, Pan, London [1985].

Saenger, P. (1989) Physiologie de la lecture et séparation des mots, *Annales ESC*, 44ᵉ année (4): 939–952.

Sahagún, B. de (1956) *Historia general de las cosas de Nueva España*, A.M. Garibay (ed.), Porrua, Mexico.

Said, E. (1983) *The World, the Text and the Critic*, Harvard University Press, Cambridge, Mass.

Saïd, S. (1985) Usages de femmes et sauvagerie dans l'ethnographie grecque d'Hérodote à Diodore et Strabon, *La Femme dans le monde méditerranéen*, Travaux de la Maison de l'Orient 10, Lyon: 137–150.

Saint-Lu, A. (1981) La Perception de la nouveauté chez Christophe Colombe, *Etudes sur l'impact culturel du Nouveau Monde* I, L'Harmattan, Paris: 11–24.

Sartre, J.-P. (1960) *Critique de la raison dialectique*, Gallimard, Paris.

Saussure, F. de (1974) *Course in General Linguistics*, tr. W. Baskin, Fontana/Collins, Glasgow.

Schama, S. (1987) *The Embarrassment of Riches. An Interpretation of Dutch Culture in the Golden Age*, Collins, London.

Schmidel, U. (1957) *Das VII. Theil America. Warhafftige unnd liebliche Beschreibung etlicher fuernemmen Indianischen Landschaften vnd Insulen...*, De Bry, Frankfurt.

Schmitt, J.-Cl. (1982) Les revenants dans la société féodale, *Le Temps de la Réflexion* III: 285–306.

—— (1987) Le Spectre de Samuel et la sorcière d'En Dor: avatars historiques d'un récit biblique: I *Rois* 28, *Etudes Rurales* 105–106, jan.–juin: 37–64.

Schnapper, A. (1986) Persistance des géants, *Annales ESC*, 41e année (1), jan.–févr.: 177–200.

Schwartz, S.P. (1977) Introduction, *Naming, Necessity and Natural Kinds*, S.P. Schwartz (ed.), Cornell University Press, Ithaca, NY & London: 13–41.

Seeber, H.U. (1971) Hythloday as preacher and a possible debt to Macrobius, *Moreana*, 31–32: 71–86.

Severi, C. (1988) L'Étranger, l'envers de soi et l'échec du symbolisme: deux représentations du Blanc dans la tradition chamanique cuna, *L'Homme* XXVIII (2–3): 174–183.

Shaw, B.D. (1982–1983) 'Eaters of flesh, drinkers of milk': the ancient Mediterranean ideology of the pastoral nomad, *Ancient Society* 13/14: 5–31.

Sheehan, B.W. (1980) *Savagism and Civility: Indians and Englishmen in Colonial Virgina*, Cambridge University Press, Cambridge.

Silverman, D. & B. Torode (1980) *The Material Word*, Routledge & Kegan Paul, London.

Simonin, M. (1987) Les élites chorographes ou de la 'Description de la France' dans la 'Cosmographie Universelle' de Belleforest, *Voyager à la Renaissance. Actes du colloque de Tours 1983*, J. Céard & J.-Cl. Margolin (eds), Maisonneuve et Larose, Paris: 433–451.

Smet, P.A.G.M. de (1985) *Ritual enemas and snuffs in the Americas*, CEDLA Latin America Studies 33, CEDLA/FORIS, Amsterdam/Dordrecht.

Smith, P. (1980) Positions du mythe, *Le temps de la réflexion* I: 61–81.

Snyder, J. (1976) Jan Mostaert's West Indies Landscape, *First Images of America*, F. Chiapelli (ed.), Vol. I, University of California Press, Berkeley: 495–502.

Spivak, G. (1985) The Rani of Sirmur, *Europe and its others*, F. Barker *et al.*, University of Essex Press, Colchester, Vol. I: 128–151.

Staten, H. (1985) *Wittgenstein and Derrida*, Basil Blackwell, Oxford.

Stradanus, J. (n.d.) *Venationes Ferarum, Auium, Piscium, Pugnae Bestiarorum et Mutuae Bestiarum*, s.l.

Sturtevant, W.C. (1976) First visual images of native America, *First Images of America*, F. Chiapelli (ed.), Vol. I, University of California Press, Berkeley: 417–454.

Sturtevant, W.C. & D.B. Quinn (1987) This new prey: Eskimos in Europe 1567, 1576, and 1577, *Indians and Europe*, C.F. Feest (ed.), Herodot/Rader Verlag, Göttingen and Aachen: 61–140.

Sued-Badillo, J. (1986) El mito indoantillano de las mujeres sin hombres, *Boletín de Estudios Latinoamericanos y del Caribe* 40: 15–22.

Taussig, M. (1987) *Shamanism, Colonialism and the Wild Man: A Study in Terror and Healing*, University of Chicago Press, Chicago & London.

Thevet, A. (1983) *Les Singularités de la France antarctique*, selected with introduction and notes by Frank Lestringant, La Découverte/Maspero, Paris [1577–78].

—— (1985) *Cosmographie de Levant*, edition critique par Frank Lestringant, Droz, Geneva [1554].

Todorov, T. (1982) *La Conquête de l'Amérique: La Question de l'autre*, du Seuil, Paris.

Troike, N. (1982) The interpretation of postures and gestures in the Mixtec Codices, *Dumbarton Oaks Conference on the Art and Iconography of Late Post-Classic Central Mexico*, E.H. Boone (ed.), Dumbarton Oaks Research Library and Collections, Harvard University, Washington D.C.: 175–206.

Tugnoli Pattaro, S. (1981) *Metodo e sistema delle scienze nel pensiero di Ulisse Aldrovandi*, CLUEB, Bologna.

Turner, V. (1967) *The Forest of Symbols, Aspects of Ndembu Ritual*, Cornell University Press, Ithaca, New York.

Tylor, E.B. (1871) *Primitive Culture*, John Murray, London.

Tyrrell, W.B. (1982) Amazon customs and Athenian patriarchy, *Annali della Scuola Normale Superiore di Pisa* III, XII (4): 1213–1237.

Vandenbroeck, P. (1987) *Beeld van de Andere, Vertoog over het Zelf*, Royal Museum for Fine Arts, Antwerp.

Vernant, J.-P. (1979a) *Religions, histoires, raisons*, Maspero, Paris.

—— (1979b) A la table des hommes: mythe de fondation du sacrifice chez Hésiode, *La cuisine de sacrifice en pays Grec*, M. Detienne & J.-P. Vernant (eds), Gallimard, Paris: 37–132.

—— (1981) Le Tyran boiteux: d'Oedipe à Périandre, *Le Temps de la Réflexion II:* 235–255.

—— (1985) Le Dionysos masqué des *Bacchantes* d'Euripide, *L'Homme* 93, XXV (I): 31–58.

Vespucci, A. (1984) *Il Mondo Nuovo di Amerigo Vespucci: Vespucci autentico e apocrifo*, a cura di M. Pozzi, Serra e Riva, Milan.

Veyne, P. (1983) *Les Grecs ont-ils cru à leurs mythes?*, Des Travaux/du Seuil, Paris.

Vidal-Naquet, P. (1981) *Le chasseur noir: Formes de pensée et formes de société dans le monde grec*, Maspero, Paris.

Voltaire, F.-M. (1963) Essai sur les moeurs, ed. R. Pomeau, 2 vols, Garnier, Paris.

Wagley, C. (1977) *Welcome of Tears: The Tapirapé Indians of Central Brazil*, Oxford University Press, New York.

Wagner, R. (1986) *Symbols that Stand for Themselves*, University of Chicago Press, Chicago & London.

Weiss, G. (1975) *Campa Cosmology: The World of a Forest Tribe in South America.* American Museum of Natural History, Anthropological Papers 52 (5), New York.

Whatley, J. (1984) Food and the limits of civility: The testimony of Jean de Léry, *Sixteenth Century Journal* XV (4): 387–400.

Whitehead, N. (1984) Carib cannibalism: The historical evidence, *Journal de la Société des Américanistes* LXX: 69–87.

Wilbert, J. (1986) Warao Cosmology and Yekuana Roundhouse Symbolism, *Myth and the Imaginary in the New World*, E. Magaña & P. Mason (eds), CEDLA Latin America Studies 34, CEDLA/FORIS, Amsterdam/Dordrecht, 427–457 [1981].

Wilbert, J. & K. Simoneau (1978) *Folk Literatures of the Gê Indians* I, UCLA Latin American Center Publications, University of California, Los Angeles.

—— (1982) *Folk Literature of the Mataco Indians*, UCLA Latin American Center Publications, University of California, Los Angeles.

—— (1984) *Folk Literatures of the Gê Indians II*, UCLA Latin American Center Publications, University of California, Los Angeles.

Wittgenstein, L. (1958) *Philosophical Investigations*, Basil Blackwell, Oxford, 2nd edn.

—— (1979) *Notebooks 1914–1916*, Basil Blackwell, Oxford, 2nd edn.

Wittkower, R. (1977) *Allegory and the Migration of Symbols*, Thames & Hudson, London.

Wright, M.R. (1981) *Empedocles: The Extant Fragments*, Yale University Press, New Haven, Conn. and London.

Name index

Subject index

Abarimon 79, 90, 122, 123
Abioi 73–4, 76
Abominable 88, 90
Adam and Eve 47, 50, 107
Aegipani 78
Aeneid 179
Africa 29, 51, 78, 86, 90, 179
Agriophagi 79, 88
akalakui 142
Akephaloi 75, 83, 106
Albanians 90, 140
Alexandros legend: Blemmyae 106;
    fish-eaters 87; Gog and Magog 80;
    influence 82; Kynokephaloi 84;
    lantern-eyed people 140; red-footed
    men 124; Wild Man 46, 47
Algonkin 178
alterity 1–2, 41, 124, 160, 169, 179–83
Amazons: Columbus's account 105–6;
    island of 104; lack of breast 89;
    Ralegh's account 100, 107; tradition of
    110–11, 174
Amenadiña 155–6
Amyktyres 77, 104, 141
Anaconda 143–4
anality 119
Andaman Islands 71–2, 82–3, 85–6, 141
Androgini 90, 106, 141, *see also*
    Hermaphrodite
animal: alterity 8, 41; symbolism 53,
    59–60; trials 59, 115
'animalisation' 59
Ankosturaña 154, 156
Antarctic Pole 131
anthropology 6, 7, 14, 115, 166, 174
Anthropophagi 78–9, 84, 88–9, 105, 107,
    111
anthropophagy 6, 8, 46, 53–6, 111, 163,

see also cannibalism
Anticaudae 122
Antichrist, The 106
Antipodes 120–33; American habitat 115;
    displacement of feet 90; language
    articulation 91; Patagonian associations
    110; sixteenth-century records 105
Antoikoi 126
Antwerp 23
anus 141, 147
Apalai 158
Apollonius von Tyrland 45
Arab peoples 54
Arapaho 128
Arawaks 22, 55, 112
Argentina 127, 144
Arimaspoi 74, 75, 78, 85, 140
Artabatitae 79
Artibiratae 124
articulation 129–30, 148–9
Aruto 113
assimilation 159, 163–6, 181
Astomoi: body openness 90, 91, 120; diet,
    77, 88, 141; illustration 118; in India
    77, 79; lack of mouth 89, 141
Atlantes 78, 88
Atlantis 1, 7
Augilae 78, 88
autopsy 176–7
Aztecs 23, 32, 52

Babylonia 90, 140
Bali 50
Barasana 142–6, 162
Battos 128
beggars, wandering 43, 44, 51, 58, 97
Blemmyae (Blemmyes): displaced eyes
    90, 141; Isidorus's account 80; Kaliña